The Attack
of
The Mustard Seed

—

Ten Sales Management Essentials

—

Just as the blueprint for the life of a future plant is somehow mysteriously contained in that little pod... so is the blueprint for the life of a successful sales team embedded in this story

JOHN W. CEBROWSKI

Acknowledgments

A sincere thank you to my distinguished Advisory Board of managers and professionals whose insights were deeply appreciated. The Board included Arthur K. Cebrowski, Sarah Beth Cliatt, Anna Mackley Cobb, Ed Crowder, Allen DuBose, Edward Durant, Dr. Mary Esseff, Peter A. Garbis, Dr. Vernon Grose, Catharine Guajardo, Oscar Guajardo, Teresa Hartnett, Roy Huffman, Dr. Blair Jobe, Sister Mary Veronica Keller, O.P., William R. Kitchel, Catharine W. Lewis, Phyllis McDonald, G. Allen Metz, Patrick Niro, Josh Ridker, Zbigniew T. Rurak, Stuart Safft, Seth Stein, Dr. Steve Thomas, John Walsh, and Paul Wiegand. It was exciting and encouraging to be on the receiving end of so many pertinent suggestions that ranged from subtle to obvious—from simple to complex—and covered everything imaginable in terms of substance and delivery.

A special acknowledgement to my wife Amanda who provided much support and encouragement—and offered numerous ideas for the early drafts.

And appreciation to Charlie Romeo, the co-author of my first book, *The Sales Manager's Troubleshooter*. Charlie provided the 'Put the Horses in the Barn' idea for Essential #1—which set the stage for naming the remaining nine Essentials.

And special recognition to David Gainer of the Kansas Department of Commerce and Housing who provided the inspiration to lend a Kansas theme to the story.

This book is dedicated to Helen S. Cebrowski, my mother, whose lifelong pursuit of excellence in all matters has been a constant inspiration. She is a model of outrageous success. Her vigorous spirit, steadfast work ethic, and high expectations are woven throughout this book.

-The Attack of the Mustard Seed-

© Copyright, 2000, 2001 John W. Cebrowski

ISBN: 1-59113-027-1

Printed in the United States of America

Fairfax, Virginia

Story Contents

Introduction

Long-Dormant Firm Attacks Market With Outrageous Success

Tiny upstart sprouts... becomes darling of Wall Street

NEW YORK – Certus Industries, Inc. fourth-quarter profits surged 3700 percent astounding analysts. Net income for the three months ended Dec. 31 rose to $1.85 a share from .05 a share a year earlier. The stock, the most active issue on the NASDAQ yesterday, closed up 14 ½ points to a record high.

The old, respected company with a history of survival struggles had market-watchers fully expecting an imminent takeover by one of the industry giants.

President & CEO J. Thornton Pimm III credited the turnaround to ...

That little company could be you. But how...?

•

There exists a hard core of essentials which if executed consistently and with precision—that can help make you outrageously successful—especially in today's frantic business environment. For any manager or business owner who is leading top-line revenue-generating efforts there are ten such essentials.

Some of you may be thinking right now, '*Hey, I firmly believe there are twelve*', or '*No, I'm convinced there are seven, and they are such-and-such*'. And then others may be thinking, '*John, I agree, you've nailed the ten essentials*'. However, I wrote this mainly for the reader who neither disagrees nor agrees with me—but for that vast middle ground who may never have given this subject much thought. Regardless of where you stand, strength of conviction regarding essentials is imperative to outrageous success.

Essential means 'absolutely necessary' and 'indispensable', and these ten *are* absolutely necessary and indispensable. These essentials represent wisdom. They are core values.

There are numerous other aspects to a manager's job—but to achieve outrageous success these ten essentials *must* be in place.

Two thoughts prompted this story. The first is that there are many managers and business owners—intrapreneurs and entrepreneurs—who harbor a deep hunger to win big. There always have been and there always will be. This story reveals the essentials and discloses the how-to.

Secondly, many managers and owners, though cognizant of essentials, do not maintain a firm grip on them. Bombardment by a constant stream of new and promising management concepts, technology and e-business pressures, and every-day operational stress cause people to inadvertently let go. This story is intended to be an inspirational reminder to hold on tight.

The book has three structural elements. The first is the story format because the hunger for compelling tales is a basic human instinct. Stories embody and embed knowledge, and give us a way to connect experiences to universal truths. The second is the deliberate country-style atmosphere and jargon to stress the grass roots, fundamental nature of the essentials. And the third is simplicity because simplicity is powerful and refreshing. Simple methods and the application of unpretentious, traditional qualities habitually result in the greatest successes in management—and in life. *But be alert—* because stories deliver subtle messages, unfamiliar atmosphere and jargon hint at unique insights, and the path of simplicity, as good as it is, is cluttered with complexities.

There are five social themes quietly woven into the story via the characters, dialogue, and quotations. The first is the value of the knowledge and experience of senior citizens in our society—too often disparaged or underutilized. The second is the value of diversity—too often given lip service or politicized. The third is the prominence and value of family—too often fractured or minimized. The fourth is the value of Native American wisdom—too often misunderstood or not respected. The fifth is the value of faith in God—too often forgotten. The themes are here because they are consistent with achieving outrageous success.

The ten essentials are highly effective throughout a company—so spread the word in your firm. You'll see that's exactly what our hero, Ol' Bert, does.

Whatever inner-fire drives you—achievement, financial reward, promotion, or survival—this story will stoke the flames. The ten essentials are hard work. But our hero is a friendly old guy who will suggest how to execute. We all have dreams about overcoming huge odds and achieving something special—things the ordinary world will never understand. So go ahead and use him as a model. After all, he's the one who leads the turnaround at Certus.

Here's a tip. Relax and read this like a story, letting it unfold freely in your imagination. Place yourself *in* the story and measure the contents of the story against the truth of your own management life. Then react accordingly.

In addition, use this book in conjunction with a library of other management books. That's why many chapters highlight selections from our hero's extensive library. An annotated bibliography of key selections is included to help you explore each essential in more detail. But keep *The Attack of the Mustard Seed* out-front of all your resource materials because it deals with essentials.

You'll find the Summary a convenient reference that highlights key points and lists from each Essential.

In closing this introduction let's not forget one important question. What is outrageous success—or what are its dimensions?
Here's how our hero would answer that question.

❑ Outrageous success means consciously pursuing and overcoming huge obstacles. There is nothing outrageous about facing minimal challenges.

❑ Outrageous success means regularly venturing into risky markets or competitive strongholds and winning. There is nothing outrageous about tramping over previously covered ground.

❑ Outrageous success implies doing things very differently. Exploring. Experimenting. And then winning. There is nothing outrageous about cautious tinkering or incrementalism.

❑ Outrageous success is breaking the sound barrier with your quickness of thinking, decisions, and actions. There is nothing outrageous about grinding clockwork.

❑ Outrageous success implies results that cause the phone lines to light up and the media to wake-up. There is nothing outrageous about predictable news.

❑ Outrageous success suggests being able to execute the unexpected and regularly create marvelous surprises. There is nothing outrageous about meeting basic expectations.

❑ Outrageous success refers to results at sustained record levels. One-shot wonders and single seasons of glory don't count.

❑ Outrageous success indicates laser-like profitability pursuit, return on investment, and wealth creation that turns heads in the financial markets.

❑ Outrageous success means making substantial bucks for all the risk-takers, all the sweat-generators, and all the stakeholders.

❑ Outrageous success refers to a reputation in the marketplace as the quintessence of service and support, setting new frontiers of customer and sales partner satisfaction.

❑ Outrageous success means becoming a person of high and diverse value to your employer and all the other communities of people in which you participate.

❑ Outrageous success insinuates a personal reputation in the firm so strong that the balance of management seeks your counsel—and executive recruiters salivate.

❑ Outrageous success means realizing the promise of e-business so well that e-gurus hold you up as an e-model.

❑ Outrageous success suggests a very personal intangible aspiration—a thirst that burns in your heart that's seemingly impossible to achieve—that you miraculously pull-off.

❑ And outrageous success brings an inner excitement and deep satisfaction that signals arrival at higher plateaus.

What would you add to the list? Go ahead, there's more.

❑ _____

_____

_____.

❑ _____

_____

_____.

❑ _____

_____

_____.

While you're at it, go back through that list and check off those dimensions that you are pursuing or have tried to pursue in your company. Put a '+' in the box of those you've pursued and implemented, a '✓ ' for those you'd like to implement, a '?' for ones you never considered but find appealing, and an 'x' for those you don't want to consider.

Caution: Be prepared for your definition and dimensions of outrageous success to mysteriously change while you are in the midst of pursuing them. Pursuit will do strange, unexplainable things to you. Accept the change—being honest that some startling new self-insights and motivations have been discovered.

Here is a final question for you to answer to yourself before you get into the story. Why would you even *want* to pursue outrageous success? There *is* a price to be paid. It demands sacrifices and trade-offs. Lesser levels of success may meet personal and professional needs. So—maybe you should put this story down and go on to something else.

But—if you're driven, or in case you ever change your mind, all you have to do is pull this story off the shelf. The ten essentials are here for the taking. They are tangible mechanisms to help you get where you want to go.

If you're wondering what the book's title, *The Attack of The Mustard Seed,* has to do with all this—just wait until you read the third essential.

The bottom line of this story is that it will give you a firmer grip on the essentials and help you achieve *your* definition and *your* dimension of outrageous success. What's in this book might be seen as improbable, implausible, and impractical—but fortunately it *can* and *does* happen.

Grab a highlighter and enjoy!

In character, in manners, in style, in all things, the supreme excellence is simplicity.
Henry Wadsworth Longfellow

Our Opening Scene

Once upon a time in a small city far, far away there was a little company named Certus Industries, Inc.

Mr. Pimm was the President and Chief Executive Officer. His grandfather had founded the business naming it Certus because in Latin 'certus' means *'something to be depended or relied upon, or trustworthy'* and that's the reputation the grandfather wanted for the company.

The company had struggled for years, astutely altering its products and services with the times, always surviving by the skin of its teeth, and never losing its trustworthy reputation.

Now however, competition was overwhelming the little company, and many prospects would not even talk to Certus salespeople. The competitors were big, awe-inspiring multinational corporations from all over the world.

Because Mr. Pimm had first started working at Certus Industries as a salesman right out of college, and because he had downsized the company, he now also filled the role of sales manager. His occasional travels with his salespeople reminded him of his early days in sales.

One day, while visiting his bank to ask for another working capital loan, the banker, a longtime family friend, suggested to Mr. Pimm that maybe it was time to bring in a dedicated sales manager for one last chance to save the business. The banker, who was a tough and smart old codger, said, "no sales manager—no loan." And in the next breath he happily added that he had read a recent article in the newspaper about a long-retired sales manager who had been a legend in his time. The article had been written because this retiree had lent his talents to lead a charity drive whose results had been phenomenal.

Slowly leaning across the desk, the banker slid Mr. Pimm the article and suggested he try and find out if this man was available. Mr. Pimm read that the man was living in an upscale community in a distant county.

The banker's idea didn't seem feasible or realistic. After all, this retiree had been out of the market for so long that he probably thought that a mouse was a rodent. Plus, it was difficult for Mr. Pimm to admit that there may be someone better than he to lead the company's sales efforts. He felt his pride getting in the way. However, his will and determination to save the business and his need for the loan were so strong that he said he would investigate.

Later, Mr. Pimm read that the man in the article, 'Ol' Bert' as the story referred to him, was originally a farm boy from western Kansas. It seems this farm boy had joined the Marines after high school, fought with valor in the Pacific, took some adult education classes after the war, and embarked on an incredible sales and management career with companies big and small. The article talked of him being one of the original 'Tin Men' selling aluminum siding in Philadelphia. He had also sold, or managed the sales of, grocery products, machine tools, mini-computers, airplanes, and insurance in his heyday. And before he retired, he had contributed his expertise to the start-up of a successful auto dealership. It seems the legend was built on the results he had achieved for his employers, the five books he had authored, his motivational speaking engagements, and his advisory roles for several sales-related Hollywood movies. Supposedly, there was nothing this fellow Ol' Bert didn't know about sales or management.

The very next day Mr. Pimm drove to the distant county for a visit, located the fashionable community, and found Ol' Bert peacefully rocking on the front porch of a meticulously maintained old Victorian home. He was living with his two widowed sisters. The sisters were grateful for the presence of their wise and watchful brother—and he in turn was appreciative of their personal attention and delicious homemade apple pies.

Mr. Pimm's greeting was a bit clumsy but the old man quickly made him feel at home. They moved inside into the sitting room and one of the sisters graciously brought them some lemonade. Towering over the old retiree, Mr. Pimm was a picture of executive pomp and anxiety. Quickly and nervously Mr. Pimm informed him of his situation and need.

The little old man impressed Mr. Pimm immediately with his poise, sharp questions, and vitality.

Ol' Bert had had no plans to leave this beautiful home, except in a box. However—when he heard that there was an opportunity to return to the profession he so dearly loved, he could scarcely contain his enthusiasm.

Mr. Pimm, with hands clenched at his sides, asked if Ol' Bert would please take the job for the sake of the company's employees and the economic well being of the small city the firm helped support.

Looking up from the antique desk in the fashionably decorated room where the two of them had been meeting, Bert said, "The challenge appeals to me, but I warn you, I'm nowhere near the manager I used to be."

Mr. Pimm responded, "If you're half the leader and manager they say you are, that is more than enough for me. I can't afford to pay you much, but I will do the best I can."

Ol' Bert grumbled and snorted, looked down at his clasped hands and said nothing. His mind was whirring with the possibilities. The silence was painful for Mr. Pimm. Finally, Mr. Pimm said that the company had an old '93 Chevy

8

four-door sedan, and he would be happy to let Ol' Bert have it as a company car. He quickly added that personal office space could be made available. And then a moment later he threw in two weeks vacation.

Ol' Bert, who hadn't used the pause intentionally as a bargaining ploy, was nevertheless convinced of the desperation and sincerity of this man.

He glanced up at a beautifully framed inscription hanging on the wall. Mr. Pimm followed his glance, and they both read it in silence.

> *"Far better it is to dare mighty things, to win glorious triumphs, even though checkered by failure, than to take rank with those poor spirits who neither enjoy much nor suffer much, because they live in the gray twilight that knows not victory or defeat."*
> **Theodore Roosevelt**

The old farm boy then excused himself to discuss this with his sisters who had been in the kitchen discreetly trying to listen-in. He was in the kitchen for what seemed an eternity to Mr. Pimm, who paced slowly back and forth across the sitting room, clasping and unclasping his hands, his mind scrambling for other options if this man should say 'no'.

Returning unhurriedly to the sitting room, a mischievous smile crept onto Ol' Bert's face, and he said, "Okay. Yep. I'll take charge of sales. This could be fun. I'll pack up, move out, and get to work. It's time to plow and plant and grow your business. My sisters can take care of our home and I'll be close enough to visit regularly. I'm sure you can help me find a simple place to live near your business."

Mr. Pimm was elated—but also a bit nervous that he was making a sound decision. He turned to acknowledge the sisters who were now standing in the kitchen doorway, smiling and nodding their support.

The two men shook hands briskly.

It would be many months before Mr. Pimm would fully comprehend the treasure chest he had just unlocked.

9

It Begins

Word spread quickly throughout the industry and the sales profession that Ol' Bert had been lured out of retirement. The press, aware of the reputation of this cult hero, made a big play of the fact. <u>Sales</u> <u>&</u> <u>Marketing</u> <u>Management</u> magazine even featured Ol' Bert as a cover story, playing up his historical exploits and management innovations.

The financial community, also aware of this well-known personality, reacted in anticipation of his impact. Certus, which had gone public only three years prior and was listed on the NASDAQ, jumped 2 1/4 points with the news.

There was only one salesperson left in the company when Ol' Bert finally arrived. Her name was Leslie. The rest had skittered-off like rats. Ol' Bert immediately liked Leslie's smarts, spunk, and strength of character. She had been with the firm for only ten months, but had seven years of prior marketing and sales experience, and was a graduate of Columbia University where she had majored in psychology and dabbled in theater.

Upon learning of Ol' Bert's return to 'the ranks' Leslie thought to herself that this was a wild desperation play. Frankly, she had been a bit disappointed that she hadn't gotten the manager's job, but Mr. Pimm's sincere explanation of the firm's need for experience and the potential for future opportunities had consoled her. When she saw that Ol' Bert had a twinkle in his eye and a way of cocking his ear to whatever Leslie said it convinced her there might be something to this old-timer. He had charisma and wisdom that Leslie found fascinating. She also knew that Mr. Pimm would never make an investment that didn't make sense.

Ol' Bert assumed this job would be easy, that he could share some ideas with the management staff, simply help Leslie close a few deals to get the ball rolling, then hand the responsibility back to Mr. Pimm and Leslie.

The office space he selected, formerly a storage room, was small and drab. Sagging bookshelves lined two of the walls, floor to ceiling, jam-packed with the huge array of professional books Ol' Bert had brought with him. He named this cramped working space—this mini-library—his 'Wisdom Pantry'. He liked to discuss the contents of his favorite books with Leslie, who provided an attentive ear. The third wall he filled with all the plaques, awards, and memorabilia that were a reflection of his storied history. He kept the dusty blinds of the only window in the office drawn. Ol' Bert liked it dark because it was easier on his old eyes. A decrepit coffeemaker sat on the windowsill. There was one brass lamp on his desk with a black lampshade that cast strange shadows. His computer, the one he had brought from home, was the biggest and baddest that money could buy. The monitor sat there like a giant sentinel with screen-saver chirping. Ol' Bert might have been old, but he understood that his know-how and experience combined with technology was a potent combination.

One eccentricity he allowed himself was an old black rotary dial phone, a precious keepsake from a past employer. He used it as a 'hotline' to Mr. Pimm's office. It would ring every day at 5:00 and Mr. Pimm would ask how many orders Ol' Bert and Leslie had received that day. On some days they could report success, but Ol' Bert would get very sad when there were no orders to announce.

Ol' Bert was small and wiry, with a shock of neatly trimmed white hair. He looked lost when he sat in his massive high-backed leather chair. He loved to tell Leslie sales stories about the old days in addition to discussing his books. He was proud that part of his heritage was American Indian, and knew that the oral narration of story and culture were essential aspects of both native and sales traditions. He firmly believed that storytelling built bonds, motivated listeners, preserved important customs, celebrated life, and of course, entertained.

Mr. Pimm was a sharp but conservative manager who sat in his office most of the day and studied all the sales, financial, and production numbers. He liked big numbers best, and he was developing a special feeling for Ol' Bert because he had solved a couple of sticky sales problems and prevented the loss of the company's biggest account. He began to feel ever more confident that Ol' Bert had one last gasp of management magic left in him to 'hit the numbers'.

Mr. Pimm knew that past and current results were a reflection of new technologies, global sourcing and manufacturing patterns, fickle market demands, profit-chewing sales channels, price-slashing rivals, and resource-rich mega-competitors—but he was becoming convinced that good sales leadership could help turn things around. Others on the Certus management team had also gained trust and confidence in Ol' Bert because of his focus on profitability, his intense listening, his vigorous help in solving some of *their* problems, the respectful way he cultivated interdepartmental cooperation, and his refreshingly honest assessments. To them, in many ways, he stood in stark contrast to stereotypical sales managers.

Ol' Bert and Leslie had been working hard for about a month to increase the sales of Certus products. They had several wins, but candidly not at a level that anyone would describe as outrageous.

One day, in spite of some improvement, Mr. Pimm decided to confide in him. He called him into his office, and said, "It looks like the prudent thing to do is to sell the company to one of our big competitors. Projections indicate that Certus can last only six more months—two quarters. I've taken all the corrective action steps the Board, the rest of the management team, and I can think of. I've invested in all the technology we could afford. I've latched onto all the concepts the brightest minds of the business world have generated. I'm tired of operating on the edge. And I'm personally worn-out. Better for us to get out while the getting is good. Why keep fighting the inevitable?"

Mr. Pimm's eyes glistened, and his hands shook as he told Ol' Bert the news. It was a brutal business world in which Certus operated. He knew Ol' Bert had tried hard, had brought in some additional business, and he thanked him sincerely.

The seemingly hopeless situation and Mr. Pimm's emotion and exhaustion caused old motivations to well-up in Ol' Bert. His drive and intensity, shaped by a lifetime of struggles and competition, began to galvanize and energize the old mind and body. His attitude and commitment suddenly hardened. The old competitive juices began to flow.

He was mad at himself for not approaching this task with the necessary focus and intensity from the very beginning.

He instinctively knew what needed to be done—and that was to execute the essentials that had made him outrageously successful in the past—and he knew he could transform Certus in the process. Mr. Pimm's announcement had awakened him from his unconsciously informal approach. He had done it before! He could do it again! His essentials—his irreducible essence of management—flashed through his mind.

- Put The Horses In The Barn
- Pound Some Stakes Into The Ground
- Plant Somethin' Special
- Know How To Git Where You're Goin'
- Use The Best Ways For The Best Yields
- Lead With Heart, Brains, And Courage
- Aid Everyone In Learnin'
- Ask The Neighbors For Help
- Treat Folks Like Kin
- Dig In And Do It Right

Because of the fact that Ol' Bert had grown up on a farm on the high plains of western Kansas and had such a deep love for his origins he had always put his irreducible essence in the vernacular of farming and gardening. He found it lifting to put his work in the context of this larger parallel—a parallel so basic and honorable—to which all could relate.

Squinting at Mr. Pimm, Ol' Bert rose slowly and without blinking cracked-off each of his essentials like a rifle shot, saying that each essential was both an obtainer and a sustainer of outrageous success. He said that all the new e-business and new-age business concepts in the world laid on top of imperfect essentials only resulted in more complex imperfection.

He was accepting of the fact that the labels he gave his essentials may sound 'hokey' to others, but to him it was a way to make them memorable.

"They sound simple—yet serious and intricate," said Mr. Pimm, impressed.

Bert replied, smiling, "Some famous writer once said, *There is nothing quite so complicated as simplicity.* In business and in life, Mr. Pimm, only what is simple can succeed. And yes, the ten essentials are intricate—but they are not so sophisticated that *any* manager in *any* business function can't use them. The essentials apply equally to mom-and-pop businesses and Fortune 500 corporations—and from sales to operations to finance to marketing to HR—to wherever.

"That's good, because we're just a small business—and we're just a plain bunch of uncomplicated, hard-working people," Mr. Pimm offered, a bit self-consciously.

"This economy is *driven* by small business—by hard-working people like those here at Certus," Bert emphasized. "And the dilemmas that you face are the same dilemmas faced by those starch-collared VP's on those expansive corporate campuses. They may huff and puff about other stuff, but it all boils down to the same essentials for *everybody.*

"Okay—but what the heck do you mean by *outrageous* success?" Mr. Pimm continued, wanting to make sure he fully understood what was being proposed.

"Outrageous? It means something kind of thoroughly incredible and amazing. It is the only level of success acceptable to me. You've ignited a hunger and a desire that only outrageous success can satisfy. I will begin sharing the *full* wealth of my talents and know-how immediately.

"Mr. Pimm, every business situation—ominous or ordinary—requires exceptional resolve on a continuing basis. I commit to you my full, spirited resolve to implement these essentials and *plant them firmly* in Certus's culture."

Mr. Pimm—these are *perennials*—perennials to be tended and nurtured season-to-season and year-to-year.

"As the person in charge of sales, I apologize for not providing that full, exceptional resolve from the very beginning. Clearly, my retirement dulled my passion and my 'edge'.

"The first step on the way to outrageous success is to recognize the enemy—and the enemy is *always* the imperfection or the lack of one or more of these essentials. Obviously, I personally have fallen prey to the enemy. Mr. Pimm, never make the mistake of considering the competition the enemy. The competition is only the competition.

"I've never faced a time constraint this tight—but together—as a team— what seems an imminent disaster is an chance for all of us to grow professionally and personally.

"As one of my personal idols, Henry Ford, once said, *Business is never so healthy as when, like a chicken, it must do a certain amount of scratching for what it gets.* The enemy—*and* the competition—are in for some rivalry and racket from this tough, old rooster that it never imagined."

Mr. Pimm was startled. He had never seen this intense, combative side of Ol' Bert. It was encouraging. It gave him sudden hope.

"Okay—I'm with you—while there's still a chance. I accept your apology—and you have my full resolve in return," said Mr. Pimm, breaking into a nervous smile. "Let's go do it!"

Ol' Bert knew that a good storyteller had the ability to perform the story while narrating it. He knew it was time to walk the talk. The door closed shut firmly as Ol' Bert walked out of Mr. Pimm's office with renewed purpose.

Essential #1
Put the Horses in the Barn

Two days later, Ol' Bert walked back into Mr. Pimm's office to announce that the first thing he needed to do was to hire two horses. "Can't plow if I don't have the horses," was the way he introduced the subject.

"Horses? You're older than I thought," Mr. Pimm responded with a laugh.

Ignoring the slight, Bert emphatically responded, "Yep. Horses. I don't need the bevy of salespeople that were here before. I've done a needs analysis, studied our markets, our marketing tools, our sales partner network, our e-business initiatives, and the size and scope of our task. I now know that I need two horses. In other words, I need two additional top-notch salespeople to complement Leslie."

"How can you possibly do it with just two more?" asked Mr. Pimm in disbelief. "Our task will require many more. Look how many have quit."

"No. If I can find the two that I have in mind, that's all that I'll need. I believe in running with the leanest organization—and the meanest horses I can find. I believe Leslie is one. Need just two more, Mr. Pimm. And besides, we don't have the budget to pay for more than two. I read an article several years ago in Harvard Business Review that said, 'Very small groups of highly skilled generalists show a remarkable propensity to succeed.' That stuck in my brain like wild honey. The history of outrageous sales success is a history of horses, few in number, but gifted with greatness.

"Where are you going to find them? We've always had trouble hiring good people. This I've gotta see," Mr. Pimm said with growing skepticism. "And besides, that will take time. We only have two quarters." Mr. Pimm's hands began to shake.

"Just watch me. Listen to my plan, Mr. Pimm."

Ol' Bert, even though he was many years senior to Mr. Pimm, always called him Mr. Pimm.

"There are no shortcuts. None. Nil. And don't worry. Leslie and I will be engaged in other critical processes in parallel to the search."

"How will you do this hiring?" Mr. Pimm asked, coming forward in his chair, his interest piqued.

"I'll use my special 'Twelve-P' system," Bert said, smiling confidently. Seeing Mr. Pimm's head cock quizzically, Bert added, "Let me tell you about it. Do you have some time later today?"

"Yes, yes, for you, of course," Mr. Pimm agreed heartily.

"Thank you. Why don't you come down to my office at six and I'll describe it. It's never failed me."

"You're on," Mr. Pimm concluded.

At 6:00 p.m., the meeting began in Ol' Bert's office. Ol' Bert knew the president liked to keep his finger in sales, and frankly, he enjoyed sharing his management lore with him and showing-off his 'Wisdom Pantry.' Ol' Bert made the boss feel comfortable by brewing up a pot of Mr. Pimm's favorite hazelnut-flavored coffee. Mr. Pimm, sitting on a small hard-back chair across from Bert's desk, took the mug of coffee that Bert handed to him. Then Ol' Bert sat back in his big chair and paused for effect.

"Hiring is a manager's most important task—because success starts with staffing. All else flows from it. Top-quality horses are out there, Mr. Pimm. You and I both know that, and horses are what I'm after. *The company with the second-best organization ends up second place in the market.* And second place is not my destination. Did you know a former CEO of PepsiCo said that? Now if a huge, successful company thinks like that, shouldn't we?"

He let that sink in, and then Ol' Bert went to his whiteboard and carefully wrote:

Preparation

"That's what the first 'P' stands for," he said, and sat down.

"A little up-front noodling, I call it. I like to think about our customers, sales partners, and markets first when hiring someone. After all, those are our biggest assets.

"I imagine what it's like to be a buyer or sales partner and try to understand what *they* would want in the salespeople from Certus who will be working with them. Customers and partners *like* to deal with people like themselves, who mirror their values, who understand their business, and who can be responsive to their problems. I confirm my imaginings by going out and talking to people, probing and listening closely. And I do it by observing customer operations carefully, because what you hear isn't always the whole story.

"I also think about my best people. I inventory the skills of my existing horses to remind me of their talents and to alert me to abilities that I am missing. I want a comprehensive pool of competencies on which to draw. Of course now,

18

in this case, I only have one saleswoman, but I ask, 'Why is Leslie good?' And she is, no doubt about it. But what does she do? What's inside her? What makes her tick? I've noted her skills and attributes. And let me tell you, never forget what made your past staff members great. I remember all of mine as if it were yesterday. All this helps me define an initial picture of what I'm looking for.

"Speaking of yesterday, I can't ignore Certus's sales chronicles. The past can be a wonderful teacher. I've been intensively studying your sales team history, looking for organizational and personnel lessons.

"Of course, I'm a big believer in diversity. I don't want clones. Yes, there are common threads that are critical, but some differences in styles and skills will let me match different people to different market needs and niches. So I think about special needs, like experience in an emerging market or a language capability, or a specific undergraduate degree. I had a cloned sales unit once, and it cost me a ton of business. I had no flexibility. Never forgot that lesson.

"I also try to create a balance between those with a speculative planning bent and those with a practical execution bent, between thinkers and doers, between romantics and pragmatists. The blend turns out to be unitive, rather than divisive. Diversity results in a harmonious fusion, particularly in times of crises—like right now.

"Then I think about what's changing in the market, the industry, and here at Certus. I hire for *what will be*, not for *what is*. I must project myself into the future, anticipating needs.

"Then I review my personal list of core values, critical character elements of success, that I've built up through the years. I've learned to *never* hire anyone who doesn't possess these elements, and I have the scars to prove it. I know it sounds impractical, but I believe idealism in hiring is synonymous with outrageous success. Every manager should have a list of character elements in which he or she deeply believes. My beliefs and someone else's beliefs may not be the same, and that's okay. What's important is that the manager *has* a list of character elements. My personal list includes authenticity, candor, caring, empathy, fidelity, integrity, resiliency, self-assurance, and self-discipline. Many people call those character elements *fiber*.

"Any manager must be able to articulate his or her list, describing why those elements are critical. To simply mouth the words is insufficient. I test myself before the launch of every hiring effort by explaining each character element out loud to peers. It's amazing how my self-test has illuminated flimsy elements—ones that are no longer gut-grabbers—and new character elements to which I've become solidly committed. My list is fluid because experience teaches. And notice that they're all 'internals'—not 'externals.' Would you like me to explain my list?"

19

"No, no. I understand. That's inspiring. Go on, go on," Mr. Pimm urged enthusiastically.

"Now. Here's a little-known secret," Bert continued. "Shared character elements are what enable a team to 'click.' Shared fiber is the basis of good team chemistry and the catalyst for outrageous success. It's why I firmly stick to my list. Simple as that."

"Son of a gun," was all Mr. Pimm said, having learned something new.

"The next thing is to review the compensation plan and the perks that can be included, such as equity or investment programs. Many sales managers don't structure their potential compensation offerings until they're in the middle of negotiations. By that time, the pressure is on, they can't think straight, Human Resources feels pushed and agitated, no one can be creative, and you often give away the farm. A measured, careful analysis of compensation options up-front saves all that anguish. I want to have this neatly in the drawer from the get-go. We still may negotiate, especially with horses, but at least I've got the foundation in place.

"The last thing I do with this first 'P' is form a selection team," Bert continued. "A team approach to hiring ensures thoroughness. This is too important to leave to one person—even me! The HR Director and I have identified the select few managers and supervisors in the company, irrespective of their job function or title, who have exhibited a gift for spotting and hiring top talent. We found three whose track record is enviable. They're on my selection team. Here's the list. You'll be amazed," Bert said, and he handed Mr. Pimm a piece of paper. Mr. Pimm raised his eyebrows in pleasant surprise. "It takes the gifted to spot the gifted. I know these three will be a big help.

"Oh—the receptionist is on our team also. You may think it's a stretch, but you would be amazed at the behaviors and impressions a receptionist can gather when a candidate comes into our office. And by the way, congratulations, you're also on the team, Mr. Pimm. I'll explain your role later.

Ol' Bert went back to the whiteboard and wrote:

Position description

"The second 'P' is a term that is passé in many quarters, but I need a 'P' word, so bear with me. This is 'the job.'

"To begin with, I've got to confirm our company's primary market approach. Is Certus first-to-market, a fast follower, the highest-value provider, a low-cost provider, a best-service provider, or a niche server? Sales teams of companies taking different market approaches *must* work in ways that support the marketing approach. The differences in required skills and attributes have

20

selection implications. The nature of the product or service is not the issue here—it's about business philosophy. Marketing says we've always positioned ourselves as the highest-value provider—and we plan on continuing that approach. Correct?"

"I concur," said Mr. Pimm.

"Okay. Next—I've got to ask others, and myself, *others* being just as important, what work we want the new people to do and in what environments they'll be operating. I look at things like developing specific macro and micro markets, implementing sales channel strategies, executing high-level conceptual presentations, leading the resolution of problems, making presentations to large buying teams, planning special sales campaigns, coaching sales partners, and many other activities. The position description also ties closely to our sales department strategies, so the description must be developed with strategy in mind. One affects the other, so at this stage I'm also considering what our over-all sales strategy will be so that the two new people 'fit' its execution, just like they need to 'fit' the marketing approach. Not all top-notch horses can execute a given strategy or market approach with equal skill.

"You wouldn't buy a horse if you didn't know what you wanted the horse to do, would you? To plow or to race? It may be that a plow horse is better suited for the job at hand rather than a thoroughbred. It's utterly impossible to recognize the best horse for the job if you can't match a job's requirements to a horse's capabilities. The same applies to top-notch people. Makes sense, doesn't it, Mr. Pimm? But you'd be surprised how many managers don't follow that simple rule.

"I usually end up with a list of ten to twenty bullets that form the position description. Then I write out what each bullet means, and *why* it's important. That process acts as verification.

"Another thing. I can't assume that the two new people will be doing the same things that the former salespeople did. As a matter of fact, I'll *guarantee you* that they will be doing *many* new and different things," emphasized Bert. "I've been studying our products, the markets, the expectations of the other departments here at Certus—all the information I gathered with the first 'P.' It all helps define the position. I want to take the salespeople's external *and* internal value-add to a higher level. This job will be *very* challenging.

Ol' Bert began pacing around, unable to sit still while talking about these matters.

"Another reason I need a solid description—and this is just a firm foundation, by the way—is that the best candidates count on being told, or will ask, what is expected of them. I *must* be able to answer that question cleanly. Realistically, they and I both know that no sales job can be completely defined, but I want to make sure they understand the priorities—certainly seventy to eighty-five percent of the job. I intentionally leave part of the job vaguely defined because horses can tolerate ambiguity, and they like open spaces. Not only are they *willing* to race and flex their talents, but they get skittish and chafe in overly structured, tightly fenced organizations.

"Oversimplifying a sales position or describing it in vague generalities and without rationalization of the work scares off horses. They can sense that they are being 'conned,' or they sense a lack of challenge and growth opportunity. Many managers simplify and soften job responsibilities so that they won't frighten off candidates with big or complex workloads—so they believe. On the contrary, self-respecting top-notch horses *want* big and complex responsibilities! Yep," finished Bert, laughing, as if he knew a special secret.

Next, he wrote the third 'P' on the board:

Profile

And he went back to pacing.

"When I hire someone, a mental image of capabilities and attributes comes to my mind. My image is based on my experience, my beliefs and values, observations, and the counsel of other managers. But—I *never* rely on that. That's how other managers get into trouble. We must have a fresh *written* profile. The selection team and I must be able to precisely explain what a top-notch horse looks like, so we'll know one when we see one.

"As a team, we'll figure out, *in detail*, a profile of the two new hires," Bert said. "The previous two 'Ps' are a big help, of course. The written profile is a candidate 'specification.' The 'spec' will probably end up containing a couple dozen points that include everything from the aforementioned fiber to education, amount and variety of experience, prior responsibilities, collateral duties, and computer competencies. I always look forward to the ideas of the other selection team members. Boy, they usually put up some pretty stringent ingredients. I love it! Most profiles are too simple. We won't make that mistake. We will get together as a team and brainstorm the profile. The HR Director has agreed to facilitate that meeting. It's not a *totally* democratic process, because after all, I'm the hiring authority.

"We'll segment our profile into three areas—knowledge, attributes, and skills. Knowledge is what our candidate should already know and understand. For example—knowledge of marketing and sales—knowledge of spreadsheet and presentation software, government procurement procedures, logistics, and today's macro business issues—knowledge of leasing, trade finance, and sales partner management—knowledge of self—and familiarity and opinions on a broad array of national and world events."

"National and world events? Bert—what does that have to do with business?" Mr. Pimm asked skeptically.

"More than you think, Mr. Pimm", Bert answered coolly. "Customers prefer to deal with interesting, multidimensional salespeople—not narrow-minded product-pushers."

Mr. Pimm acquiesced with a slow nod.

"Attributes are the personal qualities and characteristics that the candidate should possess. For example—tactful assertiveness, a seismic sensitivity to situations, a fascination with human behavior, love of proximity to power and decision making, a healthy dose of impatience, infectious enthusiasm, an unquenchable appetite to influence, a riveting charisma, a hungry and resourceful mind, a disdainful attitude toward competition, and a passion for games."

"Games! What?" Mr. Pimm interrupted again, more vigorously this time.

"Yep! Games," Bert said, laughing. "Board games, court games, field games—any competitive contests that demand nimble thinking under pressure and where progress is little by little, where advances are a point or a square at a time. Sales work most often requires clever, little-by-little advances and a tolerance for occasional backward moves, in the same way."

"Okay, good point. Now tell me about skills," Mr. Pimm said, steering Bert back to a subject that he felt was more practical. "What surprises do you have for me here?"

Bert took Mr. Pimm's lead without hesitation. "Skills are the natural or acquired talents that the candidate already possesses, things that they can or should do with proficiency. For example—platform skills, social skills, organization skills, detective skills, writing skills, language skills—and conceptualization skills and synthesizing skills—and being able to strategize on both emotional and analytical levels.

"The profile, which contains all of our brainstormed attributes, will ensure that nothing falls between the cracks. Of course, we'll prioritize the list.

"At the end, we'll test our profile against our existing top salespeople. In this case, Leslie. The action serves as a 'reality' check, to make sure the profile is useful. I'm *not* looking for a 'match'—I'm just trying to make sure nothing critical has been missed. I'll also benchmark the profile against other horses that I've hired and coached in the past.

"In the end, the profile will be a detailed description of the kind of people we want here at Certus.

"By the way, we'll update this profile whenever we decide to look for more horses. There's too much change in business nowadays to get ourselves stuck in a profile-rut."

Ol' Bert went to his bookshelves, grabbed a few books, and then wrote...

Process

"I've put together a detailed series of steps to walk a candidate through. Here, look at this," Bert said, and he handed Mr. Pimm a document from the top of his desk. "This process checklist lets the candidate and me know where he or she stands and what's next. It's a simple one-page matrix that identifies all the proposed steps in our hiring process, the people who will take part, and the timing. It's adjustable, of course, because I'm sure experience will show me that we need to add or drop a step as we move from candidate to candidate. This draft checklist includes résumé reviews, phone screenings, screening interviews, initial interviews, second interviews, facility tours, lunch with some of our staff, an executive interview—which, of course, is you, Mr. Pimm—reference checks, education checks, employment checks, psychological testing, cross-cultural assessments, an employment agreement review, offer-letter mailings, compensation negotiation, and acceptance-letter reception. We'll work on it some more. These are just sample ingredients.

"A written process ensures thoroughness. As you can see, it follows a logical sequence and requests confirmations and sign-offs all along the way. The team will also have an opportunity to tweak this process. A process helps keep *me* consistent. As an experienced manager, I've discovered that *I* need this more than anyone does. Experience and overconfidence can let anyone inadvertently drift.

"I have found that sharing a copy of my process with candidates displays our professionalism and differentiates us from other firms the candidate may be considering. People want to know 'what's next'. The structure sends a good message. The very existence of a checklist provides some insights into our values and work culture."

"The interviews, of course, are a critical part of the process. I really prepare for them. I have a core of questions written down beforehand. A foundation of ready-to-ask questions in black and white sharpens impromptu questions and strengthens the entire interview. I maintain a file of questions that I have built up over the years, questions that I've heard friends use, questions I've learned by going to interview seminars, and questions out of the many good selection books that I've got here, such as *96 Great Interview Questions to Ask*

Before You Hire, Hire The Best…and Avoid The Rest, Interviewing and Selecting High Performers, and *Hire with Your Head*. As I pluck some questions and process ideas out of these books, I bend them to my liking. I also share these core questions and process ideas with others on the selection team. It helps all of us—because if we ask the right questions, the answers matter.

"Selection team, wait a minute," interrupted Mr. Pimm. "You don't expect *me* to interview all the candidates, do you?"

"Of course not. But you *will* be talking to the finalists. HR, other selection team members, Leslie, and I will be doing most of the initial interviewing. We're still ironing out the details.

"Hiring is so important that a manager should never do it alone. I'm sure HR, you, Leslie, and the other team members will see some things that I miss."

"But shouldn't Leslie be out selling?" Mr. Pimm challenged.

"Of course, certainly," Bert answered calmly. "She'll be talking to select candidates after hours, on Saturday morning, during regular hours—or whenever."

"Saturday? Whenever?" Mr. Pimm questioned in disbelief. "Never happen!"

"Certainly it will," Bert said with a laugh. "Top-notch people are sensitive to their current responsibilities. We let them know we're flexible. They respect that. It's their choice. Leslie will be seeing pre-screened people, so we won't be wasting her time.

"Plus, you should *always* give your *best* people a lead role. Horses tend to identify with, and latch onto, each other. Your best people will recommend candidates who mirror their own image. Top horses don't want to dilute the herd they run with. 'Best' fosters more of the 'best.'

Continuing, Bert said, "One final comment on interviewing. A favorite technique of mine is to use two or three mini-cases—little vignettes—and ask candidates how they would handle those situations. The answers provide wonderful insight into analysis and actions. You get to see how the candidate is likely to perform—and it displays their values and priorities. My mini-cases are built around major elements of the job—*real* historical and current situations. They vary in their degree of difficulty, and they differ in their settings. As you might guess, responses vary from remarkable to middling to humorous to downright sad. I have a repertoire of eighteen favorite cases. I'll share them with the team.

"I've also created some log sheets for all of us to use to record observations and impressions during the interviews. We can't afford to rely on memories alone when it comes time to recall interview responses and finalize our picks.

Back at the whiteboard, Ol' Bert wrote:

Poking around

"There are several secrets here in regard to the fifth 'P,'" he said.

"What do you mean, poking? We're not hogs poking for acorns," Mr. Pimm joshed.

"No, but that's where I got the idea. Back on the farm. Nothing more persistent than a hungry hog," answered Bert.

"Here are the secrets. The first secret is for the manager to be personally involved, not delegating the search. Sure, others will help. It's a team effort, but the sales manager—*me*—has got to stay out front, poking around. I've got to be into the search up to my elbows—*leading*.

"The next secret is to be *constantly* on the offensive and nosey, and not sit back and wait for an ad, an agency, a Web site, or HR to deliver candidates to you. Complacency is a killer. You have to nose around in unusual places with unlikely people to find uncommon talent. Look where no one else looks. The trick is to turn a hundred rocks as opposed to ten, to dig deeper and scan farther afield. Everyone knows all the obvious sources of salespeople, such as traditional networking, contingency and retained executive search firms, the eCruiting jungle, and print ads. So you've got to be a better 'poker.'

"For example, once I asked a checkout cashier at my local supermarket if she, or anyone she knew, would be interested in a sales position. It just so happened that her sister-in-law was looking for a new opportunity, and she turned out to be a superstar. Another time, I was at a Chamber of Commerce picnic, and one of the volunteers at a game booth impressed me. He turned out to be a President's Club winner. And once I even called up someone whose picture had been in the business section of the local paper. Wow! She was great.

"Another time, I found a guy as a result of personally visiting a local outplacement firm. And once, I approached a retiring triple-A baseball player whom I had seen interviewed on TV. Another time it was someone who caught my eye in church. And another time I discovered some top talent when I was a guest speaker in an evening class at a local community college. I can go on and on.

"*Outrageous* sources. 'Poking around' is approaching unlikely people you *don't* know, as opposed to traditional networking. That's the secret. It just takes a little nerve to ask and not to make any assumptions about anyone. Being friendly and inquisitive helps. There was *never* a time where the person I approached wasn't pleased that I had inquired. It's perceived as a sign of respect—as a sign that the person made a positive impression on you.

"What you have to do as the hiring manager is constantly put yourself in 'target-rich' environments, places where there are people interacting with people, so you can observe 'people skills.'

"A subtle element of this constant offensive poking, Mr. Pimm, is that it uncovers *passive* horses—people who aren't actively looking—and *semi-passive* horses—people who are a little twitchy about their current situation but doing nothing. Combined, they form the *biggest* part of the total pool of horses. This constant poking also results in referrals and expands your pool of traditional network contacts.

"The next secret is to work closely with Human Resources. Many, but *not all*, HR people are naturally great 'pokers.' Fortunately we have a great one here. Sometimes you've got to prod HR a little because they have other business functions to worry about. But the squeaky wheel gets the oil. Of course, they are always more responsive if you come with the first four P's already executed. Speaking of HR, I'm also in the habit of contacting HR departments at companies I hear are downsizing and offering 'packages' in the process. There are *always* some horses that take the package and search for greener pastures.

"The final secret is to be a *patient poker*. It's the hardest secret to execute. I do it by comparing a candidate to my best people. If I can't honestly say that a candidate appears better or equal to what I've got, I 'pass.' It makes no sense to hire people who are less than your best, or don't have the clear potential to reach that level and carry the load. That only drags the sales unit's average capability lower. For example—assuming that I already have a '9' on board, the average of that '9' + a new '10' becomes '9.5.' Or, the average of that '9' plus another '9' would still be '9.' Or, the average of that '9' plus a new '8' would drop the average to '8.5.' What would *you* do? Doesn't it make sense to go after the '10'? I want my average capability to *constantly climb!* Plus, we can afford to hire two '10s.'

"I've found that my ability to recognize ability has gotten better because I've disciplined myself through the years to talk to a lot of people. I'm always poking at people to find people. In order to be outrageously successful, Mr. Pimm, you *must be* an outrageous poker.

"We're halfway through the 'P's.' You okay?" Bert queried.

"Oh yes—yes—of course. I really like the precision, the structure, and the creativity—*and* the teamwork," Mr. Pimm quickly added. "But this seems so sophisticated for such a small firm. I don't know. Is it too much?"

Bert was quick to say, "I always worry it's too little, considering what's at stake. I see sophistication as an imperative, as unrelated to size. A seed is also a *very* sophisticated and complete package—but it's the same seed whether on a five-thousand-acre farm or a five-acre farm. True?"

They both looked at each other for a minute—then Mr. Pimm slowly nodded. Bert then wrote the sixth "P" on the whiteboard:

Persuade

"Number six. Think for a minute. Why would *anyone*, especially a horse, want to join a tiny firm that they hadn't heard of? *And*, why would someone want to join a struggling outfit like Certus that is ready to go out of business? These are *tough* questions. We've got to be able to address these questions confidently, regardless of whether top candidates ask them. Believe me, even if they don't ask, they're certainly thinking about them. It's a free-agent world we live in.

"We've got to *sell* Certus, Mr. Pimm, and when I say sell Certus I mean its people, culture, commitment, environment, technologies—everything about the company. We have to persuade horses that this is a great place to work—that we're a winner. Remember, we're competing with many household-name, deep-pocketed outfits. It's not easy.

"What we have to figure-out is what the top-notch horses are looking for. We must dig to understand their true motives, or hot buttons. Sometimes they're forthright—sometimes they're not. I think I know the answer to what they want, but it's shifting sand, because values in our society are always moving, and everyone is different. Then we must show them that we have what they need and want.

"Top-notch sales professionals of all ranks want to see, feel, and believe that what is important to them can be found at Certus. Mr. Pimm, what top-notch people look for, and the degree to which they must see it, *is not the same* as what lesser types look for and need. Horses are looking for such things as a participative work culture, a champion's attitude, innovative processes, courageous leadership, the availability and usage of leading-edge technology, and robust compensation, including equity or major incentives. *And* they're searching for eye-popping products, first-class recognition programs, the freedom to invent and implement, a commitment to personal development, and the ability to make a real contribution. *And* they're scanning for intellectual challenge, the operational excellence of the rest of the company, responsibility and accountability, refreshing adventure, and being a part of something bigger than them—something grand!

"We must show them that there's a *gap* between what they're currently experiencing—what someone else may be offering—and what we can deliver. The bigger the gap, the more likely we'll corral the horse.

"Of course, what they're looking for varies from one top-notch prospect to the next. I can remember once talking to a real winner, and I finally wheedled out of him that he was really concerned about inventive marketing support and our level of marketing sophistication. Once I could show him that, we had a deal.

"And we have to figure out what top candidates are looking for from the *very beginning* of the interviewing process. Top horses aren't patient. We must *facilitate their discovery* of who and what we are—we can't hope that they'll discover all this on their own. That's the secret!

"I must—*we must*—put ourselves in the horse's shoes. I know what I would look for, or what would attract me to discuss another opportunity. Back at my retirement home, you *connected* with me emotionally, whether you knew it or not. After all, I was pretty comfortable there with my sisters. You know, one of the hot buttons was *you* personally. Your sincerity and personal commitment to your business really shone through—it touched me deeply. I am going to ask you to share that with final candidates."

Mr. Pimm looked pleased. He smiled at Bert.

"The interviewing team must be *consistent* in describing the values, attributes, and deliverables of Certus to top-notch people. Horses keep their eyes and ears open to inconsistencies—which translate as smoke and mirrors.

"Just as we want to differentiate our products to customers, *together* we must differentiate our company to top horses. Our story must be uniformly compelling. To help make it compelling, let's look at our assets, and I mean *real* assets, not romantic visions and fluff. What have we got here? Of course we have a famous brand name in Certus. My reputation will be a draw, as well as the continuity of the Pimm family leadership, a chance to be a part of a turnaround, the compensation package, our industry-leading production technology, our research relationships with two leading universities, our prize-winning engineer in R&D, and the micro-business sales philosophy I'm implementing. Fully developing this asset list will be one of the tasks of our selection team. It will be fun, because we'll all come out of it feeling better about what we are a part of. What's good is that the list will also have value for all the other departments here at Certus." Laughing, Bert said, "It's amazing how many companies don't go to the trouble of formalizing and articulating their assets in detail.

"But we must be careful while we're persuading. We can't oversell. Our persuading is more a case of fully discussing who and what we are and the value to be gained by being a part of this organization. Top-notch people can tell the difference between enthusiastic persuading and hard selling. If there's too much hard selling, they begin to smell a rat, and they're gone. Yes, everyone likes to be courted, but it can be overdone. Speaking of 'courting,' we've got to communicate our sincere interest in the horses and *project* our vision of *their* contribution, *their* future, and *their* outrageous success. People go where they are made to feel special, wanted, and can envision their success—and they *stay* if those feelings and visions persist.

"We have to inquire about *them*, and *their* credentials, and *their* achievements, and *their* desires—not just talk about us. This 'P,' persuade, isn't just about us. Our empathy must demonstrate that we truly understand *their* lives. I believe people make these kinds of decisions based on their emotions and rationalize them logically afterwards.

"Now, we'll probably lose a few top prospects, Mr. Pimm. I want to warn you so you're not disappointed. We can't corral every horse, but we can improve our chances, and that's what this 'P' is all about—stacking the odds in our favor."

Ol' Bert refilled Mr. Pimm's coffee cup, then wrote:

Precautions

"You okay? I'm ready to describe the seventh P. It's dark reality."

"I'm fine, fine. This sounds like I better hold on to my wallet," Mr. Pimm said, and he sighed.

"You've got the idea. We need to be careful in our interviewing and in making our decisions because we can get a bite in the butt that would take a long time to heal if we're not alert," Bert said as he grimaced.

"What should we be careful about?" Mr. Pimm asked.

"There are innumerable precautions. Here, follow me through this list." Bert handed Mr. Pimm some papers with his precautions listed.

"First. Never, never, never yield to hiring people who don't meet the profile. Compromise is incompatible with outrageous success.

"Next, a manager shouldn't take a cookie-cutter approach. It can be dangerous. Mix up the team's composition. A varied sales team fuels a variety of ideas, strategies, and styles and can provide a competitive advantage, as I mentioned with the first 'P.' Plus, searching for look-alikes can cause you to inadvertently pass over some really promising horses. A wide field of vision, not tunnel vision, is key. A manager who wears 'blinkers' often hires also-rans, not winners.

"Next, the 'bar' that a manager expects candidates to clear is often the measure of a manager's self-image of his or her own skill and capability. Many managers use themselves as the 'bar,' and while they may have been good at selling, it may prevent them from hiring even better people. A bad, bad mistake. I want people who are better than I—*as I am today*."

"Better than you? C'mon, really?" Mr. Pimm challenged.

"Of course. Why not? They're out there. How do you think I got to be as good as I am? I surrounded myself with people who were better than I am. I'm not interested in *protecting* my self-esteem, I'm interested in *growing* it," Bert chuckled matter-of-factly. "Think for a minute. Implicit in the act of not hiring people *better* than you is hiring people *worse* than you, and that feeds the Law of Diminishing Performance. Bad! I'm intent on feeding the Law of *Escalating Performance*."

"Doggone-it! You're right, Bert," Mr. Pimm acclaimed.

"Then next, let's recognize that hiring takes time. That's another reason why launching the hiring process for two horses is the first of the ten essentials I'm implementing. The horses will come.

"Next, we need to be cautious of first impressions, even though research has demonstrated that first impressions are valid. Interviewees are smart and better prepared these days. They have received coaching and read books. Sales and sales management applicants are particularly expert at making good first impressions because it's built into the profession. It's one of the reasons you should always have several interviews with candidates.

"Let me tell you—the impressions of horses 'hold.' The facades of also-rans finally fall.

"And speaking of impressions—matters regarding fiber leave their greasy fingerprints on everyone. The 'prints' of unsavory characters are seen in the uncomfortable twinges that we get in our gut as we talk to a candidate. You've *got* to listen to your gut. Sometimes you just get 'a feeling' that something isn't right. Call it chemistry, call it smelling something rotten,' call it a red flag, or whatever. *Listen* to those signals. They are always right."

"The next precaution has to do with the horses out there who have been fired or downsized out of previous employers. If—*if*—they are horses, it's often because they chafed under tyrannical managers or systems. Or they were transformers stuck in stagnant environments. Or they were dynamos stuck in a vacillating or political culture. Or they made the mistake of joining up with a shabby outfit. They didn't 'fit.' They are sometimes the very best. Maybe someone along the line did not know how to lead and manage them. It happened to me."

"What? You mean it?" Mr. Pimm asked. He was stunned.

31

"Sure. You show me a horse who's never been fired or nudged out, and I'll show you a horse who compromised his or her values—or didn't run to his or her potential—or opted for self-preservation in a warm stable—or prefers to run at a bush-league track," said Bert.

"So the precaution for us is not to assume that just because someone got fired in the past means they're not for us. However—there are many who deserved to be fired or pushed out because they had performance or attitude problems. They can be culled out easily. The tales of woe they spin about previous jobs, their mediocre results, their wishy-washy dispositions, and unconvincing presentations make them easy to spot.

"Next point. We need to watch the number and depth of a candidate's questions. To me, a lack of either is a signal that someone can't be open, is afraid to show her hand, hasn't prepared for the interview, lacks curiosity, or she simply doesn't have the intellectual oil for the job. I look for someone to push and challenge me during the interview. Voltaire once said, *Judge a man or woman by his or her questions rather than by his or her answers.* I believe it.

"Then, we need to watch for those who agree with everything we say. To me that implies a lack of personal conviction or fear that they'll lose the opportunity. I always love to throw a ridiculous comment or in-house jargon at someone like that to see if they continue to numbly smile back.

"We need to be careful of those who speak in generalities and use highfalutin academic words as if that will impress us—or they dodge and dance—or they won't answer questions with facts and figures—or they aren't expansive. Those are all bad signals.

"I'm cautious of people who can't tell stories, paint verbal pictures, or use anecdotes or humor in discussing their past. Those traits are requisites in good communicators.

"Next. The candidate's level of listening is a signal. Is he or she talking, talking, talking—selling, selling, selling—trying mightily to impress me? Our customers and sales partners don't value glib slicksters. Rather, I watch for those who are intently absorbing and chewing on my questions, *balancing* the delivery of their vignettes with respectful attention."

Mr. Pimm interrupted, saying, "You know I agree with you, Bert. These points are all familiar, but to see them all together—it emphasizes what you're saying about precautions. Your next couple of points I see written here hit personal raw nerves," and Mr. Pimm read from his list. "'When candidates talk solely about themselves, with no reference to resources, colleagues, or superiors in relation to their accomplishments, you worry. We don't need macho Lone Rangers here. I need—*we need*—team players.' My gosh, that is certainly important to me as president of this company. Hmmph!

"And next, here, where you noted a simple thing like posture telling you a lot. How it communicates respect and interest. You're right on.

"And then this one, another simple thing, their personal image and presentation say a lot. If they don't make a professional impression on us, they are certainly not going to change for our customers. You know, Bert, in the end it's always the simple things, the details, isn't it?" remarked Mr. Pimm, more to himself than to Ol' Bert.

Bert paused and was pleased that Mr. Pimm was really getting into the subject. He concluded by saying, "Finally, Mr. Pimm, I'm always antsy about people who don't volunteer tidbits about family, faith, community, or country. To me, that's also fiber. I don't ask questions about those things, but I share *my* values in bits and pieces during the course of the interview. That sometimes generates sharing in return. But you know—and this is uncanny—I've found that horses share those things on their own, even before I do. They do that because they're concerned about their 'fit,' and they want you to know who they are and what they stand for. They're not in line for 'a job.' The stronger the fiber, the stronger the fabric, the stronger the finished goods—and then the stronger the company.

"The selection team will edit this precaution list. I'm sure they'll be able to add to it."

"Bert, you make a great point with these precautions," said Mr. Pimm. "We can't afford *any* mistakes."

Bert wrote the next 'P' on the board:

Pick

"Decision time, Mr. Pimm. At this point, we'll get the selection team together again. Armed with thorough preparation, a detailed position description, a solid profile, a scrupulous process, a lot of poking around, well-crafted persuasion, and mindful of the precautions, the picking should become almost self-evident. But—*not always!* The best part of this step is listening to everyone's comments about the finalists. The observations and notes that come out of the give-and-take can be rich with new insights. I absolutely love this step.

"Yet, sometimes—often, in fact—the decision is obvious. But it's still imperative to get the team together and recount everyone's impressions.

"HR has agreed to facilitate this discussion. I'm not sure yet whether we'll use a qualitative model or a quantitative model."

"What do you mean?" Mr. Pimm asked nervously. "It sounds like you're making it overly complex. We either like a candidate, or we don't. Right? We don't have much time."

Reaching for the pitcher of ice water he always kept on his desk, Bert, who acted as if he had ice water in his veins, said, "Not quite. The gut plays a role, but it's a more complex analysis. You're a football fan, aren't you? Do you realize the data, film, interview notes, analyses, and stack rankings that the pro teams go through prior to draft day? They have millions of dollars at stake—just like you do, Mr. Pimm. Why should the picking for Certus's key players be any less precise? Yet, so many companies do just that. It always amazes me."

Ol' Bert's logic and composure calmed Mr. Pimm.

"We'll have the selection team grade every finalist. We could do that qualitatively, assigning a rating of 'excellent,' 'good,' 'fair,' or 'poor' to each profile criterion, which, of course, are prioritized. We could also do it quantitatively by assigning a top score of five down to a low score of one. A total will give us a 'score' for each candidate. It lends some rationality to a decision. It's not a decision-making tool on its own, but it's a great input.

"An important part of this analysis is not just to help us pick a candidate, but also to help us understand *why* we feel good or bad about a candidate. We'll look at the data, everyone's interview log sheets, and listen to the selection team's observations and evaluations. We'll give ourselves time. We'll factor in the chemistry and the 'gut level' feelings that are so important to hiring decisions. We'll balance our analytical thinking with subjective 'fit.' And then once I hear everyone out, I'll make the decision."

Bert then wrinkled his forehead and stared off into the distance, reflecting. "You know, in my experience," he said, "all of the top horses I ever picked turned out to be what many today would call prima donnas—prima donnas that run together—like the teams that pulled the chariots in those old epic movies, like *The Gladiators*, or *Ben Hur*. Did you ever see teams of horses that looked so haughty, self-assured, and invincible, Mr. Pimm?"

Mr. Pimm squinted, thought, and slowly said, "No, as a matter of fact, never."

"Additionally, I hire *people* before I hire *sales*people," emphasized Bert. "Give me a rock-solid citizen with the core values and profile in place, and I can teach and coach a triple-crown winner. I'll be looking for solid people during this effort," finished Bert.

"Speaking of people," Mr. Pimm asked. "Do you ever hire anyone without experience?"

"Of course, but *not* in our current circumstance. Let me give you an example that applies to other circumstances. Remember when we talked about 'profile,' I said that questioning skills were critical to sales? I've found that folks who come from backgrounds that required a lot of diagnostic interrogation, a search for evidence, exploration of symptoms, or probing for information, can adapt to sales questioning skills quickly and easily. I can take *every other* profile ingredient I gave you and come up with commensurate background skills to look for in inexperienced folks. It's the skills, knowledge, and attributes that are critical. We may look for some 'yearlings' when this crisis is over."

"Interesting. You've got this down to a science," said Mr. Pimm.

"Yep! I sure do," Bert said, back at full speed. "In conclusion, we'll document the discussion and use the comments to go back and 'tweak' our profiles and processes for the second position to be filled."

"I'm with you Bert. What's next? My confidence is climbing. It's refreshing to listen to someone who believes strongly in something. I wish more people had such deep convictions. Please continue," Mr. Pimm urged.

So Bert wrote on the board again, laughing peacefully.

Priming

"This is so simple, but again, many managers miss it," he explained. "The first few weeks or months the new employee is with the firm should be a *rigorous* boot camp. An intense and formal indoctrination into our products, services, technologies, markets, policies, practices, and processes. There won't be any pampering. I guarantee it. I never delegate this activity. Sure, others help, but the new people need to see their manager leading from the get-go. They need to see me—out front—doing it better—setting the example—practicing what I preach.

"Before cutting anyone loose, we've got to get them primed. When I cut these two new horses loose for the first time, believe me, they'll be primed to run at full speed."

Laughing again, Bert said, "I love to watch the expression on customers' and sales partners' faces when they see that the new rep is far and away beyond their expectations. You know, Mr. Pimm, customers expect new salespeople to have 'fumbleitis' and to be just about worthless. Well—not mine.

"I like to give them all sorts of tests. If the scores aren't satisfactory, it's back to the books and hands-on practice and role plays until they get it right. I let candidates know about our 'priming program' early in the interview process. Of course, they all say they can handle it, but none of them have any idea how intense it will be. But you know, everyone who has left me for one reason or another through the years has thanked me for the rigor of our initial priming programs. They hate it when they're in it, but they love it afterwards, especially when the commission checks start to come.

"The new horses come out of the gate only once—one chance to position themselves for a long, tough race. I aim to improve their chances. I want to make the best better. That's the bottom line."

Then he wrote:

Plan

"And here's the tenth 'P,'" Bert said, then sat down. "All these things I've told you about are spelled out here in the hiring section of my organization plan." With that, Ol' Bert turned his massive computer monitor toward Mr. Pimm to show him that he had all this written down. He scrolled through the previous nine 'Ps'—preparation, position description, profile, process, poking around, persuade, precautions, pick, and priming.

"This is too much stuff to keep in your head. It must be documented. All the things I spoke about regarding the other 'P's are in my plan.

"I must do everything possible to make horses want to join and stay with Certus. This document ensures my comprehensiveness. I look at it *every day* to remind me where I am and what I need to do next. I love to tinker with it. It inspires me. Team building is fun. Even with a full staff, just looking at it causes me to question and challenge the status—the organizational health—of my team, and then to take an action step to do something about it. A manager's hiring plan is also the basis for his retention plan, and that's my super-shrewd eleventh 'P,' Mr. Pimm," and he wrote:

Prevent

"Prevent horses from walking out of the barn. I treat my horses as if I am *always* in the process of hiring them. No matter how long they've been with me, I am hiring them *over and over* again. It's an attitude. You with me?"

"Son of a gun, Bert. That's a marvelous philosophy," said Mr. Pimm, clearly pleased and comfortable. "I'm impressed with the finesse of your Twelve-P-system. After listening to all this, I can see there's a lot more to you than meets the eye."

Chuckling, Bert acknowledged, "One of my life-guiding pearls of wisdom comes from writer John Morley, who once said, *Simplicity of character is no hindrance to subtlety of intellect.*"

They both laughed.

"Preventing involves explicit managerial effort as well as attitude. It's constantly looking your people in the eye—sniffing and listening for changes in tone, views, and vocabulary—watching behaviors—and being alert to shifting motivations. And then doing something about it—*quickly reacting*—if you see, hear, or smell something funny.

"I'm sure you've watched the Kentucky Derby, the Preakness, or the Belmont on TV. Picture the care, the gentleness, and the respect bestowed on the winner by the trainer, jockey, owner, and hangers-on. *That's* how I treat my people. I expect every effort they can possibly give, like Affirmed did in seventy-eight, but I treat them with great respect in return."

He then pointed out a framed picture of the last Triple Crown winner, autographed by jockey Steve Cauthen, with his twelve 'P's neatly printed on the picture's mat.

"Very nice. But just a minute. Where's that twelfth 'P'?" Mr. Pimm questioned alertly.

"Ah—thanks for reminding me."

Pruning

"Fortunately, the twelfth 'P' is not needed right now.

"When there's a nonrepairable mismatch between the employee and the job, a manager must move *quickly* to put that individual in a more appropriate spot, suggest they find other employment—or terminate them. People and company situations are *always* changing—which is how mismatches develop. Managers must be vigilant—and brutally honest—about staff. Even 'horses' can become nonrepairably mismatched—and be given a different job or led *out* of the barn and cut loose. Pruning is imperative for both individual and corporate health. Pruning should *always* be in the plan.

"We're under way, Mr. Pimm. It's happening. I mean to help you turn this company around. My reputation is built on the team I put together, and I mean to enhance my reputation.

"One manager is as good as another until he has made his first hire—then the separation begins. Goodness sakes, this is probably the last shot I'll get at doing this, so I aim to do it better than ever."

"Amen," said Mr. Pimm.

Bert concluded by saying earnestly, "Certain horses require sweet-talking, others require admonishment, and some, the whip. I want the exceptional few that must be restrained.

"I have a goal to have both of our new 'horses' in the barn and primed within six weeks. Not having a goal is a common hiring mistake. Maybe you don't always hit the goal, but you *must* have one, and you must hold yourself accountable to it. I think the goal I've established is realistic, given our circumstances and resources.

"Speaking of goals, I have a meeting with Leslie tomorrow morning at seven-thirty to discuss our goals and expectations—what I call our 'stakes in the ground.' We'll pound them in. 'Pounding the stakes' means commitment, and commitment is now a part of our culture, Mr. Pimm.

"You'll be hearing about our 'stakes' very soon.

"Thanks for coming down to my Wisdom Pantry to hear about my 'Twelve-P' system. Why don't you call it a night? I have a couple of things to wrap up here."

When Ol' Bert was finished, Mr. Pimm just sat there in silence, chin resting on his hands, staring at Ol' Bert—then staring at the whiteboard—then staring at the computer screen—then staring at Ol' Bert again. He had soaked it all in. It was so logical. It was professional and thorough. All he could say was, "Hmmph," and nod approvingly. He got up slowly and walked out, still nodding, feeling more confident that his decision to bring Ol' Bert on board had turned out to be a wise one.

Essential #2
Pound Some Stakes Into The Ground

*The old master liked to have discussions in his office where both he and his
people could be comfortable. He knew it took time, but he always worked hard
to create a warm and welcoming atmosphere—business-like but inviting—where
people would feel at ease and above-board, not anxious and guarded. Ol' Bert
knew that was a simple secret for creating an environment conducive to success.
His door was never shut—and his coffeepot was always percolating some
gourmet blend. This morning it was French Vanilla.*

*He had prepared some materials to share with Leslie, having learned a
long time ago that a ready-made handout went a long way towards establishing
the importance of matters to be discussed. Otherwise, people treated exchanges
casually and then had no ready reminder of important points. He handed Leslie
a couple of pages, and an accompanying disc.*

"Leslie, it's time to pound some stakes into the ground, stakes for you and
me to reach for," Bert announced with a bouncy smile. "And we also need to
pound some stakes to keep us 'in-bounds'. Stakes are easy-to-identify markers
of both destinations and boundaries. In other words, it's time to talk about goals
and expectations, the second essential for outrageous success."

"We'll pound all the stakes very carefully because the smallest right
decisions now lead to the largest payoffs over time."

"Okay, Bert. I'm ready to go," Leslie responded in high spirits. She was
aware that Ol' Bert had already started to look for two new 'horses', was
pleased to be included in that process, and was looking forward to what came
next. This was becoming a solid working relationship.

Handing her the document and the disc, Bert said, "I call this 'A Guide to
Stake-Pounding'. I have found this guide to be very helpful. One of my old
managers gave it to me a long time ago, and I've tinkered with it through the
years. Some day in the future you can share the guide with people who work for
you.

"Let's read and discuss the guide together, okay? Let's start with Part 1—
The Basics—eight simple reasons to manage our efforts according to stakes,"

Bert began. "But watch yourself here because the apparent simplicity of this guide can dull your alertness.

"First point. All professionals, you and I included, are purposeful by nature. We live and work to reach our stakes. You or I can pound stakes on our own or on a suggestion from others, like from Mr. Pimm. Without stakes— professional or personal—we just wander aimlessly. Right?"

"Sure sounds logical," Leslie said matter-of-factly.

"Next point. Stake-pounding is so basic that it is a necessary condition for my leadership and management—and for your account and sales partner management—to occur at all. If there are no stakes there's nothing to manage or work towards," Bert went on.

"Sounds straightforward to me," said Leslie, nodding.

"Third point. Your performance, my performance, and Certus's performance improves when we all have stakes and we all know what they are. The very existence of stakes sparks better results. Stakes puuush—and prrrod— and strrretch us," Bert dramatized.

"Yes, yes—I can see that," said Leslie, starting to get into the flow of the exercise.

"Next. The pursuit of worthwhile stakes is more likely to lead to purposeful activities and high integrity behavior. Conversely, the lack of stakes leads to free-spirited management and shotgun selling that can lead to trouble. Believe me. I've done that," said Bert, sheepishly.

"Yes, I can relate to that also," Leslie, said, eyebrows raised and teeth clenched, now beginning to feel personally touched.

"Number five. Both you and I can get so wrapped-up in daily activities we can lose sight of the reason for the activities. If we get caught in activity traps we don't grow as professionals. Stakes keep us growing, helping us realize our professional and personal potential," Bert said looking her straight in the eye.

"You know, I think I've been in many of those activity traps," said Leslie, glancing aside, remembering something from the past. "And I'm *certainly* interested in growing."

"Now here's a *real* key point. Both you and I can get so wrapped-up in urgent things we can lose sight of the important things. Stakes keep us focused on what's important," said Bert, dragging out the word important.

"You're right, Bert, but the word important has always puzzled me. How do we know, or I know, what's important?" Leslie asked. "And is what I think important—*really* important?"

Bert nodded, smiling, "Yep—it puzzles many people. Important things are significant or consequential, things that *strongly* affect the course of events— like the ten essentials for success I have been telling you about. The ten essentials are consistent with The Law of The Farm, a natural law that governs work. And since I come from the farm I can't think of a better example. I got the idea from a Steven Covey book, *First Things First*. The Law is about an approach to life and work based on timeless truths. It's about *natural* priorities and focusing on them at the right times. Can you imagine not plowing, planting, watering, cultivating, and harvesting at the right times? Of course not! Those are *natural* priorities. There are absolutely no options with those activities—no 'ifs', 'ands', or 'buts'. Those activities are *important!* The stakes we will pound must be consistent with The Law of the Farm.

"Okay, I think I can understand that," Leslie smiled. "But remember, I'm a city gal from Hartford. The closest I ever came to a farm was my dad's backyard flower patch and trips to the supermarket."

Bert laughed. "Of course, of course! Then let's also call it The Law of The Garden. Same activities—different words. Scratching. Seeding. Sprinkling. Weeding. Tidying. Picking. How's that?" he teased.

"Thanks, Bert," Leslie smiled, shaking her head at his mischievousness.

He went on, saying, "The decision-making process associated with crafting stakes, the oversight of management, working with colleagues, constant exposure to learning, and your personal experience all help separate what is important from what is not. I also think of scrutinizing what's important like my momma scrutinized the flour she sifted to make pies. Occasionally she picked out and discarded something she didn't like. We'll sift and pick the same way, leaving in what's important."

"Okay, I can visualize that as well. My mom's a pastry chef," Leslie offered.

"Seventh point. We need standards against which to measure ourselves. The buzzword nowadays is 'metrics'. You, Certus, and I will succeed only if we know what to measure. How do you know if you ever arrive at your destination if you never knew where you were going in the first place? Hmmm?" Bert asked.

"Of course! That seems like common sense," Leslie agreed.

"Yep—common sense," Bert wistfully added, shaking his head. "There is a big dose of common sense in pounding stakes, but common sense is sometimes in short supply. Never forget Harriet Beecher Stowe's view that *common sense is the knack of seeing things as they are, and doing things as they ought to be done.*

"She's one of my favorite authors, Bert, because of the clarity of her writing. I'll follow her lead," Leslie volunteered.

"Good for you," Bert smiled.

"Eighth and final point. Failure for either or both of us can consist of failing to reach our stakes. But not having stakes is far worse—it can contribute to the death of a business. And that's what we're trying to avoid here at Certus.

"Whoa! That's an attention-getter," Leslie added. "I'm sold."

Bert finished by saying, "As someone interested in theater you'd appreciate this quote from Anna Pavlova, the famous Russian ballerina, who once said—*to tend, unfailingly, unflinchingly, towards a goal, is the secret of success*. And of course, I like to add, a secret of *outrageous* success."

The two of them then bantered around some questions and opinions prior to proceeding. The old man was good at executing interim 'checks' to ensure understanding.

"Now let's look at Part 2, Suggestions on Stake-Crafting," Bert went on. "I know you're familiar with some of these points, but the review will do us both some good. I personally go through these points prior to every stake-pounding session. It keeps me alert and on-track—and causes me to think.

"First, a stake should be a specific statement of a destination. It is acceptable to state that a stake will be '$1,000,000 in sales' but not to state that 'We will improve sales'. A stake should also have some kind of time element as a part of it. It is necessary to say that 'our stake of $1,000,000 will be achieved in three months'."

"Yes, I'm familiar with those points Bert," Leslie nodded.

"Good. Stakes should also be explicit. Our stakes should be so definitive that, later on, when Mr. Pimm, you, I, and others try to agree on whether or not the stake was actually reached, we can find easy agreement," said Bert.

"Ummm, yes, I can see they must be clear. I can remember some humdinger arguments we had around here in the past about whether someone did what they said they were going to do," Leslie agreed.

"Stakes should be of ascending difficulty. Let's first define those stakes that deal with ordinary things. Then we'll turn to major problems that need solving," Bert stated.

"I can understand that," Leslie added. "If we started with major problems, we might not have the time or resources to get around to many other goals—err—stakes. Whew, that could be a killer."

"Stakes shouldn't stress the obvious, but rather should be characterized by innovation and exceptional improvement. Stakes that are merely routine won't excite anybody, certainly not me. Those stakes that are merely a repeat of the past or an incremental improvement won't do much for the company, you, or me. Incrementalism can trap us in mediocrity," Bert stated.

"I know what you mean, Bert. You tend not to pay attention to stakes if they are blasé or uninspiring. I think that's one of the problems we have had here," Leslie admitted.

"Leslie, there are three categories of stakes to think about—close-in stakes, farther-out stakes, and over-the-horizon stakes. The close-in stakes, for the immediate three months ahead—or for shorter periods—are roll-up-the-sleeves, get-the-business, bull-work destinations.

"Farther-out stakes, from three to six months, are usually prepare-the-ground type activities. Those are market development, pre-positioning, and lining-up-the-targets type of stakes.

"Over-the-horizon stakes, beyond six months, are surveying and scoping-out kinds of stakes, more research and planning than doing," said Bert. "A lot of sniffing around."

"Ummm, okay, that makes sense. I think I'm with you," Leslie said, feeling ever more comfortable.

"By the way, the time frames I just spoke of only make sense for *our* business and *our* current circumstances Leslie. Don't get hung-up on my three-month, six-month example. When I was in the airplane business each of those timeframes was much longer, as you can imagine.

Bert went on, saying, "When we pound stakes in the face of uncertainty with incomplete information, we'll define the stakes within ranges of outcomes. The ranges should be tight, not so broad that they are meaningless."

"I didn't know we could do that," said Leslie feeling lightened. "I thought everything had to be a hard number."

"No. Ranges are acceptable, providing you or I don't overdo it and use ranges as an 'out' or escape hatch. Ranges should be used on an exception basis," Bert cautioned with a wink.

"Next. We'll examine history and the markets before pounding stakes. The best kind of stake is one that starts with a thorough look at the results from past weeks, months, and years, and the current situation. We're putting ourselves 'on-the-line'—we're risking and hazarding ourselves just as gamblers play for 'high stakes'. But our due diligence will reduce our risk."

"Ohhhhh, you've hit a sore spot," Leslie winced. "I always felt that our targets in the past were assigned on a whim. We never knew the rationale. The targets just flew in like birds on the wing."

"Don't worry about that anymore," Bert consoled. "The only flying that'll be going on here will be us and our high-flying results!"

"Next point. Many stakes are hard to attain. That's okay. Every set of stakes, even when crafted and pounded by experienced stake-pounders like me, includes some stakes that may not be achieved due to unforeseen, complex, or road-blocking circumstances. We have to face unpleasant reality from time to time," Bert said. "Not unlike droughts or floods faced by farmers and gardeners."

"I'm glad to hear you acknowledge that. Lack of that recognition can deflate a salesperson and crush her motivation," Leslie admitted.

"Every stake we accept means we have rejected some other stake. We must have a reason why we chose one stake over another, and we must be able to explain why," said Bert.

"Ah, I never thought of that, but you're absolutely right," Leslie agreed.

"An error in setting or choosing stakes will produce an error in activity. The effects of choosing the wrong stake or stating it improperly will produce a chain reaction. Bad stakes produce bad activity—good stakes produce good activity. Makes sense, doesn't it?" Bert asked.

"Makes huge sense to me, Bert. That's crystal clear," said Leslie. "But you know I never heard it before. I'm getting your point now on the value of reviewing this guideline."

"If any of our stakes are conditional, we must state the conditions. We might be able to set some stakes as conditional upon certain events, such as the launch dates for new products—or the completion of a customer's new facility—or a certain sales partner winning a government contract. But conditions shouldn't be stated to lay the groundwork for excuses or blame—only to reflect reality.

"We must also be prepared to move our stakes to keep them realistic. But movements should be triggered by exceptional, not ordinary, changes in the environment. Bumps and thumps happen out in the market and here at Certus all the time. We'll wait for a minor earthquake to move stakes," Bert solemnly said.

That sounded awfully firm to Leslie. There clearly wasn't going to be any playing around here with these stakes, she thought to herself.

"Any legitimate customer or colleague demand must become a stake for the team. The demand for some product, service, or assistance should be firmly fixed as a stake. Stake pounding is a real-time, on-going activity. It's not just a once-a-quarter or once-a-year chore," Bert emphasized.

"Boy, I'm really beginning to see how this will help all of us. It's certainly going to help me personally, now and in the long run." Leslie was becoming more enthused.

"And then, stakes should reflect real effectiveness, not 'grandstanding' or stuff that's on a tangent to our reality. Real effectiveness means pounding and reaching a stake that makes a *real* contribution to Certus, not just a self-serving result," said Bert.

"I understand. No selfish pursuit of some off-the-wall opportunity—and no false rationalization of deals. Enough said," Leslie agreed, as someone who had been-there-done-that.

"Next. Stakes that show promise of aiding profitability should replace stakes, which don't promise the same. As Lee Iacocca once said, *volume times zero isn't too healthy.*

"And *we* are an important part of the quality of the stakes, Leslie. A good stake is often good because a proven performer pounded it. Credibility breeds credibility. Don't ever forget that," Bert admonished in finishing.

"Don't worry. I understand. This has been a great help."

"What's next?" Leslie inquired.

"The actual stake-pounding—figuring out where we're going.

"Yogi Berra, who was a perfect Hall-of-Fame catcher but an imperfect linguist said it best—*If you don't know where you're going, you'll end up somewhere else.* Stake-pounding, or stake-setting, is a forward-looking process, Leslie, done by imperfect managers and salespeople like you and me.

"Our major emphasis will be on developing an understanding of *precisely* where we'll be going—so we *don't* end up somewhere else. I understand that for you this may be a wholesale departure from the past. Our culture is changing, Leslie."

With that, he paused deliberately and turned back to Leslie for her reactions and questions.

Leslie said, "We never had the kind of stakes you're talking about. Yes, we had some sales targets, but we just tried to sell as much as we could. Plus, people wanted what we had to sell. We were always busy."

Bert said, "Well, this is one of the things we'll be changing because we want to succeed outrageously. We're going to be selling with a purpose and helping our customer's buy, not just taking orders like the sales team did in the past. Being *busy* doesn't guarantee success. Yikes! As a matter of fact it hurts! Rather than being busy, we'll be working according to The Law of the Farm—or Garden. Did you ever hear anyone refer to a farmer who was plowing as being 'busy'? Or a gardener who was weeding a flower patch as being 'busy'? Of course not! They're plowing or weeding.

"Leslie, never confuse motion with action. Motion is synonymous with aimless wandering. Action is synonymous with crisp pursuit of precise destinations.

"Okay, now let's take a look at our ultimate destination. Mr. Pimm and I discussed what the company needs to sell to avoid shutdown in six months. See

JOHN W. CEBROWSKI

this number on this paper? It will be a challenge, but I sincerely believe we can do it."

Leslie looked at the number with wide-eyed amazement. She gasped. She thought it was impossible, but Bert did not seem to be too excited. As a matter of fact, he was rather calm. She was surprised that he wasn't squawking and griping, but his demeanor and acceptance gave her confidence.

"Stakes are shaped by the objectives of the business, Leslie. Since Certus's objective is turn-around to survive we'll put our stakes in that context. Turn-around and survival will be our main stake-selection criterion. As time elapses and the situation evolves we'll put our stakes in the context of the revised objectives. Remember earlier you asked how to separate what's important from what isn't? Stakes we consider important *must be* aligned and consistent with what's *important* to the business—with current business priorities. We'll challenge our stakes ruthlessly.

"Another thing. In order for the company to turn itself around you and I must have certain *daily* sales stakes because time is critical. That way we will be able to react to shortfalls day-by-day. We'll both have daily stakes so we'll both be ready for Mr. Pimm's 5:00 o'clock call. We'll also have some weekly stakes. Because we're in a turn-around mode we'll be checking ourselves very frequently.

"Frequent measurement aids achievement. When the crisis has past we may shift from daily and weekly, to weekly and monthly stakes. We'll see. Frequency of measurement should vary by stake, and with the situation. But you know—I've found that an outrageous success mentality is synonymous with nonstop, real-time assessment of metrics. I absolutely *love* to keep score. And because visibility helps—we'll keep a big scoreboard here in the Wisdom Pantry for everyone to see—a scoreboard that displays the status of *all* of our stakes."

"Now—how do you think we should split-up the company sales stake between you, I, and our two new horses?" Bert asked for starters.

Leslie was incredulous. Mr. Pimm had *never* asked such a question before—and it was so trusting in lieu of the fact that the two new people weren't yet on-board. She couldn't believe that this manager was actually asking her for her opinion. It made her feel good.

Bert went on to say, "Since you have a pretty good understanding of our markets, the competition, and our existing customers you probably have some ideas. Remember, we also need some farther-out and over-the-horizon stakes. This way we can be laying the groundwork for subsequent quarters while we are *exceeding* this quarter's stakes."

46

"Exceeding? You've got to be kidding, Bert," Leslie said with disbelief and a bit of a challenge. "We'll be lucky to come close!"

"No. *E-X-C-E-E-D*," said Bert, reaching for his ice water. "I meant what I said. Salespeople who simply work to reach stakes, rather than exceed them, never amount to much. And of course, your commission and my bonus would be less. Therefore, I've decided our stakes will be 10% higher than what Mr. Pimm has assigned us. It will give us a head start and a potential cushion for the next period. A 10% kicker is also very *possible*, and *any* possibility is a hint from God—so said some theologian.

"Leslie, I hope you don't mind me bringing God into our discussions. You'll learn that I'm not overly concerned with being politically correct, only correctly successful. Some English army chaplain once said something like— *nobody worries about God as long as he can be kept shut up in churches, synagogues, or mosques. He is quite safe inside. But there is always trouble if you try to let him out.* You'll find that I regularly let him out—at risk to self.

Leslie slowly nodded, respectfully, taken-back a bit by the simple openness.

"Here's another way to look at the 10% kicker. When you run a race you run *through* the finishing tape, not just run up *to* the tape. Running up *to* the tape, up *to* the number Mr. Pimm assigned us, causes us to decelerate. The last thing we'll be doing here is decelerating.

"Look at the up-side," he said playfully, "We're lucky we've had a few early losses. It relieves us of the pressure of trying to have an undefeated quarter. This doesn't mean you and I *always* need to step-up *all* stakes we have been handed. I love St. Thomas Aquinas' saying that, *Not everything that is more difficult is more meritorious.* The measure of merit lies in the value of the result to the objectives of the business, not to one's self. I only make stakes more difficult if they benefit the business. In this case, raising the bar 10% passes that test.

"No one can *ever* assign you an outrageous stake, Leslie. It's simply impossible. You may be assigned *very tough* stakes from time to time, but outrageous stakes can only come from within. Only *you*—with help from above—can author outrageousness. You may even want to take this higher than my 10%. Hmmm?"

"No way! I'll settle for *your* outrageous stake this time," said Leslie. "Maybe next time."

She continued boldly, saying, "Excuse me Bert, but you *are* kind of up-there in years. You're probably as old as my grandpa. Where do you get the attitude and energy for all this?"

47

"I'm probably older," Bert smiled. "I live by a phrase from an old Dylan Thomas poem. *Do not go gentle into that good night. Old age should burn and rage at close of day.* I've always thought managers need to see themselves as a locomotive burning up the tracks to the end. I want to go out in a rage, knowing I left nothing behind, wearing out, not rusting out. And practically," he said with a wink, "It's a good way to stay employed in today's topsy-turvy world."

Bert went on, saying confidently, "This first quarter's stakes won't get us completely out of the hole, but on our way. We can do it if we work together. Next quarter we will have an even greater differential between the company's stakes and our personal stakes because we'll have a full team. The sales department will *pull* Certus out of its slump. You and I—and our two new horses—will lead the way.

"Leslie, here's another gem from history to seal this point—*while we pursue the unattainable we make impossible the realizable.* We won't be looking back. That memorable gem came from some writer by the name of Robert Ardrey."

Oh, my gosh! Maybe I should have quit with the rest of them, Leslie thought to herself, thinking about all the other departed salespeople.

"Bert, tell me more about those long-term stakes you referred to earlier," Leslie asked with growing apprehension. "Seriously, shouldn't we just concern ourselves with the next three months?"

"NO!!! That would compound the problem! Certus would find itself back where it was," said Bert, taking another drink of ice water.

"Long term stakes are the farther-out and the over-the-horizon stakes. I also call them 'roll-the-clock' stakes because they deal with the future. We roll-the-clock so that we are *simultaneously* working in the next two reporting periods as well as the current period. We work on three reporting periods at once. Operating stakes for the current period. Positioning stakes for the next farther-out period. Surveying stakes for the period over-the-horizon.

"First it was 'exceeding', now it's 'simultaneously'. Holy cow!" Leslie could picture the workload building up. He just laughed softly and reassuringly.

"Those longer-term stakes are our insurance for *future* reporting periods, Leslie. We will both agree on measurable, predictive activities that generate solid prospects and expand current customer business so that when subsequent quarters begin we will have an ample supply of opportunities to satisfy that reporting period's stakes. We'll follow the '2-to-1-Stake-Rule'. For every two forward-looking stakes we'll have one backward-looking how'd-we-do stake. For example, you and I will agree on how many promo pieces to mail and to whom, how many new contacts to make, how many prospect profiles to complete, how many customer studies to perform, how many seminars and

48

factory visits to conduct, how many demos to execute, and so on. Those are forward-looking, predictive, roll-the-clock stakes.

"The benefits of thinking and working long term include gaining insights into market trends, getting 'a feel' for customer plans, planting awareness of our products and services, sowing relationship seeds, biasing customer specifications, creating a basket of potential 'pull-in' opportunities, and many other things."

"All right. It *is* logical, no doubt about it," Leslie conceded.

"Ahhh—but beyond logic, there is also a certain spirit of adventure associated with looking out ahead and staking-out possibilities. Can you recall the magnificent vistas in the *Dances With Wolves* movie? Remember when Lt. John Dunbar leaves Fort Hays, Kansas for his assignment at an abandoned outpost on the fringe of the frontier? The prairie rolls and fades in a beautiful panorama of hills and ravines. His destination was over-the-horizon in the same way that many of our destinations will be beyond our view—but within our imagination and within our power to explore and establish ourselves."

"That's an understandable image, Bert. Yes, I can see how we need to establish an early presence, or pound stakes, at remote locations."

"A word about priorities though, just so there's no confusion. While stakes for all three time frames *are* important, our primary focus must be on the current period. As essayist Thomas Carlyle once said, *our main business is not to see what lies dimly at a distance, but to do what lies clearly at hand.* It's a matter of balance—of prudent focus."

The two of them then proceeded to pound some operational stakes for the current reporting period, positioning stakes for the following quarter, and then surveying stakes for over-the-horizon. They referenced the stacks of market data, historical records, and databases that he had gathered for the occasion.

They created total sales stakes, stakes by product, stakes by major customers and major markets, stakes for the sales partners, stakes for major sales activities, stakes for problems to solve, stakes for information to obtain, new customer and new market stakes, competitive account conversion stakes, customer retention and churn-reduction stakes, market-share and wallet-share stakes, customer satisfaction stakes, and stakes for many other things. *All* the stakes were metric-able. They didn't overdo it because they knew there were only two of them, but they were rather aggressive.

Bert convinced Leslie that to be outrageously successful took outrageous stakes—and that what got measured got done. They agreed on all the stakes and all the stakes were consistent with The Law of the Farm and The Law of the Garden—and were aligned with Certus's objectives. They also agreed on how, when, and in what format they would track their performance against each stake.

49

The process wasn't easy, but they both learned a lot about the business and each other in the course of the effort. He told Leslie the stake-pounding process got easier every time. There was mutual satisfaction at the end of their session.

Bert then said, "Okay, we *own* the stakes—the goals. They're ours. Stakes are commitments. That's why they're pounded in. We're accountable for reaching them, but I'll e- mail a copy to Mr. Pimm for his information and 'OK'. We want to make sure the big boss is familiar and comfortable with our stakes. And, I wouldn't be surprised if he has some inside information that will help us achieve one or more stakes. We'll also share our stakes with the other department managers, but we'll do that together, in person. They may also possess some information critical to us. Our stakes will affect many people here at Certus. We're part of a team. Our leadership and our stakes may prompt other managers to create new stakes or modify their existing stakes—and then share their stakes with us.

"Our sharing also results in a confirmation of the validity of our stakes. Our best stakes will draw intellectual energy, support, and resources from other managers like iron filings to a magnet. Our weakest stakes won't result in any level of attraction—which is a red flag to go back and reevaluate those stakes.

"Now I need to share my expectations—'the boundary stakes'—with you," Bert said. "Destination stakes and boundary stakes go hand-in-hand, like biscuits and gravy. I'd like to tell you what I expect from you and what you can expect from me.

"Then it will be your turn. I would like your opinion on what you expect from me and what I can expect from you. Communication of what is expected is a characteristic of the best organizations. Even with only two of us, neither has room for guessing.

"On poorly run business teams, managers and staff don't know what is expected of each other. By sharing our expectations we will understand each other much better, be able to more comfortably work together, cut out needless anxiety, improve our chances of reaching our stakes, and have some fun in the process."

Leslie was a little tense about this expectations stuff. It was new. Responding, she said, "I don't understand exactly what you mean by expectations—by 'boundary stakes'. It sounds like rules."

"Let me start," said Bert. "It's like the barbed-wire fences in the fields back in Kansas. Or the dainty little picket fence that maybe your dad had around his garden," he tweaked.

Leslie just shook her head, smiling.

"Think of expectations as values or philosophy—things that are important to me about our working relationship and our relationship with our other colleagues here at Certus, and with our sales partners and our customers. Expectations are behaviors and attitudes of mine that you can count on. It's stuff in which I deeply believe. Okay? Does that help?"

"Okay, I think I'm with you," Leslie nodded. "Please go slowly."

"Here are my expectations of you." And Bert turned his monitor so they could both see his cleverly animated slides, and he handed her another disc, which contained a copy.

"First, I expect results. Execute. Bring in the business. Do what you say you will do. Reach your stakes.

"Next. Work hard *and* smart. Run to your heart's content, but don't forget to give yourself time to reflect. Give yourself fifteen minutes of quiet time, at a fixed time, for some pensive introspection during each workday. I give myself that breather every day.

"Then. Build a name for yourself inside and outside the business as a problem solver. But if you run into something incredibly nasty bring it in here, presenting alternative solutions, fragmented suggestions, or opinions when you present the issue. That will help *me*—and others—help *you*.

"I expect you to come up with new and bold ideas. Think about how we can do things differently. There are no sacred cows or pet chickens here at Certus. We need some courageous strokes to survive and succeed.

"Pay attention to quality in all things that you do—big and little—tangibles and intangibles—concepts and details. Do nothing second rate.

"No surprises. Keep me informed about good and bad, especially the bad. And let me know what ugly stuff you *anticipate* and the reasons why. I may be able to help.

"Share your feelings. They're often more important than the facts. Feelings are priceless early warnings. Don't hesitate to speak up regardless of how silly you think your feelings are.

"Be on time with everything that has a deadline. We're racing the clock, and both of our plates will be loaded, so there's no time for delays.

"I expect that you will exhibit integrity in all matters with everyone. No game playing. No far-fetched commitments. No smoke. No soft-shoe.

"You okay?" he checked.

"I'm with you—keep going," Leslie said, confidently.

"Next. Think 'e' at all times. Use our technology tools to the fullest. Help save the trees.

"If you don't have something that you need to get the job done—tell me. I'll do my darndest to help you get it.

"Assign yourself personal responsibility for attitude control. Don't expect me to cajole.

"Align yourself instantly to new realities. We all have to be able to turn on a dime and recommit when something unexpected happens.

"Adhere to company practices, policies, and processes. If one causes a burr under your saddle make a suggestion to improve it or eliminate it.

"Act like you own the business. Take whatever actions you deem necessary to service and satisfy our customers. Let me know after you've done it. To emphasize this point, here's your personal Decision Maker's License," and he handed Leslie a driver's license-sized plastic-laminated card. The 'license' was neatly embossed with Certus's recently revised mission statement, objective, and logo. It was signed by Ol' Bert and Mr. Pimm.

Leslie stared at it in wide-eyed amazement, swallowed hard, looked at it again, and finally nodded understanding.

Smiling, he let her regain her composure, then continued.

"Use all your talents. If you use all God's given talents you'll find that they become multiplied in their use. Where you thought you had two, you'll find five.

"Emphasize action. If something coughs or misfires don't dawdle or look around for sympathy. Fix it. If you stumble, get up and dust yourself off. Leave skid marks and race on.

"I expect that you—and I—will make mistakes. Don't be paralyzed by mistakes. Mistakes teach us. Simply learn the lessons and don't repeat the mistakes. Don't worry—I won't confuse the error with the person who errs.

"Next. Give your full support to our colleagues here at Certus. Exceed *their* expectations. And hear them out when they offer opinions. They have much to offer.

"I expect you to pay attention to what goes on around you—noticing not only the obvious but being sensitive to the subtle. Be curious about nearly everything.

"On the personal side. If you begin to think you're not loving what you're doing—first admit it to yourself—then tell me—and then I expect that together we'll figure out what you should do next.

"Similarly, I expect you to give me feedback in any area that you believe will help my personal efforts—and our mutual efforts. There is no need to soft-pedal any criticism. I expect candor. I'm not thin-skinned.

"Then. Don't walk through this job without leaving worthy evidence of your passage. Leave a legacy to be proud of.

"Next. Because I'm interested in your success as a total person, not just a salesperson, I suggest you never be entirely at leisure, but either be writing, teaching, politicking, volunteering, praying, or doing *something* for the public good.

"Finally, have fun and stay loose. Don't take yourself too seriously. Look for the humor and wit in everyday events. Make others smile and laugh. Okay?"

"Yes. Certainly. I can handle all that," said Leslie, sounding relieved.

"Now—this is what you can expect of me." And Bert slowly and deliberately continued with his boundary stakes.

"You can expect a regularly refreshed vision of where the sales team is going.

"You can expect intense focus and concentration on the task of saving Certus and having it succeed outrageously.

"You can expect a balance between an upbeat buoyant attitude and a downbeat pragmatic outlook in regard to our efforts.

"You can expect democratic decision-making most of the time—but also expect no-discussion directives from me on occasion—and in those cases I'll give you an explanation.

"You can expect vigorous efforts to take obstacles and hurdles out of our way.

"You can expect quick, straightforward, easy-to-understand answers to your questions—or referrals to where you can find the answers.

"You can expect real-time developmental and evaluative coaching. Candor runs both ways. I'll be as quick as I can be to give you useful feedback. But be forewarned—some of it may sting.

"You can expect confidence and trust in your actions. I'll support you, both inside and outside.

"You can expect an open door, an open environment, and an open willingness to listen. I'll always make time for you.

"You can expect a steady flow of changes in processes, practices, and policies for our mutual benefit. I'm a transformer who likes to tinker.

"You can expect that I'll always have an unquenchable thirst for new ideas from all sources.

"You can expect no hidden agendas. What you'll see, hear, and feel is what you'll get.

"You can expect that I'll quickly let you know what's going on elsewhere within Certus so you can plan and work accordingly.

"You can expect that I will help you advance your career and your personal goals to the extent that you let me, and to the extent that you seek my advice.

"And you can expect quick and robust recognition for a job well done."

Ol' Bert paused and gave Leslie a chance to think and feel at ease with his expectations.

"Now—does that help define our environment—the boundaries of our relationship? Any questions?" asked Bert.

"Wow. That's neat. No questions, Bert. Thanks. I never had a manager that shared all those thoughts with me," said Leslie. "However, I didn't think there was anything outrageous about what you said. You're not asking anything I can't deliver."

"No, I'm not, and that's a good sign that you feel that way. It proves you're a 'horse'. A person who wasn't a 'horse' likely wouldn't have responded the way you did. I also recognize, as writer Margaret Deland did, that *a pint can't hold a quart. If it holds a pint, it is doing all that can be expected of it.* That's all I'm asking of you. Again, outrageous stakes can *only* come from within. Only *you* can author destinations and boundaries that are tighter, more stringent, more difficult, or more challenging than what someone hands you. Only you can grow yourself from being a pint to something larger."

"Yes, I can understand and accept that Bert," Leslie acknowledged with pride.

"Why don't you take a crack at your expectations of *yourself*—and your expectations of *me*," Bert prompted. "I realize I'm putting you on the spot here without much advance warning—but I'll give you many opportunities in the future."

Leslie then haltingly articulated several of her self-expectations and expectations of Bert. He carefully listened and recorded them as Leslie revealed her opinions and feelings. As he had suspected, she was hard on herself and gentle on him, but he said nothing.

"Either one of us can pull-up and move the stakes or pound in new ones—update our goals and expectations—at any time," Bert concluded. "It's simple. Just walk in and let's talk."

"Really? Thanks, Bert. I'm ready to go," enthused Leslie. "I like this expectation sharing idea. There's no mystery. No puzzle. I feel much better about where I stand and what I need to do. Plus, you know how *I* feel. Let's get started. Let's go!" Leslie was fired up.

"Good! But we've still got work to do with the other essentials of outrageous success," said Bert.

"We know what stakes we're going after, and the boundaries of the pursuit, but now we need to plant somethin' special. In other words—we need a sales department strategy. How about if we discuss that in two weeks at the same time? I think we've done enough for today, don't you?"

"Yes. Sure. Sounds great. But what does planting have to do with strategy," asked Leslie, feeling more positive about what was happening.

"You'll see," said Bert, who then gave her copies of several old magazine and journal articles about strategy, and pulled several books off the shelf that discussed strategy. He handed the huge stack to Leslie.

"Here's some homework for our meeting in two weeks. Please read it."

"Homework?" Leslie was flabbergasted. "You've got to be kidding. We never had homework before. Bert, I don't have time, I..."

"Yep! Homework," Bert interrupted, smiling. "I'm not kidding. I'm confident you can find time. You'll enjoy the materials. I've marked-up and highlighted all the key spots so you don't
have to read through everything. It will make our discussions more enjoyable. Thanks for your cooperation."

"Bert, how did you decide to spend your career in management?" Leslie asked, in a spirit of newfound respect for the old-timer as a result of their stake-pounding discussion.

"First, I became a salesman because I liked to talk and listen and mix it up with people. When I became real good my bosses made me a manager. I was good at that too, because I discovered I liked to help people. I discovered I got antsy when I saw things not being done as good as they could be done, and I found I liked to fix those things. I discovered I liked to build and guide winning teams. I discovered it was rewarding to use *all* my God-given talents, leading activities for the benefit of my employer and the community in which I lived. And somewhere in the middle of all that I remembered something one of my teachers told us—something from the famous Greek philosopher Plato—*All things will be produced in superior quantity and quality, and with greater ease, when each man works at a single occupation, in accordance with his natural gifts, at the right moment, and without meddling with anything else.* That passage kept me on course and deepened my commitment to management," finished Bert with that sparkle in his eye.

Everyone who had a chance to see the sales department's 'destination stakes' raised their eyebrows. The review with Mr. Pimm and others did in fact cause some prudent adjustments, but the comprehensiveness and aggressiveness still left a couple of people chuckling in private disbelief—with a 'I'll-believe-it-when-I-see-it' attitude.

JOHN W. CEBROWSKI

However, Ol' Bert, later picking up some of those expected reactions from the grapevine just kept plowing forward, unperturbed.

Meanwhile, a flow of candidates had started. HR said they had never seen anything like it so soon after the launch of a hiring campaign. There even seemed to be a couple of potential horses in the group. The recruiting effort, also, had other people talking because the selection team had been spreading the word.

When Ol' Bert wasn't out in the field, he was seen buzzing around the company like a bee, chatting in his unique animated fashion, encouraging and energizing everyone.

Business was slowly improving. There weren't as many of those 'empty' 5:00pm calls with Mr. Pimm. His graphs and charts had slowed their downward spiral and gave signs of leveling off.

The general attitude throughout the company was a little more buoyant. People seemed to have a little more pep in their step and vigor in their voice.

Essential #3
Plant Somethin' Special

"Lance, it's wonderful having you on the team", Bert said, grasping Lance's hand with both of his, squeezing and pumping as hard as the old man could.

Leslie stood there beaming, looking up at the towering, lanky newcomer. She had interviewed Lance a couple of weeks ago and was really impressed by his market development background, computer skills, and subtle humor. Gosh, we need some humor in the midst of this crisis, she had thought.

A nephew of Ol' Bert's who managed a big resort in Hawaii had first-hand knowledge of incentive trip participants. The nephew had been talked into keeping a lookout for 'horses' on behalf of his old uncle. Turning that rock turned-up Lance.

This was a horse if there ever was one—a unanimous impression of everyone on the selection team. Lance had twelve years of experience as a salesman, market team leader, and National Account Manager with a Fortune 100 company. He had been chafing at the bit for more freedom of expression and growth, and when he met the Certus team, he saw and he felt that both opportunities were here.

"Lance, this is a terrific week for you to start," giggled Bert, tickled that he had found one of the two 'horses' he needed. "We're about to decide what to plant."

Lance had been an engineering major and president of his fraternity at Grambling. Originally from a small town in southern Louisiana, Lance knew all about planting—rice and sugar cane—on his grandparent's farm.

After some welcoming banter, Ol' Bert kicked-off the meeting. "Leslie, why don't you start by sharing with Lance some of your thoughts on the reading homework?"

Lance turned to Ol' Bert, eyes wide open. "Bert, you didn't mention homework when we were interviewing," and kiddingly got up as if to leave.

Both Leslie and Ol' Bert laughed, making Lance feel good. The bonds were forming.

"Do you two know what it feels like to take a gulp of fresh air on a cold morning?" asked Leslie, scanning Ol' Bert's 'Wisdom Pantry' with admiration.

"It stimulates you and makes you want to do things. Well, that's how it felt when I read those materials you gave me, Bert. I thought it would be boring, but instead it cleared away the cobwebs and made me consider things I have never reflected on. Those readings took me to a whole new level of thinking."

"I thought they might hit you that way," nodded Bert, chuckling to himself, feeling good that the desired affect had been achieved. "That's why I read and collect all these books. There are a lot of smart people out there—much smarter than I. I've learned a great deal from them. I never had benefit of a college education, but I sure appreciate the value of knowledge and new ideas. It's one of the reasons I used to go to at least one high-and-mighty sounding seminar every year. It was like taking the old tractor in for a yearly overhaul."

"This book, *Competitive Advantage* had some good ideas," Leslie said, flipping the pages, then handing it to Lance.

"Yep—written by good old Mike, Michael Porter," nodded Bert. "I went to one of his conferences once. I sat there with my mouth open the whole time. Never knew anyone could know so much."

"So did this one, *Strategic Management*, and this one as well, *Strategic Skills for Line Managers*," added Leslie, skipping over others stacked in front of her. "All these old *Fortune* and *Harvard Business Review* magazines and other periodicals also had some neat ideas," and she handed them to Lance. "I'm sure glad you highlighted the important points, otherwise I never would have been able to get through them. It's heavy reading, Bert," Leslie admitted.

"Yep—it is heavy, a mixture of academic and practical ideas, but the good ideas float to the top like cream from a good Kansas cow," Bert laughed.

"But, Bert, these books were not about sales, I was a bit confused why you gave them to me," Leslie added.

Bert laughed softly, saying, "The *first* books we need to read are the books *our customers read* so we can get on their wavelength and talk their talk. Decision-makers read these books. They're concerned about these subjects—as we should be. Plus, they deal with strategy."

"Bert, how did you ever get time to read all this stuff? I never seem to have time for the newspaper," Leslie wondered.

"Yes, same here," Lance chipped in, relating to Leslie's experience.

"It comes down to disciplining yourself, and how bad you want it," said Bert.

"How bad you want *what*?" Leslie and Lance wondered in unison.

"How bad you want to achieve outrageous success," Bert said, looking at one, then the other, straight in the eye.

There was a telling pause, then low groans of understanding from each of them.

"Well, why don't we get down to business," Bert started, smiling at both, and leaning back confidently in that massive chair.

"Good strategy is a requisite for business survival and success. We all know that. And sales teams must have a strategy to survive and succeed, and to support the corporation. Adopting and implementing a sales team strategy is my job, but it affects you. And some day you'll be doing this for your own sales team. Our strategy will also be the basis of our collective reputation. Those are some of the reasons we're here discussing this together."

"Why must the team have a strategy? All our accounts are different. We'll have individual strategies for each of our partners and customers. Isn't that enough?" Leslie asked quizzically.

Slowly picking his words, Bert started. "Whoa, good questions. A sales team strategy is *a central theme* around which we'll all rally and work. It will become a starting point from which to launch our individual partner and customer sales efforts." And Bert paused. "It will serve as a common language and a common thread. It will be a specific concrete approach and attitude that we will *all* emphasize to win and retain business. A sales unit strategy is emphasis on something sales related." And Bert paused again. "A strategy will aid all of us in marching single-mindedly in one direction to a common drumbeat. It will serve as *the activity base* from which each of you will customize individual partner and customer strategies, Leslie." And then, pausing once more for effect, he got up and went to peek through his blinds.

"Strategy is the vehicle in which this sales team will ride to get to its 'stakes', just like my Chevy out there," said Bert, glancing at Lance whom he knew had missed the stake-pounding discussion. "While our strategy will be as solid and trustworthy as that car—it will be much more elegant.

"Or—it's like the first tractor, an old Model "D" John Deere, in which my daddy proudly invested. He really relied on that tractor, and it carried us through the Depression. We'll collectively rely on our strategy to carry us and help us survive the same way.

"Through the years my daddy would get a new tractor—when he could afford one that is. He struggled to get a Model "B" several years later. The initial investment in a strategy, and changing that strategy, can also be a struggle so a team must select a strategy carefully in the first place. Strategies, like tractors, are big, big investments. Strategy decisions take a lot of thought because they dictate tactics—and because they have a ripple effect on other aspects of the business. There's no casual dabbling with this strategy stuff.

"But, Bert, isn't our strategy to hit the numbers by simply blowing everyone's doors off and closing hard?" said Lance.

"No, no, there's too much blowing going on out there, like those twisters we used to get back home. Blowing and closing hard are strategies used by desperate or unsophisticated sales teams and businesses. In the end they're simply destructive," Bert cautioned.

"Remember that fella Mike, in that book? He once said, *the essence of strategy is choosing to perform activities differently than rivals do.* That's *exactly* what we're going to do. We're going to perform *sales* activities different than our competition so we *stand out.* And we'll do it without blowing. And we'll let the competition lie like sleeping dogs on a hot summer day as we sneak on by," Bert chortled.

"One of the reasons that sales have been weak at Certus is that there wasn't a sales team strategy. The lack of a strategy was one of the reasons the other department managers thought that previous sales efforts were shot-gunned. The lack of a strategy was also one of the reasons all the departed salespeople seemed confused and were drifting independently of each other—groping for gimmicks or caving on prices.

"But isn't strategy a marketing issue?" questioned Lance.

"It most certainly is. Marketing must have strategies for marketing related activities, such as pricing, branding, product mix, and promotional efforts. But sales must have a strategy for sales related activities, such as new customer acquisition, account growth, and customer retention," said Bert. "*All* business functions—Production, HR, Finance, R&D—must have strategies.

"Like other departments—we *must* be consistent and supportive of the company's marketing strategies—because we're on the same team and because sales is a subset of marketing. I've been talking regularly to our marketing manager, and he says our marketing strategy is based on product innovation and premium prices. It also seems that because we're small we can get to market quicker then anyone else with new items. Speed, innovation, and premium price seem to be marketing's strategic thrust. I like it—it makes sense to me—especially in this business—although I'm worried about premium prices right now. We'll have to figure out some way to support pricing. He and I have developed a great relationship. I respect the fact that pricing is a very complicated subject."

"Bert, can you give us a sales team strategy example?" asked Lance. "That may enable us to understand this whole subject better."

"Sure," said Bert, perked up by the question. "I remember when I was in the machine tool business and our sales team strategy was based on extensive product and applications knowledge. Man, were we smart—far smarter than any of our competitors. There wasn't a question the team couldn't answer. We were really respected. Customers and non-customers called us all the time. We were so smart our own product design people included us in their development work. That was a real ego trip for the troops. *Deep, deep product knowledge* was our forte—I called it our *Wisdom Strategy*. It worked wonders!

"Another thing—it was a small point—but it also differentiated us from our rivals. We always sent a personal handwritten thank-you note for every order. No competitor did that.

"Big idea or small idea, as long as the *action* differentiates the sales unit from rivals. Okay?"

"Okay. Thanks, I understand," said Lance.

"Bert, two weeks ago I asked you what 'planting' had to do with strategy. Remember? What do you mean?" asked Leslie, and both she and Lance leaned forward to hear another pearl of wisdom.

"The word 'plant' means that we—I, in particular—need to embed the strategy in this sales team's culture. We'll all do that by ensuring its understanding, seizing it, believing in it, and engaging it constantly—with my unflinching oversight. That's what 'planting' means. If a strategy is not 'planted'—if it's an idea just whimsically tossed out onto the market—it will never grow. It will wither and die. It will never achieve its destiny. A seed is nothing unless it is planted. But if it is sown a glorious harvest awaits. Same with a strategy.

"The word 'plant' also emphasizes the fact that strategies need fertile ground in which to mature—and *we're* the ground. Our open and positive attitudes, and commitment to the strategy, are the measures of fertility.

"Strategies must be cultivated and nurtured. They get better and better over time if they are fine-tuned and tweaked. Experience will teach. Lessons will be learned. And it's my job to make sure this refining happens. Like anything in life, Leslie, you get better the more you practice. A common mistake many managers and teams make is that they don't plant their strategy and give their strategy time to mature. They think they can harvest immediately. It doesn't work that way. It takes time to distinguish yourself in the marketplace. *Only* when you hear the market echoing your strategy can you feel confident that it has taken root. We'll listen closely. We'll be patient—but make no mistake—I'll be driving our strategy vigorously.

"A well planted sales team strategy can become a trademark for us and for Certus, and that's exactly what we want", said Bert. "We want an enviable and respected reputation—we want to be seen as the most attractive sales proposition out there—just as we were back in the machine tool business.

"We also need a strategy to *focus* our little team so we can *exceed* our stakes while staying within our resource constraints," said Bert, as he prepared to write on his little whiteboard.

61

"Lance, you'd better get used to the word 'exceed' around here," cautioned Leslie.

"Uh-huh, I think I get the picture," Lance winked back.

"A sales team strategy that focuses our energy, brings in profitable business, and aids our attainment of outrageous success must be based on this simple 3D recipe," Bert said and wrote.

DEMAND
DIFFERENTIATION
DOMINANCE

"How we choose to contrast ourselves with competition must be 'special' to customers and sales partners. Our strategy must therefore meet *demand*. The strategy must have value in the market. Our strategy must be appreciated for the pleasantness it delivers, the pain it alleviates, or a combination of both. That's a major reason it's important to have an in-depth understanding of what is important to our customers and sales partners. That's why when I say 'plant *somethin' special*', I want us to emphasize market and customer values— somethin' special to the market. It makes no sense to plant a strategy which isn't in *demand*—or which the market won't appreciate or perceive as special. Understanding of values and demand is imperative.

"For example, I value courtesy and therefore demand a pleasant 'good morning' and 'thank you' at my bank. I value prompt and correct answers to questions, and therefore demand that of the clerks at the local super-computer store. We're all consumers—we all have values and demands—and we all patronize businesses that fulfill our values and demands. What we have to figure out is what are the most important *sales-related* values and demands of Certus' customer population. We want to touch those hot-buttons—those values and demands—and the best way to find out what they are is to constantly listen, observe, and ask the customer and sales partner population. Okay?" And Ol' Bert paused, checking for understanding from his two horses.

"The second D, *differentiation*, means that we are filling a gap or niche not covered by the competition. Or, we are doing *something* at a level of intensity or level of uniqueness that they are not doing or cannot match. We are making our sales approach look different than any other supplier, and that difference can be sustained. Again, when I say we need to plant *somethin' special*, it's also to emphasize the necessity for differentiation. *The essence of strategy is choosing to perform activities differently than rivals do.* Remember? That phrase is one of my favorite quotes. Forgive me if I say it all the time.

"If *we*—are *different*—in ways *demanded* by customers—Certus will be seen as a considerably better value proposition. You with me?"

They nodded.

"And if we don't establish—*plant*—our own differentiation—by default the market or competition will do it for us. And I *assure you*—we won't like it one bit because we will end up being painted and viewed as something not of our choosing—something hurtful. Understand?"

They nodded with more vigor.

"I can remember the variety and condition of pick-up trucks sitting out in front of the general store when I was a boy and how those trucks sent a message about their owners. I was always proud of my daddy's truck," said Bert. "It stuck out from the rest because it was really clean and had no dents. Our sales team strategy needs to stick out from the competition's sales strategy the same way. And just as many of the other farmers were a little jealous—you can count on many of our competitors being jealous—either trying to put dents in our strategy by tossing verbal missiles or by working hard to make their own differentiation more appealing.

"Differentiation implies that we *understand* our competitors' sales strategies so that we can perform *our* sales strategies differently—and with *greater* appeal.

"How can we possibly know competitive sales strategy?" asked Leslie.

"By observing them at shows. By reading their literature. By listening to their ads. By studying their websites. By listening to how customers and prospects refer to them, their activities, and their approaches. By paying attention to whom they call on. By talking to people who have left their employ. By purchasing something from them. All we have to do is keep our eyes and ears open. It's simple. The signals are all around us. We must constantly watch and listen," smiled Bert. "After a while, certain words, actions, and reputations begin to bubble-up. Knowledge of competitive sales approaches is one of the starting points of strategy generation. You can't make yourself different if you don't know what the other fella looks like. I've been studying competition intently ever since I've been here."

"But, Bert, what happens if the other fella's strategy is highly valued by most of the market—if their strategy meets demand? Then what?" asked Leslie, thinking she had Ol' Bert cornered.

"Not a problem," smiled Bert. "We have three viable choices then.

"One, we can 'draft' on the competitor's strategy just like those souped-up race cars do at Charlotte or Daytona, and do exactly the same thing—let them pull us along. It *can* work—*but*—we're virtually invisible to the market since we're a small flyspeck hidden in their shadow. It can also be dangerous. We're always concentrating on someone else's rear-end rather than concentrating on what's going on in the market—and if they sputter, cough, or hit the wall we're out of the race with them.

"Two, we can tack-on a little something special, differentiate ourselves in an *extra* way while drafting, adding a little *more value* to what the market wants—like putting a row of police-cruiser lights on the roof. The attention-getter can work—*but*—that causes the guy in front to spend more time looking in his rear view mirror and making some dicey moves trying to 'shake' us. A little gamble there too, because if he falters or makes a bonehead move, we're also in trouble. And we're still looking at the same rear-end, inhaling the same fumes, and remaining partially obscured by the same dust cloud. He's still first and very visible—and we're still second and perceived in the market as second best. The problem with these two choices is we're letting competition control us—our destiny is in their hands. Viable—but not inspiring. And *certainly* not consistent with an outrageous success mentality.

"Thirdly, we can take that highly valued strategy to a *much higher* level of execution, putting the pedal to the metal, aggressively pulling out and passing him—and that takes us to the third D, *dominance!*

"**Dominance** means we execute the differentiated strategy *so well* that we end up out front by sheer power and quintessential execution—quintessential—one of my favorite heavy-book words. We rise above that competitor. We leapfrog them! We *execute* at a level of mastery and professionalism that gains us a reputation par excellence, as the French would say. We didn't have many French people in western Kansas, but I sure like their differentiated and dominating cooking, don't you?

"Dominance means the highest level of execution, the same way. We become recognized as *the absolute best* with a given strategy, significantly better than anyone else in one or more ways. Dominance means we become automatically associated with the actions and attitudes that characterize our differentiation. When customers and partners think of 'x', they will think of us—*first*. We'll engineer the best of what *they* value and demand—ensuring *we* have a monopoly over fulfilling their reasons to buy—and *we'll* be in control.

"No difference is disaster. Slightly different is dangerous. *Very* different is dominance!

"Dominance also reminds me of an old silver-screen heartthrob of mine, Mae West, who once said—*too much of a good thing can be wonderful*. And that's what dominance is, a whole lot of a good thing."

Ol' Bert got excited talking about these matters, as Leslie and Lance could tell from his animated gestures and the sweat on his shirt. But they weren't sure if the excitement had to do with strategy or Mae West.

"The 3D model also reminds me of my favorite country music singer, Lorreta Lynn. That sassy little gal believed that to be successful, *you either have to be first, best, or different.* Sounds sorta 3D to me, eh?" And Ol' Bert began to hum *Coal Miner's Daughter.* He was really in a good mood.

"Mr. Pimm's business strategy right now is to keep costs as low as possible and focus on our core technical competencies—and our market approach is to be the highest-value provider. That's a solid business strategy and market approach—and important for us to know. We *must* be consistent with the company. Consistency means that our sales team's strategy reinforces and complements corporate efforts. Our sales team strategy must therefore be cost effective, technology related, and of high value," said Bert, as he got up and began pacing around the small office, struggling to think of ideas. His obvious mental churning got Leslie's and Lance's brows furrowed with thought as well.

"Okay. Let's start with a clean slate, not worry about 'drafting', and make some notes," said Bert. "First. What do our customers and customer segments need and value *now*—and what may they *likely* need and value in the future? Evolving customers demand evolvable strategies.

"Next. What *are* our competitors' business, marketing, and sales strategies right now and how might *they* evolve? Let's put ourselves in their shoes. And *then*—let's create a 3D sales team strategy that's *uniquely* ours!"

With that, a lengthy list of competitors' reputations, the market's values, Certus's existing strategic thrusts, and sample strategies were generated. The three decided to call out for pizzas so they could work right through lunch, and that led them to analyze the various big-name pizza companies, discern various pizza strategies, and draw out analogies. Ol' Bert told them that a strategy should be based on a variety of elements. He said multiple sources of value had an exponential impact—as long as it wasn't so many as to dilute or fragment the effort. He also told them that while differentiation is a way of getting a company *into* markets it is also a way of keeping a company *out* of markets—so they must be careful because the very differences that win many customers may turn-off others.

In the end, they agreed that their sales team strategy would be based on three elements.

The first element would be the deepest and broadest knowledge of the fundamental technologies and basic scientific research relevant to their products. That intelligence would be their entrée to difficult-to-approach high-level execs. They knew top execs were intensely interested in the future of those technologies for their own strategic planning and costing purposes. They wanted to be perceived in terms of the thing *most valuable* to top decision makers, and uniquely, as far as they knew, no one else was doing this. It would enable the Certus sales staff to have vital, visionary conversations that their competitors were not having. It would be adding explicit decision-maker value well beyond Certus's products and services. Ol' Bert told them being first with a key strategic element was a bit rare, and *always* a great advantage. Their credibility would be boosted considerably.

Secondly, they would also update their modest customer contact software to a much more sophisticated customer relationship management (CRM) software and add communications tools to *extend* marketing's speed strategy and *exceed* customers' operational requirements. Differentiation is implicit in *extending* and *exceeding* Ol' Bert reminded them. They would do that by using the product of one hardware supplier on whose Advisory Board Ol' Bert was a member—using the hardware of another supplier with whom Ol' Bert had worked in a former industry association—and partnering with a well-respected mid-market software vendor and integrator that Leslie knew was looking for a beta site for a new release. They would be the fastest, most comprehensive data warehouse in the market. It would enable Certus, *enterprise-wide*, to dominate its customer-base with operating information. The portals they designed and opened would also link to Certus' back-office systems facilitating their customer and sales partner processes and objectives better than any other supplier. This second strategic element would fit nicely with the first element. They knew they weren't first with this element, but their plan was to dominate by designing their system around information and workflow that delivered value primarily to their customers and partners—*not* to their internal functions as other suppliers were prone to do. They would also fully link the standard and customizable capabilities of the CRM software and communications tools to the specific requirements of *all* their customers and partners—not just the big ones. They would recognize the uniqueness of *every* Certus customer and partner.

And third, they would leverage their people-skills and problem-solving skills by building intimate applications-intensive relationships through rigorous support of customers and partners at the lowest user-levels—with the 'worker bees'. This would be in contrast to the low regard and indifferent attitude exhibited by their competitors towards the blue-collar folks. Again, they wanted to be perceived in terms of the thing *most valuable* to the 'worker bees'. And this third strategic element would *also* be a 'first'—and would integrate nicely with the other two strategy elements.

They knew all three elements were very important to customers, so the strategy met *demand*. They also knew all three elements would cleverly *differentiate* the sales team. And Ol' Bert told them that the precision, pace, and professionalism of their execution would match the 'pit crews' at Charlotte and Daytona—making the strategy *dominating*. He told them the market rewards valued actions delivered with precision. And he also told them that he'd be one, stern, uncompromising 'pit crew' chief.

All three loved what they had agreed upon. It was special! They had followed the 3D model. Their strategy was both customer-centric and customer-facing—and it was in harmony with Certus's business and marketing strategies. They also knew the strategy would provide tangible benefits to customers—and that customers gladly pay for tangible benefits. Thus, they could rely on the strategy to help keep prices and margins up. They decided to give their strategy a name so as to have a memorable rallying cry—and to help ensure it was 'planted' in Certus's sales and business culture. They called it *The Attack of the Mustard Seed.*

"Wow—this is one outrageous strategy," Lance intoned, clearly impressed.

Bert finished by saying, "*Fortune favors the audacious* is the way some old-time author put it, and that's what we'll be. An audacious attitude is a natural by-product of an outrageous strategy. Our audacious attitude will be a replica of Marshall Ferdinand Foch's dilemma in 1914 when he said at the Battle of the Marne, *my center is giving way, my right is in retreat; situation excellent. I am attacking!* Just like Foch—when we are threatened—or when we are being hammered—or our situation is unclear—we will keep pushing forward—and keep attacking.

"And when things are going smashingly well, we will also continue driving hard.

"An audacious attitude is also very contagious—so we want to make sure our colleagues here 'catch' that attitude—as well as competitors and customers. Is everyone clear on the attitude portion of our strategy?" he finished with a penetrating stare.

"We think we're picking up some vibes about a certain degree of aggressiveness here," Lance deadpanned, tongue-in-cheek. Leslie chuckled in agreement.

Bert grinned, saying, "Our strategy is not going to do the work for us, but it's going to make the trip a lot easier. Speaking of making the trip easier reminds me of Kansas, and watching the geese fly south every fall. A writer-friend told me that by flying in a 'V' formation each member of the flock creates an updraft for the bird immediately following. This allows geese to fly at incredible speeds for prolonged distances. In fact, scientists have discovered in wind tunnel tests that geese can fly 71% further in this 'V' formation than if each goose went its own way. *That's* outrageous! The 'V' formation makes their long migratory trip easier. Our common strategy provides the same updraft enhancing our individual and collective productivity.

"Let's take off!" Bert was excited. The energy was rubbing-off on Leslie and Lance.

"One of the things we'll have to do is inform our customers and partners about our strategy. We must plant our strategy in their minds by explicitly describing the three elements to them—not just letting it all unfold haphazardly—hoping and assuming they see and feel our efforts. That's a recipe for not getting full value from the strategy.

"Secondly, because strategy must be linked to measurements, we must revisit our 'stakes' and make sure they are consistent with our strategy and that we have measurements for each of our three strategic elements. A strategy unmeasured is a strategy unfulfilled.

"Thirdly, we have to inform all the other department managers and Mr. Pimm about our strategy. That'll create synergy. I'll schedule some meetings."

"The 3D formula never changes, but our markets, customers, and sales partners change, our company's products and services change, our company's resources and people change, and our competition changes, so we—and I mean *we*—always need to be evaluating the viability of our strategy. As the rate of change in the business world accelerates, the suitability of a strategy becomes a more pivotal decision. So—the strategy we just created is *not* cast in concrete—and we may find that we must modify our strategy just at the time we have become most comfortable with the old one. You two horses got that?" Bert asked sternly.

"Yes, boss! We got it." And Lance and Leslie laughed, feeling power like they had never felt.

"Holy cow, and this was only my first week," Lance said in disbelief.

"We'll know we have an effective strategy—a solid, trustworthy and elegant vehicle—when business starts pouring in, we begin receiving compliments from everyone, all our metrics are moving in the right direction, and we begin exceeding the stakes we've pounded," concluded Bert.

He paused to calm down and collect his thoughts.

"Okay team. Now that we have a strategy, we need a plan. As we used to say at home, we need to figure out 'how to git where we're goin'. I've scheduled a meeting next week over at the State University to meet with some of the people I know in their library. They have a neat little conference room we can use to work on our sales team's plan and your individual market and account plans.

"In the mean time, Leslie, I know you've got a lot of sales activities scheduled. I'll be working closely with Lance to get him duly indoctrinated, 'primed', and up to speed, and I'll be out there selling myself. So—let's go!

"We'll drive over to the university together next week in my old Chevy. I just had it detailed. I'm anxious to show it to you.

"Thanks for your great ideas and participation today. We're on our way. We have a great team," said Bert in conclusion, exuding ever more confidence.

The strategy announcements to customers and partners were met with pleasant surprise, gratitude, new unexpected openness, and a willingness to give the sales staff more time.

The strategy-sharing meetings with other department heads and their staffs also had a profound effect. Others were inspired by the creativity of The Attack of the Mustard Seed and the voluntary sharing. It heightened everyone else's confidence in the sales operation, gave everyone hope for the business, and caused others to take steps to craft a 3D strategy in their own departments.

The sales team noted that their reward was increased respect from customers, partners, and the rest of the business. It was like they had dropped a stone at one end of a watering trough—watched the wave go out—bounce off the other end—and come back at them with greater amplitude.

Not surprisingly, Certus's performance continued to improve, as more orders somehow materialized. The production manager even put some of the part-time factory people back on full-time status. But there was still a long, long way to go.

Ol' Bert kept turning rocks looking for his next horse.

Mr. Pimm kept crunching the numbers. The 5:00pm personal calls had been replaced by an automated wireless system that prompted each of them to punch in their numbers every day for marketing and for Mr. Pimm.

A humming sound of success was now faintly audible.

Essential #4
Know How To Git Where You're Goin'

As they pulled out of the parking lot at Certus headquarters, the old Chevy coughed, and Ol' Bert handed a piece of paper to Lance with the directions to the university's library. "Lance, you're the navigator," Bert announced. "And Leslie, keep your eye out for a place we can get a coffee and a doughnut before we get out of the city."

"Bert, this car looks great, but it doesn't sound great. Maybe I should have driven us in my BMW," Leslie offered.

"No, that's a cute little thing, but I like the space in this contraption, plus I need to drive, and I wouldn't want to spill coffee on that pretty upholstery," Bert said, glancing playfully in the rear view mirror back at Leslie. "The Chevy is today's strategy—it's the vehicle that's going to get us there—and I need to drive it just as I need to drive our Mustard Seed strategy."

After a quick coffee stop, the atmosphere in the car turned noticeably quiet and glum, everyone self-absorbed. Ol' Bert had not yet found his second horse, the company was experiencing some setbacks because of competitive actions, and the plant was having some quality problems, which had been causing the three of them to play defense with customers.

Bert broke the silence by howling, "Know how to git where you're goin'." That startled Lance.

"What? Oh. Yes. Well, it says here we get on State Road #10, go to the County Courthouse, then County Road PP north to an intersection that's under construction where we get on the Interstate, east to exit 14, take a right at the Wal-Mart, go four miles, then—and I can't read this. What does this say, Bert?" and Lance stuck the paper in front of Bert's nose. Ol' Bert, who could barely see over the steering wheel of the huge Chevy almost went off the road.

"Easy. Whoa. Everyone okay? Give it to me a step at a time," Bert said, back in control.

"Let me use that episode to make a point on planning," Bert said, with composure regained. "The words *'know how to git where you're goin'* in this fourth success essential emphasizes the need for a manager to triple check his or her own understanding of the plan. A lot is on the line. Plans, like stakes and planted strategies must be carefully crafted and thoroughly internalized. I must know the plan inside-out, upside-down, and be able to communicate it to you and our colleagues back at Certus. I should never, ever, have to ask anyone what the plan is, as I asked Lance a moment ago. People should be asking *me*, and I should be able to spit it out as quick and easy as a watermelon seed. Everyone got that?" Bert asked, glancing right and then checking the rear-view mirror.

"Yes, we got it. That's a good point," said Lance. "Sorry about that direction episode."

"No problem," Bert chuckled. "I'll keep this team on the road. Not to worry."

"Bert, whose directions were those? Who gave them to you? Who told you the way?" Leslie asked.

"My good and dear friend at the library. You'll meet her. Wonderful woman." They could
tell by Ol' Bert's voice that this woman had to be someone special.

"Leslie, let me use your question to make another point about planning. The best plans are the ones you draw up from scratch yourself. Never use anyone else's plans. Yes, it's certainly the right thing to do to ask for advice. But in the end you and I and Lance must be the authors of our own plans. One of the best ways to become acquainted with the nitty-gritty of our jobs, and execute those jobs at the highest level, is to author plans on how to do those jobs.

"Speaking of authoring, I'm not naive. I know that what most business professionals think about planning is similar to the way Dr. Samuel Johnson, the famous English author, thought about composition. *Composition is, for the most part, an effort of slow diligence and steady perseverance to which the mind is dragged by necessity or resolution.* Isn't that so true with planning?" laughed Bert. "But when you've seen the payoffs you'll have sold yourself on the value of planning.

"As a former insurance salesman I always thought of a plan as an insurance policy for outrageous success. I pay premiums via my efforts to create and maintain the plan, and the plan pays handsome dividends while protecting my rear-end from disasters.

"I know you have both created plans before, but I'd like to share some fundamental principles on planning. The two of you will be operating semi-independently and need to understand the sales team's road map so that your own road maps and actions are consistent. I also know from experience that salespeople can instantly recognize a plan that will not work and that's a reason you're a part of this process—we've *all* got to buy-in at the outset. There is not enough time, money, or resource to do the job twice."

Ol' Bert used the ensuing ride to talk about planning. There was a lot of productive give and take.

At this point he said, "We all know where the sales team is going just like we know where we are going today. Our 'stakes' have been pounded into the ground. Again, the words *'git where you're goin'* underscores that a sales plan maps a long and arduous journey, that our stakes must be locked in our mind's eye, and that we absolutely MUST get there! Not *try to* 'git there, but *'GIT there*! Our destinations and resolve are crystal-clear.

Then he said, "We're all familiar with the strategy we've just planted just like we know today's travel-strategy is this old Chevy. All three of us need to be as closely attached to, and comfortable with, our sales-team strategy as we are comfortably attached to the plush seats in this Chevy. That'll happen through consistent application of the strategy, and we'll get just as warm and cozy.

"Now—while we have a map for today's journey, we still don't have a map for the business, and *that's* the task at hand—*know how you're gonna git there*. The stakes-strategy-plan sequence is often missed in actual practice. Stakes-strategy-plan, stakes-strategy-plan," he repeated. "Never forget it. It is a never-ending circle."

Ol' Bert said he had chosen today's meeting site to emphasize the mental aspects of planning and the rich array of resources that are available from multiple sources for effective sales team planning and individual account manager planning. He said he knew that many managers and salespeople were poor users of resources, and the bulk of the problem was that they didn't know what existed and where it was. He also talked about thought-provoking resources such as bookstores, websites, newsstands, historical records, federal and state agencies, special databases, market researchers, their own marketing staff, and planning software. They all had their new laptops loaded with the new software with them, so they were ready.

Bert started again, saying, "Remember how the Queen remarked to Alice, in *Alice's Adventures in Wonderland, 'it's a poor sort of memory that only works backwards'*? Well, think of planning as forwards-type memory. We all have an 'R' and a 'D' in our minds just like this old clunker-of-a-car and we need to use both.

He continued to spin-up this little planning lesson, volunteering, "I'm far from finalizing the sales team's plan. I have some ideas, and I want to use my own plan creation as a model for both of you. You'll have your own plans to create, and I want yours to reflect certain key elements.

"Plans must ultimately be in writing, but by the time we all start writing 90% of the work will be done. Plans are *not* just verbal or mental road maps. Never let anyone trap you into believing that. They are *documents*. A plan is the end product of planning—and a planning document is the plan put in writing. It's amazing what the transition from mind to paper or laptop gives rise to. How can others know what you think until they *see* what you have to say? And your own *seeing* has a way of illuminating gaps for your own benefit.

"Your sales plans aren't an exercise to satisfy me or someone else's requirement. They aren't meant to be stuffed in some binder or drawer. They're for *you* to use and reference daily—plain and simple.

"Planning is a learned skill. It's something everyone can master. If an old farm-boy like me can do it, anyone can do it.

"I've talked to the other managers back at the office to get their suggestions and views since they've witnessed past sales efforts and they have more experience in the business than I have. It's imperative to ask colleagues—both pragmatists and freethinkers—for opinions about plan content.

"And finally, a manager should always get the inputs of team members. I really value your experience and ideas. You're here because I believe you both have much to offer. And please share with each other."

He said a lot more. And Leslie and Lance soaked in every word.

"Hopefully today's road-map is the quickest, the safest, and the most economical route to the university's library. Plans need to share and balance the same three characteristics—but right now we need an emphasis on quickness and economy," Bert said apprehensively, checking with Lance for the next turn.

"Today we have one destination, so we have one plan. If we had two destinations, we'd need two plans. Ten destinations, ten plans, and so on. Every one of my stakes and your stakes requires a plan—a plan that describes *how* you and I are going to get to each stake. That's all a plan is—it's 'the how'.

"Remember that our stakes are interdependent. Since the permutations of interdependence grow geometrically it reinforces the point of not having too many stakes. And speaking of interdependence, you should view stakes, strategies, and plans with a certain degree of tentativeness as all three come together—each testing the do-ability of the other—all three firming-up somewhat together. So don't be surprised if our planning causes us to go back and tweak our stakes and strategies.

"You're each running micro-businesses out there. Tell me *how* you're going to do it.

"Got it!" said Leslie. "*When* is the best time to start planning, Bert?" she continued.

"Keep yourself from planning in the first few weeks—even a month—on a new assignment. Don't jump to conclusions. Pay close attention. Get the feel of things. Leave yourself exposed to soak up impressions and subtleties. You don't want to miss any interesting stuff—surprising possibilities that may open—like passages and tunnels in those mystery video games.

"It may get uncomfortable as the impatient eyes of bosses and colleagues glare at you—so just nicely explain yourself.

"I'm planning at *this* time because I now have a good sense for the situation. You'll never have a *total* sense for a situation—so *please* don't wait for that.

"I often think of this intentional lagging as doing a little imagining and a little chewing—and some nosing and sniffing-around—like cows patiently eating that Kansas blue-stem in those wide open spaces," and he laughed. "Let your mind wander and ruminate the same way.

"Once you've been in an assignment for a while any starting delay is unnecessary. Only at the beginning. Okay?

"Okay. Yes, but then *where* do we start with plans?" continued Leslie.

"Another good question. Well, we've already started," said Bert, "because, as I said, we have our stakes, and we've planted a demand-based, differentiated, dominating strategy. But we don't yet have the road map, *the plan*, to get to those stakes.

"The books say the next step is analysis, but that word always gave me the willies," Bert said, fidgeting for effect. "Analysis sounds like contemplating your navel. I prefer to call it good old-fashioned tough questioning—like the hard, squirmy questions my momma used to ask my daddy about how he was going to solve a problem or get us out of a nasty predicament. I saw first hand that the tougher the questions and the more honest the answers, the better it was for everyone. Never forgot the lesson.

"Hard, squirmy questions act as both windows and mirrors into stark reality. We need a balance of both—window-type questions for the marketplace and the mirror variety to look at ourselves.

"Lance, take the first three pages out of that folder and give one to Leslie, one to me, and keep one for yourself. I've noted some hard, squirmy questions we need to think about. No reason I can't talk and you can't think while we're driving along."

Ol' Bert then proceeded to ask questions regarding what he and Leslie and Lance needed to think about, pausing at length between each question, and letting them absorb each inquiry.

"Ready? Here goes."

"What's our current location, or business situation? Let's make sure we really understand our journey's launching spot. The Law of Navigation says you can't navigate without a known current location.

"What do we sell and provide of intrinsic value to our partners and customers? It's more than the physical product and service bundles. It's also intangibles and concepts. Let's make sure we can explain all that in meaningful *customer-terms*. This relates to The Law of Magnetism, which says—we draw not those that *we* want, but rather are drawn to those who want *us*.

"Who are our current customers? Let's thoroughly catalog the customer base, and that's more than the names of companies, it's *specific* people in those firms. This ties to my Eveready Bunny Business Credo—which says the people to whom a supplier's staff is wired and connected are the contacts that build business—and keep it going and going and going.

"Who are our *optimum* customers and prospects, the ones that will account for the majority of our successes, and the ones that will quickly help our cash flow? Let's follow Old McDonald's Good-Dirt Maxim—planting where the earth has proven its richness and pass up the rocky soil that has proven its poorness—eeyi-eeyi-yo," Bert sang, smiling broadly.

"What market segments, vertical markets, and niches are contestable? Contestable markets make it possible for little companies like us with limited resources to build commanding positions. General Pickett's Axiom says that head-on assaults against massed entrenched competition usually result in disaster.

"Are there any emerging markets forecasted where we can pre-position ourselves ahead of the competition? Frank Perdue's Premise holds that the eggs you snuggle and hatch are ones you don't have to struggle to catch.

"Do we know how to characterize early-adopters and the early-majority, the folks that can help us get a foothold with our new products? This relates to Barnum & Bailey's Parade Proposition, which says that someone *always* has to be first, second, third, and so on.

"How should we deploy ourselves and our limited weapons for productive effect—being aligned with Mr. Pimm's and marketing's priorities? What should our deployment criteria be? By product line? By geography? By customer size? By market or customer-class? By competitor? After all, we're an underdog. Let's follow Crazy Horse's Principle—when you're outgunned you must out-maneuver the competition.

"Let's consider the role of timing in order to engage for maximum impact—whether that be time-of-day, day-of-week, or week-of-quarter. Prospect receptivity has a temporal side. Carefully picking the time to strike is consistent with The Calendar's Dictum—and that is—*every* sales opportunity has a springtime of its own.

"What threats exist in the market? Let's prepare thoroughly. This relates to a favorite Fast Food Proverb of mine, which says—a prairie dog with only one hole is a fox's quarter-pounder. As a result, I like to *do* lunch, not *be* lunch.

"Is there any other stuff that might prevent us from reaching our stakes or possibly go wrong? We can't wait for stuff to come unglued. We've got to identify crazy but possible 'what-ifs' that come from the inside *and* the outside—and outline contingency approaches to shield ourselves. And we've got to identify and quantify the early signs that 'stuff' is starting to happen. This relates to The Law of Dispersal, which says—unexpected 'stuff' that hits the fan is never evenly distributed.

"How much money do we have in the capital and expense budget to invest? Let's figure out how to get the biggest bang for our limited bucks. And let's plan how to sweet-talk the company into investing more in the sales department's viable ventures. And I think I'm all out of Laws, Credo's, and Maxim's. Maybe you can have some fun—as I have—and come up with convenient reminders for the rest of my hard, squirmy questions.

And of course, smiling, Leslie and Lance said they would try.

Bert continued, "What products contribute best to Certus profitability? Let's prioritize our product lines and services.

"Specifically, how are our markets and our customers changing? What are the sales implications? The world is a dynamic place. Let's change with it.

"What are the buying trends in the industries we serve? Let's figure out if priorities and processes are evolving and how to take advantage.

"Why do people currently buy from us as opposed to others? Let's figure out the things we've been doing right and replicate it everywhere it makes sense.

"Who are our competitors—and that's both current and potential competitors and direct and indirect competitors? And that's not the *name* of companies—it's the values and behaviors they're providing—and the technologies and the tools they're utilizing. Let's scrutinize all that as if we were picking a chicken bone clean. Can we learn anything from their approaches and techniques? Let's be honest—they're doing many things right. Oftentimes that's hard to admit, like the neighbor whose corn is growing taller than yours is growing.

"On the proactive side, what do we do better then our competitors? What advantages of ours can we exploit? What weaknesses of *theirs* can we exploit? Let's leverage all that, and toot our horn," and he tooted the Chevy's.

"Are we competing with ourselves? Let's identify those internal conflicting agendas and processes where we are wasting our energy and blow out those fires.

"What regulatory, environmental, or safety issues affect our offerings? Let's promote how we better satisfy those necessary requirements than anyone else. And let's make sure we understand pending legislation that may impact us and what we're doing about it.

"What are Certus's corporate strengths and assets? Let's identify them for leverage purposes. How about weaknesses? Let's develop rational answers.

"What are the evident *and* potential capabilities of *all* our customer-contact colleagues, such as Customer Service and Technical Support? What steps can be taken to ensure that customers and partners get the benefit of a 'tip-top-treatment plan' at every point customers and partners' personnel or documents 'touch' Certus?

"Do we have issues with other departments as a result of the change and movement we're triggering? And do they have issues with us—which reminds me of one last Law—Richard Petty's Pit-Crew Postulate. Sparking and chafing are reduced in direct proportion to the amount of teamwork-oil that is applied between team members. A 4W-30L oil, where 'L' is a 'Listen' additive, works best.

"What does the 'W' stand for?" asked Lance.

"We," said Bert, without skipping a beat.

Ol' Bert said they'd have a couple of chart pads in the conference room at the library to think more about these—and many additional hard, squirmy questions.

By the time Ol' Bert was finished with all the questions they had arrived at the university's library. Leslie and Lance's heads were spinning.

Ol' Bert's friend, the daughter of an old service buddy who had been killed-in-action, was the chief business information services librarian. She met them at the front entrance right on time. It was an emotional greeting for Ol' Bert. She gave a warm welcome to Leslie and Lance.

The librarian escorted them inside, got them comfortable in the little conference room they would be using, then proceeded to lead a tour of the library's facilities and resources. She started with the on-line databases, all menu and key word driven, making them easy to access. Then she visited several websites that would be of interest to them and gave them a document with numerous other sites listed for further exploration. Since the library was a depository of Federal Government information, she went through numerous samples of specialized directories, handbooks, and reports. Leslie and Lance were beginning to suffer from information overload. Next they looked at numerous print resources, including special encyclopedias, surveys, books loaded with trends and statistics, and industry analyses. Having been briefed by

Ol' Bert, she focused on materials of obvious interest. At the end she indicated that the library offered a fee-based research and document delivery service based on complex databases they could all easily access on an ongoing basis.

It was clear that this was a storehouse of ammunition that would be very useful and give them a competitive advantage.

When they got back to the conference room after the tour, Bert said, "Planning is thinking, an intellectual exercise, not a mechanical exercise. What you've just witnessed should have stirred your mental juices. It certainly got me in the right frame of mind."

They took several minutes to discuss how they could utilize all they had seen and heard.

Then they discussed and took notes on all the questions that Ol' Bert had shared with them in the car—plus other questions. They ended up papering the walls of the conference room with chart pad notes. They also threw up a copy of their stakes and strategies. It was a spirited discussion, weaving the questions, stakes, strategies, and the recently discovered resources together.

When they were done, Ol' Bert said it was time to get into 'writing up the plan'. He started by saying that, "A plan is a strategy *implementation* tool. Sales team plans and account manager plans are very personal. There are *no* hard rules, but I've found three common threads through the years that weave warm comforting plans. Ever go into a fabric store? Did you know the three common types of thread are called dual-duty, quilting, and buttonhole twist? How's that for a bit of trivia? Learned it from my momma.

"I'll start with dual-duty for the first common thread, which is format. Matrices, flow charts, tables, or a spreadsheet filled with bullets work well. It makes for an 'easy read' for yourself and others. Import graphics, scan-in photos, and create charts. Be as short as you can on prose. A multiplication of words does not promise a multiplication of results. Readability and usability go down with the square of the length. And use small words. Make sure it is well organized, that it 'flows', and make sure 'plan hygiene'—the spelling and grammar—is perfect. The readability and quality of your plan says a lot about your commitment to quality execution.

A spreadsheet format encourages a short, succinct plan. We're not here to write a book—or what I call credenza-ware—or file-ware. A table or spreadsheet is also easily upgradeable and easy to work from. We don't need to create something that's going to cause major rewrites every time there's a market hiccup. Create a table or matrix for each 'stake'. Each should highlight the 'who', 'what', 'where', 'when', 'why', 'how', and 'how-much' associated with achieving a particular stake. The specificity facilitates execution and demonstrates to others that you'll handle all tasks thoroughly and intelligently.

We don't need fiction, we just need facts. These formats can be customized and be made very readable and useable. Think of them as a management art form. They can be easily toted around in your laptop for real-time inputs and reference—which is why I say 'dual-duty'—for home *and* on the road.

Then Ol' Bert gave them each a couple of sample format pages and a disk. "Not every element of a plan can be in this format, but most elements can. Massage these samples to your personal liking. Experiment.

"I'll switch to a quilting thread for the second common thread, which is content," and he handed out another outline. "Let me review these points for the sales team's plan, my own road-map. This outline is meant to stimulate my thinking and make sure I cover everything. I'd like you to know what will be in my plan so you know what I'm thinking and so you can be supportive. And, after all, you may be in my shoes someday."

"Bert, shouldn't you finish your plan before we start ours?" Leslie asked.

"No, not at all. You've each got your own little business to run. We're linked together by our stakes, linked by the sales team strategies we're planting, and linked by all of the questions we discussed earlier. After that, your plan is your own. This is a parallel, but *not* an independent, process.

"Obviously I'll have some elements in my plan, like compensation, that you won't have in yours. And you will have some elements in your plan, like how you're going to manage the XYZ account, which I won't have in mine. But we'll both need to cover some common subjects, such as new customer acquisition. Your plan will be more specific than mine will be.

"I want you both to know *exactly* what I'm planning and drafting, and why. In the end we'll all get to review each other's draft. Sharing often sparks fortuitous ideas. This is an iterative process. Okay?"

"Okay. Got it. You're right," said Leslie.

Ol' Bert then proceeded to talk-through his own plan outline, simply identifying major sections and all the things he needed to consider and include— a few of which had already been done. His intent was to emphasize his comprehensiveness, hoping it rubbed-off on Leslie and Lance.

He spoke of the steps he would take to build and strengthen the sales organization, including new hires planned and his Twelve-P process, deployment options he was considering, teaching and coaching plans, his own continuing personal development needs, and simple actions he would execute to ensure integration of the sales department into the rest of the business.

He discussed the actions he wanted to take to improve coordination and results with Certus's sales partners, including 'stakes' and strategy, communications hooks, support toolboxes, up-dating of policies, contract implementation, the exchange and measurement of expectations, training, mutual-action plans, the selection process for planned partner additions, and any necessary terminations.

He talked about key customer priorities and issues, market segment rationale, the sorting-out of strategic accounts, National Account efforts, beta site needs, vertical market classification, customer retention efforts, the necessity of at-risk account 'save' plans, new customer acquisition efforts, and attacks on certain competitive strongholds.

He shared the what, why, when, and how of communications tools he was thinking about using, including sales meetings, newsletters, e-mail, an intranet, video-conferencing, conference calls, user group meetings, an independent rep council, and distributor meetings.

He listed control processes he was considering such as quotation guidelines, procedures for RFP's (requests-for-proposals), bid/no-bid criteria, periodic business reviews, contingency handling, major market indicators to follow, a competitive information tracking system, pipeline reviews, forecast creation and management, a regular sales process audit, the timing and format of key sales metrics tracking, price exception tracking, sales partner inventory tracking, and key sales activity tracking.

He spoke about the importance of maintaining their currency with relevant technology, including their computer and peripheral assets, their Customer Relationship Management software, investigation of Electronic Data Interchange tools, various presentation apparatus they would use, and communications devices that they would evaluate.

He gave an accounting of compensation strategy, detailing what salaries were intended to cover, and how corporate objectives, teamwork, personal contributions, and special challenges would be compensated with incentives.

He outlined the operating budget, the budgets for each salesperson, capital expenditures planned, reporting processes and policies, and spending authorization levels.

He reviewed the things he was planning to do to recognize individuals, the team, and sales partners, including management citations, commendations, various performance awards, and a President's Club—and also sales department recognition of Certus employees in other parts of the business.

"That's it! That's the bulk of the stuff I have to think about. A lot of little pieces—which is why I use a quilting thread here," he smiled playfully. "To bring it all together beautifully."

"Wow, that's pretty thorough. I'm impressed! But you didn't say anything about sales tactics, Bert," Leslie noted. "Why not?"

"Tactics are your job Leslie. Tactics includes all the activities you'll use to bring in the business. It's the meat, the potatoes, and the dessert of *your* plan," grinned Bert. "And I'm here to help you whip up as appetizing a spread as my momma used to make. More on that later."

"Glad to hear that Bert. I can use your help," Leslie admitted.

"One final personal note on content. I've always put prayer in my plans as well—and I treat it as a steering wheel, not a spare tire—and as a result I've never lost my way.

"I'll switch to buttonhole twist for the third common planning thread, which is style, *how* you write your plan," and Bert handed out yet another page of comments.

"I learned all this stuff the hard way, by having past managers critique *my* plans. Believe me, a lot of the critiquing wasn't pleasant.

"First—make sure your plan is aimed at dominance. All effective plans radiate that attitude.

"Next—make sure you know what you're talking about by exhibiting *sensitivity* to our overall business situation, the macro-environment in which Certus is operating, and our constraints. Your consistency should be readily apparent. Consistency says you *understand* our reality.

"Make sure your plan is *focused* on markets, customers, products, issues, processes, and people that are relevant to Certus's current mission—which is survival and turn-around. Don't spin-off on tangents.

"Make sure your plan provides an absolutely accurate sense of the real world—that it's a triumph of reality over appearance, of what *is* over what *seems* to be.

"Make sure you don't hide behind a veil of complexity and intellectualism. Make the plan as transparent as the windshield of this car. As some author once said, *unless one is a genius, it is best to aim at being intelligible.*

"Make sure you reference other people that have been solicited for opinions or data. Reference all you learned here today—identifying all the databases, directories, and handbooks. Highlight other research you plan to execute. Continuing research displays thinking and thoroughness, and maintains your credibility.

"Make sure you highlight what's important—and highlight *your* priorities. Rationalize those priorities. Be consistent with *my* priorities, the stuff I identified earlier, and the priorities of all the other Certus departments with whom we work. Do you remember The Law of the Farm and The Law of the Garden? Stick to them.

"Make sure you are creative. We need boldness, new ideas, suggestions, and calculated risks in our plans. We're not going to climb this mountain doing it the way it's always been done. Be aggressive. Challenge the status quo. Innovation and surprise can create turmoil for competitors. Aim at being *both* interesting *and* exact.

"Make sure your plan is loaded with hard numbers, fixed dates, firm percentages, savvy probabilities, tight ranges, and other solid data. Keep the squishy-squashy stuff out. A mushy plan means you don't know where you are going. But a few assumptions are inevitable, so explicitly state them. It will clarify your thinking and allow you and others to more quickly recognize, and thus react to, any of the assumptions being wrong.

"Make sure you show *who* else and *what* else you need to get the plan accomplished. Collaboration and asset utilization is a recipe for success. If you need my help or the help of others, say so in the plan. Also, be specific indicating what other material or financial resources would be appreciated.

"Make sure you identify the major barriers that are in your way, come up with some suggestions on how to go over or around the barriers, or indicate a process you will use to try to dissolve the barriers. And point out the attendant risks. You've *got to* identify things that inhibit us from reaching the stakes—and your problem-solving recommendations are imperative.

"Make sure your plan communicates your solid commitment to 'work-the-plan' and solid commitment to results. Committed plans reflect a ton of energy, are loaded with action words, and are very direct and honest. Finally, nothing great in sales or business has ever been accomplished without passion. An outrageous plan oozes sticky passion that clings to both the author and any reader. But one must also be able to stay objective and non-emotional to correctly and timely recognize when elements need to be changed or even abandoned. Blind commitment and excessive passion must be avoided," finished Bert.

"Button-hole twist ties your plan firmly to the corporation just as it ties a button firmly to a shirt."

"Bert, this piece on style really hit me," said Lance.

"That's good. If you do it with 'style' you'll end-up proud of your plan and eager to execute it. If you find yourself so excited and stuck on what you're creating that you start executing before you're finished—it means that your plan has captured *you*—and you'll know you've succeeded.

"I'll tell you," Bert continued, "When you go through the planning process you end up understanding the business, the markets, and your customers so much better. Planning causes you to stop and think. It *is* a lot of work, but planning is the most worthwhile reflective activity that we can engage in. As old man Henry Ford used to say, *if you chop your own wood, it will warm you twice.*

"Now, let's 'chop' independently, using the resources we've seen to help us fill in the gaps. Let's get our heads together again in two hours and share our individual thoughts and progress on our drafts. We don't intend to finish anything today, only get a solid start. Okay?" Bert concluded.

"Two hours?" Leslie whined.

"Two hours," Bert repeated. "The great Sauk Indian chief Black Hawk once said, *The path to glory is rough, and many gloomy hours obscure it. May the Great Spirit shed light on your path.*" And Bert smiled reassuringly.

Two hours later they were back together, all talking at once, proud of their progress and their ideas. Ol' Bert brought a little order to the proceeding by asking Leslie, then Lance, to share their drafts. Then it was his turn. The interchange helped all three flesh-out their plans.

On the way out of the library they thanked the staff for their gracious assistance. Ol' Bert said he would be back to execute a pro-bono mini-seminar on sales and marketing for the business information services staff.

Back in the car, Ol' Bert used the opportunity to talk further about plans and planning.

"Once a plan is done you turn from a thinker to a doer. But remember, any plan or planner is faulty that does not anticipate and accept changes during the course of the 'doing'—and documenting the reasons for each change as a learning tool for us and others.

"Remember when you first learned to drive how you watched the pedals and the instruments rather than where you were going? Remember how herky-jerky you drove and all the near-accidents you had? Well, you can expect the same thing with your plans. You'll be looking at that plan more frequently at first, and then as your comfort level rises your ride will smooth-out and you'll be cruising just as we are now.

"I love to write plans," Bert said. "Outrageous ones especially. I think the reason I do is because it gives me a great feeling of confidence that I'll achieve outrageous results. I can take a deep breath, exhale, and relax a bit. Anxiety, which you know *never* goes away, is *greatly* reduced.

"Have you ever been rushed for a simple thing like a sales appointment, unsure of quite how to get there, uncertain if you had everything you needed, and fearful of being late? Doesn't that anxiety get you mad at yourself and detract from the sales call? Then consider how good, how comfortable you feel, when you give yourself time, you're well prepared, and you know exactly how to get where you're going. You handle the call in the best of spirits and without apprehension, don't you?" Bert said with confidence.

"My gosh, absolutely. I can't stand the sweaty palms and the knot in my stomach when I'm in a rushed, uncertain situation," chimed in Lance.

"Me too. Been there," Leslie added. "It ticks me off."

"Well, there's the value of a plan in a nutshell. A plan contains clear-cut routes, early-warning signs, contingency steps, and the peace-of-mind that comes from knowing you are prepared—*knowin' how to git there.*

"Who is *my* plan for? It's for me," Bert started again. "Me first," he emphasized. "This sales team plan will be my personal road-map. I have a selfish attitude about plans. Always write *your* plan for yourself first. If it's not really for you, you won't have a strong sense of ownership, and it's not likely you'll have faith in it or use it.

"I drew that map we used to get to the library today, right? Did you notice how Lance had a hard time following it? That's because I wrote it for *me.*

"However, in this case with my sales team plan, I am also writing it for *you.* I have to make sure *you* understand it, because I'm the manager. You're *not* a secondary audience. *We* are a team. If *we* don't understand it, if *we* all don't buy into it, *we* fail collectively. I've got your success in my hands. So my selfish attitude extends to you. It's a responsibility I take very seriously," Bert accentuated. "So my feeling of plan ownership is for the team, not just myself. An even *better* way of saying all this would be to say '*we* are writing all of this for *us*'. Clear?"

And Ol' Bert paused.

"Oh, yes. Clear, very clear," said Lance. "I never had a manager explain it to me that way. It makes me feel you're really concerned about my personal success."

"Lance, believe me, your success comes *well* before mine. My success comes *through* you.

"One other thing," Bert interjected slowly, "When you're in the planning process, which *never* stops, it's a good idea to keep taking peeks in the rear-view mirror at that massive 18-wheeler that's gaining on you, looking left and right for ugly weather closing in, gazing far ahead to check for potholes—and keeping your eyes and ears open for pleasant vistas and compelling sounds. Do you remember the *Forrest Gump* film? Remember how Forrest's momma told him, *Life is like a box of chocolates. You never know what you're gonna get.* Well," Bert laughed, "business is a super-sized variety box, so we're always having to react with a plan to the surprises we bite into.

"We've gone this route before, haven't we?" Bert continued, referring to their drive. "Didn't we come this way this morning? Aren't we more comfortable with how to get back? Of course we are," he said, smiling. "Well, a plan is the same way. The more you use the plan the more comfortable you become. Why I bet if we were to go back to the library in the morning we would be tempted to leave that scrap of paper behind. We would know the route. Plans are the same way. We'll get proficient with our plan once we begin using it—and therein lies an accompanying danger. We'll be tempted to leave it behind once, and then shortly thereafter we'll forget about it altogether. And *then* we'll begin to be buffeted by forces outside our control, like the nasty wind outside, and *then* we'll become totally reactive, and *then* we'll get jumpy and all stressed-out, and *then* we'll end up who-knows-where, and then we won't reach our stakes! Yikes!

"In order to avoid that, remember that a plan takes *you* on a journey more than you take *it*.

"The plans we're creating are based on a certain bunch of impressions, subtleties, and facts—all that initial sniffing around and all those hard, squirmy questions, right? But if any of that changes, as the weather and the seasons *always* do, we need to modify our plans. If a flash flood closed this Interstate we'd have to find a new route, wouldn't we? Well, if the market or competition 'closes us down' for some reason or another, we'll have to modify our plan. If a competitor drops out or a new market opens up we'd also have to amend our plan. That's why planning never stops. The environment is always changing, like the construction at that intersection ahead," Bert noted. "Always hold on tight to your roadmap."

"Now if I were to take a left at that next light—and go down that pretty country road—maybe it would get us back home quicker. Huh? No, I won't, but it looks tempting, doesn't it? You'll find distractions trying to get you off your plans as well. All distractions do is invite delays and disasters. Does that mean you shouldn't experiment? Of course not, as long as you know you are experimenting, and you know the way back to the main road. But don't start experimenting until you've got your initial plan down pat and you've got the luxury of time and no pressure—which we don't have right now.

"Well, we're not done. Next week I've invited one of our best customers to come and talk to us about our plans. Knowing the industry, she's going to tell us what *she* would do if *she* were in our shoes. I've come to know this woman well in the past couple of months, and she's sharp."

"Seriously? A customer will do that?" questioned Lance.

"Of course. Remember, we're 'partners' with our customers. We have a 'partnering mentality'. Customers can provide practical insights and ideas to keep fluff out of our plans. No one has time or money for fluff. She'll share her expectations of a supplier and a supplier's sales force. It will help us focus," Bert added.

"You're darn tootin' it will. That's a great idea, Bert," chimed in Leslie, all enthused, "But why didn't we do that first?"

"Because it may have limited your horizons. Creative planning benefits from an unencumbered and unbiased beginning."

"Okay, the agenda for next week is to get your plans in final draft stage. After listening to our guest speaker I'll talk about the fifth essential for outrageous success, using a process and tools to maximize our yields. That's the tactics to which I referred earlier, Leslie—it's the fun stuff. Then we'll finalize our drafts but that doesn't mean you shouldn't work from them right now. As General Patton said, *a good plan violently executed now is better than a perfect plan next week.*

"It's been a very productive day. Thanks for your ideas and really mixing it up," Bert concluded. "So let's stop and get some dinner. They've got good chicken-fried steak up ahead."

"Oh, that sounds healthy, Bert," Leslie tweaked. Then she added, "Lance, why don't you and I send a little thank you note to the librarian tomorrow."

Ol' Bert kept quiet and roared into the restaurant's parking lot.

After dinner he gave them each a gift copy of *The One-Day Marketing Plan* and *A Whack on the Side of the Head* to aid their planning efforts.

When they got back to Certus it was dark and everyone was gone. Ol' Bert's office was littered with worrisome notes from other Certus staff members seeking out his wisdom and calming guidance. He had become a magnet for others in the company during the crisis.

He dashed-off several e-mails in response. He pulled some materials out of his files, made copies, and laid them on the desks of a couple of the inquirers. He checked out a few websites to get some answers for one of his colleagues. He edited a new policy that someone had asked him to review. And he called a couple of candidates whose phone numbers and résumés the HR director had left. Then he went home.

His self-discipline and unassuming high-energy style was unmistakable to the rest of the management team. He was cultivating the culture, little by little.

His example was causing everyone else's activity to quicken like his percolating coffee pot.

Essential #5
Use The Best Ways For The Best Yields

The meeting with the customer guest-speaker was delayed because of help Ol' Bert was providing to other managers. Also, Mr. Pimm had asked him to spend some time with Certus's marketing team to work on an upcoming product launch. While all that jumbled Ol' Bert's plans he was happy to assist. The detour was balanced by the fact that he had found and hired his second new horse. He was delighted! Mr. Pimm was ecstatic!

Luke had grown up in Boise where his father had run an independent sales agency. After graduating from the University of North Dakota, where he was a history major and a tough defenseman on their NCAA championship ice hockey team, he went to work for his dad. Most recently he had been working for a big wholesale distributorship outside of Dallas. Ol' Bert had spotted a well-written article that Luke had contributed to <u>Industrial Distribution</u> magazine. The following Saturday morning Ol' Bert flew in, hungry and taking no chances, and rang Luke's home doorbell. The rest was history.

Leslie and Lance thought that the boss liked Luke because he was short and aggressive. They liked him because he was promotion-minded, a conceptual thinker, and understood hybrid-channel selling.

The delay worked out well, because by the time the meeting with the customer guest-speaker did occur, Luke had been able to get some of Ol' Bert's legendary 'priming' and be brought up to speed on the 'stakes', the planted strategies, and the 'road-map' efforts-to-date.

When the customer's presentation on expectations in Certus's conference room was finally accomplished two weeks later, it was well received. The bottom line was that customers expect vendors to understand their business, manage their satisfaction, act as their advocate, and be knowledgeable about applications. There was unanimous agreement that the customer's comments would help them focus their plans. The event also helped to seal the relationship with this customer. A first-class luncheon capped the event.

After the luncheon the little sales team went back to Ol' Bert's office. It was clear to the three horses that this was going to be a customer-driven culture. They loved it. The mood was up-beat.

"It's time to talk about yields—bushels per acre—or orders per effort," Bert said. The discussion had been pre-planned.

Bert introduced the subject by saying, "Certain ways of selling—certain sales processes—are proven and productive and more effective than others. There *are* best ways. It's a fact.

"The same applies to sales tools and to management tools. There *are* best tools.

"Our know-how and experience, plus the know-how of others, educates us and suggests what processes and tools will work best for Certus.

"It's *our call* to decide what sales process and tools are best for us, but what's best for us must *first be best* for the customer, so—one of the things we must determine and confirm is the *buying* process for Certus products. That's a subtlety many companies miss. They try to force-fit people's buying into their company's selling process, when the opposite should occur. Or they don't even think about their customers' buying processes at all. We must match our selling process to our customers' buying processes. The customer comes first.

"Please clarify what you mean by buying process," Lance asked.

"It's the mental and emotional—and logical—progression that buyers go through. It's a progression of thoughts and action steps—from unawareness of a need, to a feeling of discontent or want, to a clear awareness of a problem or opportunity, to deciding to do something about it—to considering options, to creating criteria, to shopping—to settling on preferences, to evaluating, to decision making, to actual purchasing, and then to reinforcement of the decision. That's the theory, but buyers don't always express themselves in those words.

"Often they use conventional phrases such as 'we don't see the need for that', 'we're frustrated', 'we know we've got to find a better way', 'we've formed a committee to look into so-and-so', 'we're studying our alternatives'—and words such as, 'we've drafted some specs', 'we're planning to look at some stuff at the next trade show', 'we've narrowed it down to four vendors', 'the executive committee is studying the proposals'—and expressions such as, 'the CFO will make the final call', 'we've cut the P.O.'. And then, 'results have proved our decision to be a good one'.

"You see what I mean? Either way—the theory or the conventional—those words tell you and I where a buyer is in their buying process. We must *always* know where *they* are positioned in their buying process—so that we know where we *should* be positioned in our sales process. If a buyer senses that you don't understand where they're positioned in their buying process, you can *really* aggravate the daylights out of them."

"Yes—yes, that's understandable, Bert," Lance agreed with growing enthusiasm.

"You and I and everyone else who ever buys anything go through such a process," Bert continued. "There has been a lot of research on the subject of buying. There are slight variations on that progression I just rolled through, but they're all pretty similar. Sometimes that whole progression takes place in a matter of seconds—like when buying an ice cream cone. And sometimes that process takes place over the course of many months—like when buying a new home.

"Business buyers go through a similar progression—a similar buying process. But be careful, because sometimes the buying process gets tangled up with purchasing *policies*. A purchasing policy could be that a buyer is required to obtain three bids before making a decision, or required to get six signatures to obtain approval, or required to accept the low bid. Policies are necessary safeguards and controls. Occasionally they're burdensome—for *both* buyer and seller. Policies are most often a part of the decision making step or the administration associated with the actual buying step.

"Don't get hung-up on policies. We need to understand our buyers' buying processes first—policies second. Understanding of our buyers' buying process will guide us how to act, how to respond—how to sell! You with me so far?"

"Yes, yes, we're following you," they each responded in turn.

"After understanding buying processes, then the next step is settling on a *sales process* for ourselves. We're a recently assembled team—four courageous, some would say crazy professionals—that is in the midst of a nasty situation. We need a sales process—a sales process to overlay on that buying process. The feeling of harmony, when you overlay the processes and you're on the buyer's wavelength, is unmistakable. It's like milking the cow at the first instant the cow realizes it needs to be milked. Believe me, the cow *really* appreciates it.

"Every company or sales professional has a sales process whether it was acquired consciously or accidentally, but few sit down to regularly dissect it, challenge it, try to tune it, articulate it—and then apply it and manage its consistent overlay on that buying process. It's key to outrageous success.

"Some people would say a sales process is determined by the nature of a product or service. For example, is the process to sell cars the same as the process to sell construction equipment? Some people would argue 'yes' and some would argue 'no'. I'll let the academics argue. I would say 'yes', that the process is basically the same, whether it's a personal or a professional sale. The people who argue 'no' often get sales process confused with sales tools, sales activities, levels of contact, or the complexity of a sale. I always thought of sales as a process the same way as I thought of planting as a process. Planting is planting, period."

91

"Time out", Lance interrupted. What do you mean, 'sales process'? Do you mean *how* we sell? I want to make sure we're all on the same page."

"Thanks for interrupting. Sometimes I make assumptions and go too fast. By sales process I mean a standardized procedure—a series of steps that lets us *execute and manage* a sales effort from beginning to end. For example, planning a contact, establishing a business reason for the contact, creating attention, fact-finding, achieving understanding, establishing credibility, building needs—then, providing information, reaching situational agreement, influencing the buyer's selection criteria, recommending solutions, answering questions—then, getting commitment, obtaining agreement, following up, and reinforcing the relationship. There are seven, eight, or nine steps that overlay—that 'fit' the buying process—like two gears meshing together.

"Whoa. Wait a minute. You didn't use the word 'close', " challenged Luke.

"No, I didn't, and I never will say it. It's an obsolete sales word as far as I'm concerned. We close *nothing*. We *open* doors, we *open* accounts, we *open* business relationships," Bert emphasized.

"Okay—so *open* is the new word. It's a word that signals a beginning, not an ending. I must admit it grabs me," Luke consented.

"Thanks. We, as a team, must be consistent in our application of our process—the best possible process—for the sake of productivity—for improving our yields! My coaching will be based on our agreed-upon sales process. I'm not here to coach freestylers—I'm here to coach a *team* that uses a common playbook loaded with 'best plays'.

"Sounds professional. I can respect that," said Lance, glancing at the others.

"One of the challenges," Bert snickered, "is that the implementation of our sales process will vary from prospect to prospect. *I GUAR-AN-TEE IT!* In some cases steps can be condensed or are seemingly left out, and in other cases, steps must be modified, extended, or seemingly added. That's because no two buyers buy exactly the same way. In practice, application of our sales process is like that wheeze-box accordion played by one of my favorite country music singers, stretching-out or compressing to make the right sound. That never-the-same reality is what makes sales and sales management an artful challenge. Outrageous sales success is *not* the result of a cookie-cutter approach", Bert emphasized.

"Sales teams and companies who take a cookie-cutter approach with their process often have a problem surviving. But in order to modify your process, or 'play your process', you must *possess* a process and *understand* both your process and the customer's buying process in the first place. Makes sense,

THE ATTACK OF THE MUSTARD SEED

doesn't it? You can't play what you don't understand—and when I say understand I mean understanding at the unconscious competence level—like driving a tractor but not really thinking about driving it. Surprised you with those big words, didn't I?"

"Bert, nothing you say surprises us," Lance offered.

When Ol' Bert shared his wisdom there was always a calm, magnetic intensity that surrounded him. The voice and aura, so like the legendary Obi-Wan Kenobi of the original Star Wars movie, drew his people in with confidence and concentration.

"Now! More homework. I would like the three of you to work on confirming our customer's buying processes and work on identifying a standardized Certus sales process that we should adopt. I want you to agree on a sales process that improves our yields—and that can be integrated into our software. Your task will be complicated by the fact that we're involved in both small sales and very large ones. I know you're aware that the processes for small sales and large sales can vary. I understand the complexity of what I'm asking you to do, but you've got the experience to lead this, and not just follow my dictates. Brief me—*with* documentation—when you're done.

"Use my mini-library here. I've got books on almost all the sales processes and methodologies that have ever been devised, such as *SPIN Selling, The New Conceptual Selling, Solution Selling, Consultative Selling, Customer Centered Selling*, and much more. These books represent *a lot* of very creditable third-party know-how.

"Go out and interview several customers and partners to get more information on buying processes. Share a generalized buying process, as you currently understand it—as I described earlier. Ask customers for reactions and their perspectives. Listen. Seek clarification as necessary. But let me warn you—these won't be easy discussions. While some customers will be comfortable talking at this level—many will think you're playing 'head games' with them. Don't worry about that. Don't be deterred. Be patient and understanding. Expect to hear a variable mixture of process and policies. Either way, you'll come away smarter—and respected. There's a lot of know-how at hand out there.

"C'mon, this is not usual stuff you're asking us to do Bert," said Leslie. "Seriously, it's not that I'm nervous about it—I know we all appreciate your confidence—it's just that it's not a normal activity for salespeople."

"No, it's not usual or normal," Bert, replied calmly. "Neither you, me, our situation, or our destination stakes are usual or normal. This is *unusual* and *abnormal* stuff that will get you, me, and Certus to an *uncommon* level of success."

Ol' Bert could see and sense their pumped-up reaction to his cool perspective.

He continued, "You saw earlier today how helpful customers can be. *And*—talk to many non-customers because those are the folks we're trying to convert to customers. Call it 'research'. People love to help researchers. Document what you hear, see, and feel. You'll get fragments. Bits and pieces. Put it all together. What you're doing is called 'process mapping'. Our sales process map should mirror the buying process maps you'll uncover.

"Let me add one very big point. This is not a one-time project. The task of searching-out and understanding buying processes never ends. You will get to be very good at this.

"How much time do you need?" asked Bert.

"Give us two weeks," snapped Luke, confidently. "We can do a lot of it after-hours—plus, I know the three of us have already been trained on various sales processes."

"That'll do," chimed in Leslie and Lance with growing enthusiasm.

"This is great," said Leslie. "We'll have a chance to contribute rather than just be told what to do. And it will be *our* very own sales process—and we'll be comfortable using it because we all designed it and bought-into it."

"Exactly! You'll be the process *owners*, and I'll be the process *coach*. I'm asking you to do all this because you're all a lot smarter than I am," Bert said.

"Maybe—but I have a feeling you're a wily old coyote," said Luke, smiling. They all nodded in confirmation.

Grinning in recognition that they had him pegged, Bert said, "I'm in love *with* process, not *a* process. I don't feel heavily invested in defending a particular process. If you feel we need to adopt the best elements of a couple of different processes and take a hybrid approach, we'll do it. If you want to add some of your own process ideas, we'll do it. If you feel we need to bring in a consultant or a process author to give us a refresher, we'll do it. Okay?

"That sounds great," said Leslie. And the other two concurred enthusiastically.

"*But*—all business processes are subject to change so don't think that what you suggest will be cast in concrete. Processes should always be challenged from the inside—just like some bright young whippersnapper always seems to challenge them from the outside. There's always seems to be someone—in here or out there—who comes up with a better idea. I'd be a fool not to pay attention. Do you think the method for planting and growing wheat is the same today as it was back in the 30's? Heck, no! Heaven forbid that farmers today would have to use the same old methods that my daddy did. We should always seek and be open to process improvement—and then tinker or trash—as the situation warrants."

"None of us are tolerant of awkward or unproductive processes, Bert. And we'll keep our eyes and ears open for anything new. We'll be the first to suggest change," Lance confirmed.

"And keep it simple and focused. We don't need 'process inflation' or 'process creep'," Bert suggested.

"We're with you 100%," Luke agreed, smiling.

"While you three are working on the *sales* process I'll be working on the order *fulfillment* process here with all the backroom folks. I want to keep you from getting bogged down in fulfillment and follow-up stuff—I want *you* focused on *selling*. I want to make sure the company's fulfillment process is shorter, speedier, sweeter, and simpler than our competitors. I call that the 4S's of Sensational Service. Those 4S's are absolutely imperative—and they offer *more* opportunity for differentiation. Customers come back because of the total-transaction experience, not just because of you or I or our products. Let's not make the mistake of falling in love with our personal efforts and ourselves.

"Now. Let's talk about tools that improve our yields. At each step of the sales process there are tools that are available to make each step effective and productive. For example, a written proposal is a tool that can make the recommending-a-solution sales process step very effective. Do you know that some salespeople try to sell without using any tools at all?" Bert asked. "Isn't that incredible? They just try to sell by talking. It always amazed me. It's like trying to plow with your hands. Crazy, but it happens.

"The *best* tools in the hands of the *best* horses utilizing the *best* process generate the *best* yields. I know I've got the best horses," Bert said unabashedly.

"Now we need the best tools. Yields are all about emphasis, efficiency, and expertness with the best process and tools," the old master slowly intoned.

"Bert, I think I understand, but before you go on, could you expand on 'tools' so we're all together?" Leslie asked.

"A tool is any sales activity, or aid, used by a salesperson to facilitate the buying-selling process. For example—here's a laundry list of tools. A tool could be a lap-top presentation, a stand-up presentation, a factory tour, a demonstration, an open house, a seminar, a written appraisal, test-lab results, a computer-generated analysis, a video, a piece of literature, a photo, a model, a top-executive visit, a proposal, a trial, a test drive, special 'sales', or a sample. There are hundreds of possibilities.

"Tools make both the sales *and* buying processes easier. Tools are primarily for the *buyers* benefit, not the other way around, as many salespeople think. Don't ever forget that.

"Tools should be used with forethought—not haphazardly. Different tools tend to fit in certain steps in the buying process. I always thought of a proposal that facilitates buying as a tool the same way I always thought of a grain drill as a tool that facilitates planting.

"A *certain few* tools—*or a single tool*—can work wonders to gain win-win agreement. They have proven themselves over time. They *greatly* influence yields and buyer satisfaction. This is a critical point. Is everyone with me?" Bert asked slowly.

"Yes, we used to call them 'silver-bullets'," Lance responded. "They vary from business to business."

"Years and years of experience has driven that point home to me, Lance. History teaches lessons on the desirability and effectiveness of certain tools. What has history taught us here? What tools were used here in the past? In what situations? By whom? On whom? In what manner? And which ones *greatly* influenced yields?

"For the sake of our discussion, let's say the fourth step of our buyers' process is *shopping* and that matches up with the fourth step of our sales process, which may be *influencing the selection process* of a buyer. Leslie has told me that demonstrations have proven to be highly effective in influencing potential buyers in the past, and that buyers value them greatly. She looked back over her successes here at Certus, and she has found that top-notch demonstrations were the common thread in weaving win-win agreements. Therefore, what we all need to do is use *that tool*—at that stage in the buying-selling process—and execute it very, very well. It will improve our yields and the customer's satisfaction."

"Yes, I can see that, Bert. And if we can do that matching of buying-to-selling throughout the whole process and have a top-notch tool or two at each step, we and our customers would be in sunflowers as high as those back in North Dakota," Luke offered.

"That's it! That's it! You've captured it, Luke," and Bert was pleased.

"Now, wouldn't it be fair to say that our competitors have also found a similar process and tools? Of course! They're not dumb. Now their process might not be exactly the same as ours, but their selection of certain tools can certainly be. Our task is to then use our 3D model to *differentiate* and *dominate* with our demonstrations because history has shown that prospects *demand* demonstrations. A 3D demonstration helps them reach a decision, a decision favorable to Certus, we hope."

"Yes, absolutely," Leslie chipped in, and they all nodded agreement.

"Okay, we've agreed that a 3D demonstration seems to be our most important tool—a silver-bullet, as Lance says. When one sales tool becomes so important, so critical, such a deciding factor, it becomes *strategic*—not tactical. It becomes a part of our team strategy.

"What I would like the three of you to do is get your heads together to create a Certus demonstration model that all four of us can use. Make it the most differentiating, dominating demonstration you possibly can. An outrageous winner! One that each of us can use as a model, or template, that we can blend to our individual styles, one that prospects will value more than any competitors' attempt. Okay?

All three agreed with gusto.

"Now—Leslie has told me that there are two other tools that experience has taught her work well. The first is a top-notch presentation to the buyer's decision-making team. It seems that buying-teams are making more decisions these days in our industry. What we need is a 3D Hollywood-level presentation model using the latest presentation technologies—a presentation that's loaded with *customer-relevant substance*—not just Certus sizzle. Perhaps we could get some help from our highly creative marketing communications colleagues in the process. Add that to your to-do list. Again, this will be a template for us to tweak for individual situations.

"Leslie, why don't you discuss the other point," Bert suggested.

"Thanks Bert. Let me tell you, my experience is that our response to a lead or inquiry—that very first contact—is also key to winning business. I'm amazed. Believe me. Guys—listen—we need to figure out the best tool to use to respond to leads. It seems it isn't just a matter of speed—it's also a matter of *who* responds and *how* it's executed and with *what* in hand. I've experimented favorably with an audiotape, but I'm sure there are other options. I think we can use Bert's 3D model on a lead and inquiry tool."

"You don't have to convince me," Luke said. "Let's tackle it. I've got some ideas."

Ol' Bert's openness to challenging the status quo was not lost on the three salespeople.

"Listen up," he said. "We've talked about three tools that seem to be of the highest priority. But—don't assume that they are the only priorities. And remember, it's only Leslie's experience that we've got to go on. It's a good starting point, but lets keep our eyes and ears open for other tools that can create even *higher* yields.

97

JOHN W. CEBROWSKI

"Here's a final question for the three of you," Bert challenged. "Are the tools for customer entrenchment and customer retention the same as the tools for customer acquisition?

"Leslie has seen that customers regularly call for support after they buy our product. It seems the responses to those calls greatly influence continued product usage and repeat business. The right answers delivered the right way are critical, but incredibly we have no *post-sale* tools! Is there room for an instruction booklet or CD, application seminars, in-services, an electronic or phone 'hotline', maintenance tutorials, best practice roundtables, executive follow-ups, a 'worker-bee' survey, or some other tool? We need to make sure customer questions are anticipated and answered—and loyalty nurtured. Consistent, awesome after-sale support and service as a pillar of competitiveness is rare. I aim to make it commonplace at Certus.

"Most sales teams never think about entrenchment and retention tools. We will. Let's hold onto all our customers with all our strength. I'll give myself the action-item to work on this with the Marketing Manager and the Customer Service Manager, but I'd like you to think about these matters as well and give me your ideas next Wednesday morning.

"Thanks for plunging into those priorities," said Bert.

"Now I'd like to share ten other points on tools. Bear with me. I know this is going to sound like a lecture. Here are some notes I call my 'Tooltime-Tool-Tips'—in honor of Tim and Al from *Tooltime*—that fantasy TV show from that wacky program called *Home Improvement*. Remember those characters? Here we go...

"Nail this idea down. The same tools don't work in all situations. Occasionally you have to reach in the tool-bin and take out a special tool for a unique situation. Some valuable specialty tools, like seminars or lists of references, are called upon infrequently. So when one of us decides to take that tool out of the tool-bin, we must make sure that we know how to use it and that it follows the 3D model.

"Screw this consideration in. Certain old tools may be effective if cleaned up and everyone retrained on how to use them. Let's be alert for the opportunity. That old videotape the customer referred to so positively earlier today sounds like an example of something we can rejuvenate. She said she was very impressed when she saw it several years ago.

"Ratchet this thought snug. Oftentimes a comfort level with, or a reliance on, one or two tools can get to be an issue. Getting in a 'tool-rut' can be a problem. Habits die hard. Entertainment is a tool, and is an example of a tool I've seen relied on too heavily at the expense of other options.

"Drill this notion deep. Sales managers and salespeople must also run to their strengths. Some are more adept with certain tools, such as presentations, than others. The tool user is an extension of the tool. Every salesperson has his or her favorite tool. That's natural. We all have innate skills and biases. Recognize your special talents and milk them for all they're worth, but don't let your bias cause you to neglect other proven tools. And share your talents with each other. For example, I've always been good at orchestrating factory visits. I'll show you how I do it.

"Everyone okay?" Bert inquired, because they were quiet.

"You've got us thinking", Lance said. "Bert, you sure are good at making us think."

"Good! Calm and creative thinking in the face of pressure is a requisite for success.

"Next. Hammer this viewpoint home. Laziness and short cuts get in the way of tool usage. It takes a little effort to take a tool out of the bin. The path of least resistance keeps some salespeople from using—and some sales managers from mandating—the use of tools. Proposals are a prime example. I guarantee you—we won't make that mistake. We'll avoid that by tying our sales process to our software and highlight tools that should be used at each step in our process. We'll also avoid the short-cut problem through win-loss analyses to track which tools were, or were not, utilized. You can count on me holding all of us accountable.

"Grip this attitude tight. Think about *opportunities* that are signaling tool application, such as sticking-points or clumsy spots in our sales process that slow us down, repetitive questions, explaining complex concepts or operations, presenting an aspect of our product that has hard-to-see implications, recurrent objections you have heard, frustration with lengthy explanations you have had to make, competitive weaknesses we would like to exploit, or an aspect of our product that we want to emphasize. All those situations are *screaming* for a tool.

"Saw this concept carefully. It follows then to think about *new tools*. Experiment on your own. I encourage you to create whatever *you think* is a good tool idea. I'll commit to investing in your ideas. Then you try it out. Massage it to your liking. If it works, bring it to the rest of the team. If not, trash it, and try again. The tool-bin should always be refreshed. Old worthless tools should be discarded and new more productive tools should be added.

"Tap this tactic in line. Look far-a-field in non-related businesses for tool ideas. Keep your eyes open when shopping, reading, watching TV, traveling, and looking at ads and displays. Observe what sales tools are used on you when you are buying something. Copy the good concepts. Consider how we can adapt something from a different industry.

"Tighten this nugget in place. We must think about having different tools for different audiences. The tool to use with a top executive may not always be the most effective tool to use with a product manager, a finance director, or a purchasing manager—and vice versa. If we have an 'audience gap', we must fill it.

"Sand this mind-set down smooth. Think of tools as assets—like money or talents—all of which are of value only if they are invested," finished Bert. "Let's keep our assets working."

"A key is knowing what's *in* the tool bin. Sometimes we forget. So I'll take the responsibility of being the tool-bin manager", Bert said with pride. "Tools must be managed and maintained. I can remember how we cared for all the tools back on the farm. They were our livelihood. I'll treat our tools the same way. You can expect me to challenge your use or non-use of the tools. I'll also be coaching you on their application.

"Whew—it's clear you really believe deeply in this tool business," Luke voiced with respect, then added, smiling, "I think Tim and Al and the whole *Tooltime* crew would be proud of you—and of us."

"Yep! Whether it's those make-believe Binford tools from *Tooltime* or genuine Certus buyer-satisfaction tools, good tools are critical to outrageous success," Bert chuckled.

"And here's a neat subtlety that results from this emphasis on quality tools. Competitions' tools can become *our* tools—possibly the best ones we have—by their inadequacy or defectiveness compared to our tools. Did you know customers also judge suppliers by the quality of their tools?"

That fired-up the horses even more.

"How about our sales partners," added Luke, concerned. "Will we be supporting them with any tools?"

"Yep! Glad you brought that up, Luke. I've appointed myself the chief designer of a support toolbox for our sales partners. They need sales and marketing materials and programs. That support *must* be consistent with our own tools, *must* be responsive to their needs, and *must* be adaptable because our partners have different skill and experience levels and operate in very different market conditions. We're one big happy family. It'll be a 3D toolbox, I guarantee. I'll be reviewing my progress on that front with all of you, and seeking your opinions," Bert was pleased to say.

"Now, before we break up and the three of you go to work on our sales process and silver-bullet tools, I'd like to share *my* priority management tools," said Bert.

He could see the light go out of their eyes. It wasn't unexpected, so he asked, "When a customer talks about what the customer wants to talk about rather than what you want to talk about, do you unconsciously signal reduced interest?"

"Did we do that?" Leslie flashed back defensively.

"Yep—you did," Bert chuckled. "I understand. I just want you to know I saw it." They sat on the edge of their chairs leaning forward for the rest of the meeting.

"Okay, we've talked about the customers on the outside, now let's talk about the customers on the inside. Some, like Mr. Pimm, the marketing manager and the production director are readily apparent. Some, like the IS director, the manager of production control and the accounts receivable manager are not. I must confirm and regularly reconfirm their values—their demands—and then we must exceed *their* expectations.

"I've got four primary management tools I must continually use and fine-tune to exceed their expectations. You need to know what those tools are, why they are critical, and your role in their application. Management tools ensure good 'order'—and good order makes organizations bold and outrageously successful, while disorder makes them tentative and ineffectual. We'll be as ordered and organized as one of those beautiful quilts my momma used to make.

"One of those tools is the pipeline—pipeline management.

"It's the job of the three of you to keep the pipe full of potential business and to apply the pressure to keep those opportunities moving in the right direction. If there's little or nothing in the pipe, it doesn't matter how good you are with your tools. The key measurement with a pipeline is its volume, how much is in it. Beating on an empty pipe just makes a lot of aggravating noise. So priority number one is to keep putting opportunities in the pipe, to keep the pipe full.

"Second priority—if there's no pressure in the pipe nothing flows out the end. Terrible to have an irrigation pipe full of water and not be able to get anything out, wouldn't it? Your application of our sales process and our 3D tools are what builds and sustains the pressure. Pressure is *not* maintained by browbeating customers and prospects with hot air and slick gimmicks," Bert jibed.

"It's my job to manage the pipeline—to patrol it, if you will. I'm the guy watching the pressure gauge, making sure there are no leaks, and coaching you on opportunities in the pipe as situations warrant. We all need to know exactly what's in the pipe and how far along each opportunity is—in other words—where is every opportunity in the sales process. Ideal pipelines are always full and under constant pressure. But the world is not ideal. So the pipe needs to be managed. If the volume goes down you can expect to hear from me. If the pressure drops, or the opportunities aren't moving along, you can expect to hear from me. You've all got the pipeline-tracking format in your laptops. Okay?" smiled Bert.

The three sat there rather smugly and sneering mischievously, causing Ol' Bert to ask, "What's so funny?"

"Bert, with all due respect, uh, you better get yourself a whale of a big pipe because, uh, the three of us are going to fill it to bursting pretty quickly," Luke chuckled. The other two rolled with laughter.

Bert, loving the disdainful arrogance, laughed back, and challenged, "Good. Show me." The bonds were getting stronger.

"Pipeline is real-time. Make inputs and changes on the fly. Neither the staff nor I can wait for end-of-week or end-of-month to look at the pipeline. You can count on it being under constant scrutiny back here. Business is too fast nowadays to allow the luxury of sporadic looks at market activity. However, once a week you and I will take a snapshot and have a formal one-on-one pipeline review. Here's the schedule," and he handed each a sheet of paper. "Expect some hard, squirmy questions."

And that caused them to smile even more. Ol' Bert just nodded quietly in acknowledgement.

"My second management tool is the forecast—what's ready to pop out of the end of the pipe. Everybody—and I mean *everybody*—in the company has a vested interest in the forecast. Don't confuse the pipeline with the forecast. The pipeline is simply potential. It's your job to sift through your pipeline once a week and pick out those select situations where you expect our Customer Service people will *receive* orders within a 2-week, 6-week, and 10-week window. I didn't pull these time frames out of thin air—it's what production and marketing need. Don't give me, or them, any 'probability' stuff—which I think is a cozy way of avoiding commitments. This isn't Las Vegas. Just tell us 'who', 'what', 'when', and 'how much' you are forecasting. Here's a format. Simple. We'll do it electronically. Get it to me prior to 8:00am every Monday. I'll look at it, assemble it, and send it into production, marketing, and Mr. Pimm. On an exception basis—and I mean *exception*—I may drop or add one or more opportunities. This is *your* forecast because no one knows the situations better than *you*," said Bert, glancing at all three straight in the eye.

While Ol' Bert was talking about forecasts the weight of the responsibility was clearly evident on the faces of all three salespeople. Ol' Bert could see that they were getting the message.

"Accuracy counts for everything in a forecast. Accuracy is the key measurement of a forecast, *not volume*. Forecast. Accuracy. Forecast. Accuracy," Bert kept repeating. "Forecasts are not crystal-balling. A crystal ball is not a precise instrument. Forecasts are commitments. Our forecast objective is to minimize surprises and maximize precision—so our 'stake' is 100% accuracy. I'll be tracking and publicizing our individual and collective accuracy. The only bad forecast is one that isn't accurate. And no one gets any points for business above and beyond their forecast so don't think about sandbagging. And none of us needs to hear why something didn't happen so don't bother with any explanations. Only the bottom line counts.

"Sounds harsh," Lance offered cautiously.

"Bankruptcies and lay-offs are harsher," Bert countered. "Let me tell you what our forecast policy will be. It comes from Napoleon—*To be defeated is pardonable; to be surprised—never!*"

There was a quiet pause. Everyone understood.

"My third management tool is a regular activity report. I've got to tell my colleagues here in the office and plant what's going on in the market, what competition is doing, and what we're doing. I need to tell them what *they need* to know. The best reports are based on their needs, not what *I think* they want to hear, and certainly not any smoke or self-serving tales of woe. The quicker, the more accurate, and the more relevant the information the better. I've already asked Mr. Pimm and all of his staff what they need to know. It's a combination of facts and gossip, like when my daddy would take me into town to the barbershop, and he and all the other farmers would trade stories about all kinds of stuff. I'd sit there and listen. Sometimes they'd laugh, and sometimes they'd be real serious. It must have all been important because when we got back home he'd tell my momma all of the stuff they talked about. Your inputs will be the basis of our report just as all those farmers' inputs were the basis of my daddy's report. But we'll do everything electronically. Our job is to gain *and* maintain *exceptional* situational awareness of markets and customers. We are Certus's intelligence-gathering center of gravity. The Certus staff has got to make good decisions based on serious stuff. They're counting on us," Bert emphasized.

"We're going to keep this short and simple. None of us needs make-work. Mr. Pimm and the rest of the staff respect that fact. And we're going to send in information frequently because we're in a survival mode. So—here's a list of questions and facts that I want you to fire in to me prior to midnight, home-office time, every Friday. *Anticipate* follow-up questions from the rest of staff and me, and *provide* those answers the first time around. None of us have time to bat these things back and forth. And here is a list of situations and information that demand immediate real-time reporting that I want you to fire in directly to the manager noted.

"Mr. Pimm didn't hire me to be a policeman, to check-off boxes, or proofread your inputs. Besides, I trust your judgment, and I know you understand the situation. For example, if you uncover a new competitive price or product, alert the marketing manager at your first opportunity to send a message. You can see how the marketing manager has even provided a sample-reporting format for us. If we saw a twister coming we'd yell and warn everyone, wouldn't we? Well, the same applies to this information. Copy me on your bulletin.

"We're like sonar technicians on a submarine, identifying dangers that can't be seen, providing early warning to Certus. We're also like radiologists reading x-rays—interpreting fuzzy stuff that the market can't or won't completely tell us. The smarter a company is about what's happening out in the market the more optimally it can employ its assets.

"Here is what our report policy will be," he said. "This comes from Cochise, the famous Chiricahua Apache chief who once said—*You must speak straight so that your words may go as sunlight into their hearts.* Let's do the same."

"By the way, thanks for being tolerant of my constant use of famous sayings. I use them not so you will think that I am very learned—which I am not—but I use them to help all of us focus on universal truths and remember the wealth of wisdom available for us to draw upon."

They all acknowledged, smiling.

"Back to the tools."

"My fourth management tool is my expense budget, and I hate that term 'expense' by the way. It's an *asset* budget from now on—which sounds more 'high finance' to me. Certus will survive if we collectively manage our *assets*—spending and investing where we can get the highest rate of return. I've already given each of you an asset budget for the next three months, and you know the guidelines. The corporate situation may cause it to change. Be as simultaneously smart and frugal as you can.

"I can remember how my momma used to sweet-talk people in the stores in order to stretch every nickel," Bert giggled. "I trust your judgment in getting the greatest return from every dollar. Use your own discretion to invest it where you think you can maximize the return. If you need more for an exception situation, let's talk about it. To emphasize return-on-investment and create a little competitiveness we'll do an investments-to-bookings analysis at the end of the quarter.

"You also know that it's critical to get your 'asset report' in prior to 5:00pm on the last Friday of every month. Accounting doesn't need any cash flow surprises. That's it—that's my four management tools."

"Outrageous processes and outrageous tools will..." Bert started and was interrupted by the three of them in simultaneous chorus. "...Will get us to outrageous results, we know! We agree! We're with you," the three horses cried out supportively. Ol' Bert loved it. It was coming together.

They summarized and reviewed their assignments. They agreed on timing. The fact that the team was now complete gave them all a renewed sense of confidence. They were ready to lick the world. They traded a few war stories and batted a few current issues around. The meeting concluded on time.

"All right. Let's get at it," Bert yelled excitedly, slapping both his hands on his desk so hard the brass lamp blinked.

And then the jovial atmosphere blinked. Mr. Pimm interrupted their meeting. He wanted to let Bert know that a management team meeting had been called for 7:30 the next morning. Mr. Pimm was pale. He asked Bert to come up to his office as soon as he could.

When he got there a few minutes later he learned that a few key suppliers had altered prices and terms, a key staff member had resigned, new products had failed some tests, and some accounting errors had altered the balance sheet. Mr. Pimm said he needed help to settle everyone down. Bert could see that Mr. Pimm needed a little settling-down himself.

Mr. Pimm wanted assistance, but in his panicked state wasn't sure what to ask for.

After a little calming discussion Bert could sense what was needed. An agenda for the next day was agreed upon.

Essential #6
Lead With Heart, Brains, And Courage

Mr. Pimm led the staff meeting the following morning. The atmosphere was tense but business-like, with rigorous give-and-take. Everyone was a little tight and there was a bit of sniping and harping, but Mr. Pimm kept it focused. All the current issues were duly discussed. Everyone knew what was at stake. Notes were taken. Action plans were outlined. The meeting finished as strained as it started. Mr. Pimm ran a tight meeting but he was also astute enough to know that he needed to lighten it up. That's where Ol' Bert came in.

At the end of the nuts-and-bolts session, Mr. Pimm told the management team that he had asked Ol' Bert to share some personal thoughts on leadership—a subject that fit and flowed perfectly on the agenda. The staff knew that leadership was critical—but especially so at this time—so an opportunity to discuss such an important subject would be time well spent. All had heightened respect for Ol' Bert since he began implementing his essentials.

The conference room grew quiet as Ol' Bert walked to the front, put both hands on the edge of the table, and shifted his gaze from one manager to another before speaking.

"This company and each of us are going to succeed," Bert stated slowly without a smile or a blink. "As a matter of fact, we are going to succeed beyond our imaginations. And one of the reasons we're going to do that is because of our potential individual and collective leadership. I emphasize potential because that's all it is right now—in spite of what you may personally believe. You may not see the unrealized potential, but I see it. And I feel it. I know it's there because I know each of you and what each of you is capable of doing, and I've been around a lot of managers witnessing their leadership efforts. I also know what it takes because I personally stumbled my way through it for years before I got it right. But I'm not here today to blow sunshine your way or sprinkle pixie dust on each of you. I'm up here today to help you understand what it takes to be an outrageously successful leader.

"It's time to move our potential leadership to the highest level of practicing leadership. Outrageous success cannot be administered, it must be led." And Ol' Bert paused to let that sink in. They were glued to the little old man.

He started again by saying, "Before we talk about leadership, we must talk about 'followership'. I don't think 'followership' is a real word," he smiled slyly, "but I like to make up words to suit the situation—and you get the idea anyway. You can't have a leader without followers, and you have to learn to follow before you learn to lead. How can you lead those you don't understand or activities you haven't experienced? Hmmm? You can't.

"The word follower, unfortunately, doesn't sound good to many people. 'Follower' has somehow developed a pejorative or disparaging aura. For example, people say, 'I'm not a follower. I think for myself'. Pride and ego get in the way. Well, believe me, it is a very good word. I know that the words 'associate' or 'helper' or 'aide' are heard more often than follower, but those mushy words are based on followership. Follower is the root word, the foundation concept. Sometimes we sugarcoat and play with words because we don't want to offend someone. It's a silly game, and employees know it's a game.

"Well, followership is not offensive. To be a good follower is an honorable and respected role. History is replete with millions of followers—solidly labeled as members, disciples, backers, workers, staff, crew, pupils, and supporters— who distinguished themselves.

"Everyone has a bit of follower and a bit of leader in him. We are all followers and leaders to a greater or lesser extent depending on the subject matter and the environment. An employee could be a follower here at Certus but a leader in a neighborhood or church program at home. While I'm a leader here, I am a follower in our community home association ."

Ol' Bert paused, turning his back to the group, and asked, "What are the characteristics of a good follower?" He picked up a marker to note the responses from the group, not looking at anyone as he prepared to write.

"Listens," came the first reply, cautiously.

"Committed," came the second, after a delay. And then it picked up speed.

"Follows instructions and the rules."

"Acquires the manner and beliefs of the leader."

"Supports the leader at risk to self."

"Encourages colleagues, all those around him."

"Is someone who is actively engaged with the leader."

"Backs up the leader when needed, like in a crisis or with a problem."

"Makes suggestions to assist the leader."

"Becomes like the leader—mirrors the leader's values."

"Issues supportive challenges to the leader for the benefit of all. Good following does not mean blind following."

"Seeks and accepts advice and counsel from the leader."
"Respects the leader."
"Fills in the leaders 'gaps' and soft spots voluntarily."
"Accepts the leader's suggestions with enthusiasm."
"Is honest with the leader. Tells it like it is."
"Has the confidence to act as a 'backboard'—or holds up a mirror for the leader from time to time."
"Works hard and tries to have the team succeed."
"Doesn't want to disappoint the leader or the team."
"Can be trusted to do the right things." And on it went.

Ol' Bert didn't make any comments but just kept writing as the group continued to chip-in and comment on each other's contributions. When the contributions slowed down and finally stopped, he said, "That's a pretty good list, and those are all pretty positive behaviors, aren't they? So there should be no problem with followership, should there?"

Everyone nodded agreement.

"Well—we're all followers," Bert said. "We're following Mr. Pimm, and Mr. Pimm is following the Board of Directors and the wishes of the stockholders. Truth of the matter is everyone is a follower—everyone in this whole world—*everyone.*

"We set an example for our own people based on how we follow Mr. Pimm. As the sales manager I am sending subtle and regular messages to Leslie, Lance, and Luke based on how I follow Mr. Pimm. They will follow and support me in much the same way I follow and support *my* manager. *My* followership behaviors are models for my people to emulate.

"While they emulate my followership behaviors I accept that there may be rare deviations from good followership time to time. Some of those deviations will be minor, such as tap-dancing, kissing-up, and patronizing behaviors. That's controllable. Some of those deviations may be severe, such as dishonesty, rebellion, or betrayal. Remember Judas? Remember Benedict Arnold? Remember the Watergate affair? Those exceptions necessitate swift dismissal. I minimize my people's deviations by *eliminating* my deviations. I strive to be a model follower.

"It's okay *not* to be a leader, or in a leadership role all the time. The need for good followers is just as important. But good followers are often as hard to find as good leaders.

"People who have difficulty following are often wrapped-up in their own troubled agendas and self-image. They often aren't at peace with themselves—or aren't comfortable with themselves—or at ease with how they fit in. Those people will have trouble leading. I, for one, don't want people like that in my organization. Do you?"

There was uniform head wagging.

"People who are weak followers will be weak leaders. So, let's each take a little inventory of our own 'followership' and make any corrections before we concentrate on our leadership. First things first."

"We're with you Bert," the finance director said, and everyone else agreed, comfortable with the direction that Ol' Bert was taking the discussion. Of course it made Mr. Pimm feel pretty good since Ol' Bert had just artfully encouraged everyone to line-up behind him and his agenda.

Bert then said, "I know you're all aware that I'm originally from the great and dynamic state of Kansas." And he chuckled at his pride and self-promotion. "So it was easy for me to relate to that famous movie, *The Wizard of Oz*. My leadership model has long been based on that movie, particularly three of its main characters, The Scarecrow, The Tin Man, and The Cowardly Lion.

"The movie wasn't about leadership, but remember how in the movie the Scarecrow is looking for a brain, the Tin Man for a heart, and the Cowardly Lion for courage? They went with Dorothy down the yellow brick road to find the Wizard who they hoped would present them with those gifts and get Dorothy back to Kansas.

"There is no wizardry with leadership, but my leadership model has always been based on heart, brains, and courage. To me, the model is simple, valid, and memorable. I'm not trying to convince you to use *my* model, but I *very strongly* encourage you to develop and live by a model of your own.

"Here goes.

"I believe **heart** emphasizes the need for a leader to grasp and internalize the feelings, opinions, and aspirations of his or her people. Heart doesn't mean softness, it means being firm and nourishing like water. It means interest, commitment, care, support, and listening. It means being able to inspire and influence, fuel self-motivation, and touch sparks to people's spirits. Business is business, but a manager is leading and managing people, not puppets.

"I believe **brains** emphasize the need to think, analyze, synthesize, and solve problems. It means competence—having the requisite functional knowledge—knowledge of the firm's products, services, and technologies— knowledge of the firm's markets, sales partners, customers, and competitors— and knowledge of the company's practices, processes, and policies. Brains also means understanding your people and yourself. A leader can't lead what a leader doesn't understand.

"I believe **courage** emphasizes the need for leaders to make tough decisions, take tough stands, imperil themselves personally as need be, take calculated business risks, create operating discipline, exhibit self-discipline, suggest and implement difficult changes, confront errant colleagues, and challenge wrongs and inequities."

Everyone shifted in his or her seat. This was getting interesting.

"Let me share a few personal leadership examples that follow my model and have stuck in my mind for years and guided me.

"The first example has to do with **'heart'** and centers around an English teacher that I had in high school. It was my junior year, I believe, when we were studying literature, poetry, and the famous writers. I was bored—and she knew it. At the start of the school year I said to myself there was no way I would ever be interested in this stuff. Well, let me tell you. This woman had a gift for painting and communicating a vision with clarity and inspiring me to buy into that vision—something I learned later was very important for a leader to be able to do. She opened my eyes to literature. She expanded my horizons. She did it with word pictures, with her enthusiasm, by explaining very simply why all of this was important and how it could help me later in my life. Most importantly she did it with her personal interest in me. She was the only teacher I ever had that seemed to have a personal interest in me—*me!* At first I didn't buy the subject matter, but then it just happened. She never wavered in her enthusiasm for the subject, *or for me.* The two became intertwined. I never admitted it to my classmates, but at the end of that year I loved all the stuff she had taught us. Later I discovered that she had inspired many of my classmates in the same way. She surprised us all. That teacher has always been my 'heart model' with my sales teams.

"An example that has to do with **'brains'** comes from one of my early sales managers. He was very competent. He knew how to make things happen. He had made himself very smart and had very high standards for his personal work and with all our work. Everything had to be perfect, or at least that was the way I remember it. He pushed us all to a higher level of knowledge and performance by causing us to think at a level that I never thought I could. He rarely accepted an initial plan, report, or presentation. 'Did you think about this'? 'Did you anticipate that'? 'What if this happens or that happens'? 'Have you considered so-and-so'? he would ask. They were calm, but serious, grillings. You felt like your mind had been through a wringer whenever you walked out of his office. He taught us how to dig deep within ourselves—to think! And he knew where our weaknesses were and he worked to patch them up. His suggestions were never negative or demeaning, but he just pushed,

111

pushed, and pushed our minds. The reward lay in the execution of our work, when we saw the fruits of our labors. It was a very good feeling. I believe to this day that deep and extensive knowledge about your functional responsibility and about management are the keys to being an outrageously successful leader.

"My third example has to do with **'courage'**. The war was on and I was pretty young. I'll never forget. It was September of '44. We had just landed on Peleliu in the Palau Islands. We were pinned down on the beach. There was this Marine general who commanded our amphibious corps. It seems he jumped into a landing craft himself to come ashore and personally see what was happening. He ended up behind this dune near me, stuck his head up to appraise the situation, and nearly got it torn off by a major-caliber Japanese round. Whew! He taught my buddies and me courage in that instant. He could have sat comfortably out on the flagship out of harms way, but no, he was right there. And he stayed with us. I still can't believe that he did that. As a result I've never hesitated to put myself in harms way on behalf of my people with customers and other managers. Did we take the island? Of course", said Bert, almost with tears in his eyes. "I've always stood up for my people the way that general did for me and my buddies back there on bloody Peleliu."

The room was understandably quiet when Ol' Bert finished. It was clear that everyone was absorbed in digging out his or her own personal leadership thoughts from misty-eyed memories.

Pausing to let everyone relive whatever personal reflections his examples had ignited, Ol' Bert then asked everyone in the room to share a leadership experience in their life. It took a while for someone to come forward, but finally, the director of human resources volunteered. He spoke about how a CEO with a previous employer had stood firm to prevent a hostile takeover.

The finance director volunteered how she had an experience with an employee who bent over backwards to take charge of, and solve, a major receivables problem that she herself thought was hopeless.

Then the marketing manager offered a story how the art director at their advertising agency had refused to accept the marketing manager's promotional strategy and instead led the development of a strategy that prevented what would have been a disaster for the firm.

Then there was a story about an immigrant family, a manager's grandparents, and how the mother took charge of the family when the father died.

Another about a nephew who had been disabled in an auto accident and ultimately inspired the rest of the family to accomplishments none dreamed possible.

Another about a high school athlete who gave a locker-room speech that sent an underdog to victory against an archrival.

One about a community leader who successfully challenged a harmful ordinance in the face of intense political pressure.

Even Mr. Pimm offered how the leadership of his grandfather who made imaginative and tough decisions during the Depression had influenced him.

It seemed that leadership examples were all around them. The reflection and story telling was inspiring.

Ol' Bert took the opportunity to suggest to everyone that they read *Leaders, Secrets of Break-Through Leadership,* and *Tough-Minded Leadership* to discover more leadership ideas and examples—all books that he had in his Wisdom Pantry. He said he had many more.

He then asked, "How do *you personally* feel working around a good leader? Think a minute."

Ol' Bert walked around the room, putting his hand on each manager's shoulder, repeating the question each time. The responses popped-out briskly. He told everyone to write them down.

"Eager to contribute and help out and solve problems."

"Safe and not threatened. I don't have to check my backside. It gives me confidence."

"I feel that I've lucked out—knowing how many weak leaders are out there."

"Relaxed and lightened. Work just sort of floats by."

"I feel very good. And I expect great things for my future knowing this manager will strengthen me in many ways."

"Committed to the organization at a higher level."

"Anxious to do something. Full of energy and rarin' to go. It fuels my creativity."

"Pleased and proud that I'm a part of that leader's organization. Maybe even a little cocky."

Bert then said, "Well, let's take steps to make all of our people experience those feelings."

He paused and gazed at everyone to confirm his and her attention.

"Now—you're going to tell *me*—*how* to inspire those feelings in your own people. The answers—*the answers*—to this next question will serve as your leadership guide. Get ready to think again."

Bert took up the marker.

He then asked, "What *behaviors* come to mind when you think about a good leadership example?"

Responses peppered-in quickly from around the conference table.

"Oozes mature confidence. There's an unmistakable boldness—though not arrogance."

"Knows exactly where he is going, and shares a compelling, embraceable vision. They help you see the invisible."

"I've noticed that the good ones seem to get better at it as time goes by. It seems they consciously evolve and renew themselves."

"Communicates a dependence on you, and you then feel more accountable and responsible."

"The voice is firm and unwavering, always a positive tone. Always a mature and certain delivery."

"They seem to somehow have extra energy and endurance—and pizzazz."

"Admits mistakes, but then quickly moves on."

"Is quick to spot and articulate opportunities or problems. You always wonder how she saw it. Her view must be different or she's tuned into different frequencies."

"You can tell he's thinking carefully about the matter at hand. Very reflective."

"They have a high level of self-awareness. They know who and what they are, and they are accepting of those facts."

"They keep their ego tucked in their back pocket—not emblazoned on their sleeve."

"They know when to issue an unapologetic directive and when group discussion is more appropriate."

Everyone was getting-into the exercise. The mood had become up beat. Ol' Bert wrote down the responses and asked each contributor to expand upon his or her input as much as he or she would like. And on it went …

"Strong—a strong personality. Tough to move him off of his beliefs and convictions—but he'll move quickly for solid reasons."

"Develops a sense of loyalty and team among subordinates."

"Looks you in the eye. And it causes you to perk up."

"Raises your level of alertness and energy just by being around. Doesn't even have to say anything."

"Engrossed with where he's taking the business."

"Makes you feel good about yourself. You know where you stand."

"Charismatic. There is like a… a dynamic or magnetic field around them. You're drawn to them. Hard to explain."

"Tough. Demanding—but fair at the same time."

"In contentious situations they foster dialogue, posing questions rather than making accusations."

"Their sense of timing is eerie. The right things always seem to get done at the right time."

"Looks like a leader. The way he or she carries themselves, their personal presence. Even when they're dirty or fatigued they look good. It's amazing."

"Strong principles and faith. They have an abundance of moral fortitude."

Bert interrupted enthusiastically, "You're right on, keep it up." And they did. And he kept writing.

"Knows her people, understands what makes each one tick, and looks out for her people's welfare."

"Inspirational. But often doesn't even have to say anything to inspire— their demeanor alone can do it."

"Decisiveness. Can make unambiguous choices quickly. Doesn't waffle around. But on the other hand, has this incredible capacity to suspend judgment as necessary, and tells you why!"

"There's no hesitation to confront difficult situations."

"Says tough things that I really don't want to hear, but says them in a way I can understand and accept. At the same time doesn't mind getting some people ticked-off in the process."

"Also defines reality and the future in terms you understand, very often with stories."

"Dependability. You don't have to worry about him or what he says he will do."

"Makes you feel wanted and needed."

"Keeps his people informed. You're not in the dark."

"Isn't about to be easily buffaloed by anyone—especially so-called experts."

"Has great social skills—seems to be comfortable in all kinds of situations."

"Sets the example—a positive, mature one in all matters. And when the heat's on, they shine."

"The great ones are confident making hard turns—not just gentle windings."

"Ensures that goals are understood and works to remove barriers along the way."

"Has the knack to stretch the team just the right amount without breaking it or causing it to lose confidence in itself."

"Great! Great! Right on! Excellent responses!" Bert said, smiling. Then he added, "Well, it looks like collectively we all know what leadership looks like and what it takes to be a leader. Let me add an item of my own, please. Fellow I heard of by the name of John Zenger once said, *leaders focus on emotional issues that connect them with their followers.* That grabbed me. Passionate connections provoke passionate followings.

"The challenge for each of us is to take steps to behave in the ways you identified—thereby connecting everyone as firmly as a trailer to a hitch," he whispered, pointing to the chart pad. "Just as you look for certain behaviors in a leader, your people look for certain behaviors in you. Since they don't all seek and respect the same behaviors your task is to ensure that you have all these behaviors 'covered'. Your behaviors translate to performance and profitability. An old Chinese proverb says, *A fish begins to rot at the head.* We're the heads of our respective departments. Don't look any further than yourself for a leadership behavior breach."

"Yes, you're right, Bert. But *how* do you do it? How do you become a more effective leader? Any suggestions? It's a big step from knowledge to practice, isn't it?" asked the production manager.

"Yep—it *is* a big step," answered Bert, smiling in recognition of an astute observation. "The answer *is* practice. *And* work. *And* repetition. And *more* practice. Remember Diogenes, the Greek historian and writer? He said *practice is everything.* I believe it. Leadership can be learned and strengthened, like anything else in life. All it takes is understanding what the valued behaviors are—and you've just identified them—so you've taken a big step in developing a leadership effectiveness plan.

"Also, watch how other people execute those behaviors. It's a mistake to try to *copy* something you see or hear, but you *can* adapt behaviors you witness.

"Personally, I've always seen the behaviors you identified as the ingredients—as the building blocks—of my heart, brains, and courage model. I can plug every one of those behaviors into one of those three categories—into my model."

"Bert, can you be more precise about how to become an effective leader?" the production manager persisted.

"No. I can't. And I won't try," Bert answered with understanding. "Don't waste your time looking for equations or sound-bite recipes. Leadership is far beyond formulas. *But*—I will say this. You absolutely *must* engage a challenge or take on an issue or a crisis to truly develop leadership skills. And since we're all in the middle of a challenge—*seize it*—*engage it*—*and learn from it!*

"You want more practice? In the future, look for situations where decisions need to be made, where goals need to be decided, where an organization needs to be held on course or vitalized, or where a team is sputtering or stalled, or where a setback has occurred. Or where there is an opportunity to pursue. Or where a just cause is languishing. Seek those situations out. Step forward. Throw yourself at those situations and lead them. Situations like that—combined with your vigorous engagement—results in improved leadership skills. You'll learn more in some situations than in others—but I guarantee you—you'll learn. Little by little.

"Finally, let me point out a subtlety for leadership growth. Take another look at the list of behaviors you created. Look carefully at the words you all used. Study those words. The language of leadership has its own vocabulary, and you've identified most of the vocabulary. *Use* those words as well as exhibiting those behaviors.

"For some it comes easier, for others it comes harder. We're all different. There *is* such a thing as a 'natural' leader. Desire is also a major factor. Some hunger for leadership roles more than others do. Frankly, that's good. If everyone wanted to be a leader as badly as the next person this world would be in serious trouble. Don't forget what we said earlier about the value of followership.

"Additionally, some people are meant to lead with certain subjects or issues and not with others. Sometimes the best leader in your organization in certain situations is one of your people, not yourself. Good leaders recognize that and aren't afraid to relinquish control.

"Obsessive control is an ugly enemy of leadership. So are excessive fear, politics, the hunger for power, self-absorption, immersion in personal agendas, selective apathy, premature surrender, and an unhealthy appetite to be liked or to please everyone. Believe me, I'm not naïve—I know all that stuff exists and tries to seep in and undermine effective leadership. But we must recognize it for what it is and stop it.

"Leadership can also go in a negative direction. It can decline and drift. Unfortunately, history is full of bad leaders—and so is our current society. Just pick up the paper or watch TV for bad examples. It's another reason that practice and development of the positive behaviors is imperative. Practice, practice, practice," Bert said to the production manager.

"Execution of all the behaviors you just identified is what will make your people feel good and help them perform to meet and exceed your expectations.

"Let me give you an example of practice, practice, practice. I was never a very good speaker but I knew that to be a leader I'd have to do something about my speaking. So I did. Over the course of several years I took effective speaking classes, I bought some books, I joined Toastmasters, I joined the National Speakers Association, I mimicked the styles of speakers that impressed me, and

I jumped at every opportunity to give a speech or make an introduction or a presentation. Sometimes when I'd go back home to see the folks on the farm, I'd stand out there in the fields where no one could hear me and I'd yell, shout, whisper, and chatter to the cows. I'm a lot better than I used to be," he laughed.

"In spite of my last crazy example, practice your leadership in view of everyone—*with your behaviors*—not by memo. Give yourself ample opportunity to 'meet and greet' and 'mix it up' with your people. And in this computer age remember that leadership attitudes and values cannot be practiced or shared electronically.

"Okay. Now let's get down to the heavy stuff. Let's look at what characterizes *outrageously successful leadership*," Bert announced.

The group was surprised. They thought they had already done that.

"Listen closely." And he bent over the table and in a hushed tone said slowly, "The secret is taking a certain few, *or even one*, of these leadership behaviors you've identified on the chart pad to the highest possible level of execution—to a level of supremacy.

"Isn't it true that when you think of a great leader in history, or a leader with whom you have personal experience, there is one or two or three characteristics that really shine above all the rest? Like the examples we all volunteered earlier? There are one or two points that define that leader, right? For example—remember how President Reagan was known as the '*great communicator*', how Lech Walesa of Solidarity fame was known for his *courage*, how Jack Welch of GE is known for his *candor and innovation*, how Supreme Court Justice Sandra Day O'Connor is known for her *strength of values*? And Billie Jean King for her *competitiveness and intensity*. And when John Elway of the Denver Broncos walked out on the field with his team behind in the fourth quarter was there any doubt that the Broncos would win? The team expected to come from behind simply because of his *confidence and ability!*

"Those leadership attributes fueled morale in the organizations those people led—and no assortment of tactics can lead to outrageous success when the morale of an organization is bad."

To prove his point further, Ol' Bert barked-out the names of a half-dozen recognized leaders and asked the group for each leader's most memorable characteristics. The management team nailed them all.

"The message for each of us is to take one or a couple of these leadership behaviors we've listed, ones for which we have a natural talent or deep conviction, and sharpen and shape them to their fullest possible expression—to leverage them. Personally, I have always tried to do that with knowledge—a 'brains' element from my model—and with relationships with my people—a 'heart' element from my model," Bert said.

"I know I'm not a very striking person or imposing presence even though I've tried to do the best with the hand God has dealt me. I know I'm not an inspirational speaker even though I've worked hard at it. I've always questioned my personal courage even as I've tried to strengthen it. But I know a lot about sales and management and I have a deep concern for people so I've tried to be the absolute best that I can be with those two leadership behaviors. And importantly, I always try to put myself in circumstances that *permit the use* of those behaviors.

"It's this emphasis on one or a couple of valued behaviors that many people refer to as a 'leadership style'. Without emphasis on a valued behavior or two you become a nameless testimony to leadership mediocrity—but *with it* you can become a memorable testimony to outrageously successful leadership. How do *you* want to be defined as a leader? It's your choice. You're in control. Do it," Bert directed.

"Let's *all* do it," commented Mr. Pimm. "Bert, this has been very good. Can we turn all of these notes into a Certus leadership guide? Is that okay with everyone?" he asked the management team.

"Absolutely."

"Sure."

"Terrific idea."

"Right on", came the responses from the folks around the table.

"I'll write this up in a useful format for everyone," said Bert.

He added, "Let's each pick a behavior—or two—or three—that we've listed, *right now, right this minute,* and work on them. Let's write them down to seal our commitment to the task at hand. Pick behaviors that are responsive to the needs of your own group as well as the needs of Certus.

"Particular situations require particular behaviors. You know the corporate situation. You know your own situation. You know your people. You know yourself. Pick prudently."

The room grew quiet as everyone thought and wrote. They all did it on the spot.

After the period of quiet, Bert began again, "One of the best leadership behaviors and one of the finest statements of commitment any manager can make is the investment in his or her people through teaching and coaching. That's one of the things I have been executing all along with Leslie, Lance, and

Luke. If you'd like to learn more about my approach stop by the Wisdom Pantry any time. You all know my daily schedule."

Everyone acknowledged the offer.

The management team gave Ol' Bert a rousing round of applause. The group's edginess and tightness, so evident earlier in the day, had disappeared. People literally flew out of the room to get on with their responsibilities.

After the session, Ol' Bert accompanied the finance director and Mr. Pimm to a meeting with their banker in Mr. Pimm's office. The apprehensive banker wanted an up-date. Ol' Bert used his leadership skills to help Mr. Pimm reassure the banker. His wisdom and people skills added credibility and calm to the proceeding.

"Bert," said Mr. Pimm, after the others had left. "I've been following you closely ever since you started implementing your ten essentials. It seems to me the essentials could be applicable in any business and in any business function."

"Yep—they are totally transferable to any business," said Bert. "Heck, I first learned these essentials from my daddy. They're applicable in agribusiness, high tech, healthcare, consumer products, transportation, and real estate— wherever teams of people are offering products or services.

"I happen to be a sales manager. The ten essentials are valid for managers in finance, in operations, in human resources, in marketing, in engineering, in any department. The details of content and implementation may vary slightly, but the ten essentials are identical. All managers need horses. All departments need destination and boundary stakes. All departments need strategies and plans. And all departments thrive when they have productive processes and tools in place. That's why I like sharing the essentials in sessions such as we just held. I've been providing a distillation of my years of experience to the others all along. I'll continue to do that. I assume it's okay with you."

"Absolutely! Go to it," Mr. Pimm enthused.

"Bert, what keeps people, myself included, from being as knowledgeable and as intensely committed as you to these essentials? They seem like common sense."

"It's puzzling," Bert agreed. "Maybe no one ever explained the essentials to them. Maybe they don't understand the value of embedded guiding principles—which is what essentials basically are. Perhaps someone unnecessarily complicated his or her job. Or they're not interested. Maybe they've developed the habit of chasing magical quick fixes. It could be they

inadvertently let go of these basics while reaching for seemingly more sophisticated ideas. Maybe daily operational issues, personal problems, or some new-fangled theory has drawn them off. Or they're not hungry enough. Perhaps they're lazy. It's possible they don't have a reminder written down somewhere. Maybe no one ever told them how to convert knowledge into action.

"I've always thought of the ten essentials like the owner's manual you get when you buy a new truck. A lot of good info to get the most value out of that truck, but you'd be surprised how few read that manual.

"Heck, if I knew what keeps managers from being knowledgeable and committed to these essentials I'd write that manual and make a million dollars.

"Don't blame yourself or anyone else. So far we're all doing a fine job of remaking ourselves—a never-ending task by the way. If we stay calm and don't panic and stay the course we'll be okay. Let's be thankful the whole team is headed in the right direction."

Bert continued, "I really appreciate your support and personal example."

"Well, I for one have become convinced about these essentials. I'm with you 100%," said Mr. Pimm.

"Thank you," Bert humbly acknowledged.

And all along Ol' Bert had also been providing growing hard evidence, via sales revenues, that his essentials were creditable. His talk—plus his walk—was not lost on anyone.

The three horses remained busy bringing in the business. The pipeline was filling.

There was little more than three months left to turn things around and achieve the stakes they were aiming for. The outcome was still in doubt, but suddenly there was a reassuring story about Certus in the Wall Street Journal. Major brokerages signaled a 'buy' for Certus stock.

Essential #7
Aid Everyone In Learnin'

The morning after, Ol' Bert was pleasantly surprised to find two members of Mr. Pimm's management staff—two of his peers—waiting outside the Wisdom Pantry when he arrived at 7:00.

"Bert, we need your help," one of them gushed nervously. "We would like to talk about training. We don't have much time. You did such a great job yesterday. We know that training is one of the essentials of outrageous success in which you so strongly believe."

It was clear to Ol' Bert that both of these managers were feeling the strain. He smiled gently. "First let me plug in my coffee pot. And since I don't have a secretary let me clear a few things off of my agenda with a couple of e-mails. Then we'll kick the door shut and chat. How's that?"

Ol' Bert's attitude seemed to unburden them. He could see them relax. He wiped off his whiteboard and pulled several books off of his Wisdom Pantry shelves to get ready for a little coaching session. The three of them sat there sipping hazelnut coffee, small-talking, Ol' Bert comfortably enveloped in that massive chair. The Wisdom Pantry offered the pleasant mingled smells of a coffee boutique and a musty old bookstore.

"You ready?" he asked.

They nodded briskly.

"I'm happy to share my thoughts. I deeply believe that the success-gods are on the side-of-the-smarter so I've been executing this seventh essential with vigor ever since I've been here at Certus. But I've never thought of myself as a trainer—*never*. It always struck me that training was something for my pet retriever, Hobie, back on the farm. Rather, I always thought of myself as a teacher and a coach. Somehow, teaching and coaching seem better suited to people. I'm not disparaging 'training' and 'trainers', words that I know are fixed in our business vocabulary. I'm just trying to take this learning idea to the highest possible level. Aren't those two very nice words, 'teacher' and 'coach'?" And the two managers mechanically nodded.

"In my mind, training seems to focus on the trainer and something 'given'. I can train, train, train and still not get very far. Learning focuses on my people.

Learning focuses on something 'taken' and absorbed. I want my staff to learn, learn, learn. If my people learn, our customers will be happier, the results will pour in, and Mr. Pimm may finally be able to relax.

"Concentrate on learning. We are learning-helpers. A teacher helps learning happen the way a doctor helps healing happen. In both cases the employee-student and the patient have a heck of a lot to do with the final outcome. The teacher or doctor can't make it happen by himself or herself. Can they?" Bert asked rhetorically.

"Good teaching transfers new information and skills. Good learning is the absorption of new information and skills. Good coaching ensures correct and consistent use of new information and skills. All three improve customer satisfaction, business results—*and* mold better company citizens," Bert philosophized. "Teaching—learning—and coaching, like the flour, water, and salt in the bread my momma baked—where your employee is the yeast—and you are the baker. All those elements are inescapably blended. If any of the three ingredients is missing, or if either of the two players is not doing his or her job, the enterprise fails—everyone goes hungry.

"My objective is to have Certus survive and succeed outrageously, and in order to do that I must continually strengthen my people and myself through effective learning. I seize every opportunity to acquire *and* transfer knowledge and skills. Knowledge is my personal treasure," he said humbly, "but useful only if invested. As Socrates once said, *there is only one good, knowledge—and one evil, ignorance.*"

That stilled the room for a moment.

Then one of the managers asked, "Could you say some more about the difference between teaching and coaching, Bert?"

Bert said, "I'm not smart enough to know the fine points. Both result in learning, and that's what I'm interested in, so I don't get hung-up on the subtleties between the two. But I've always thought of teaching as imparting new knowledge and showing people how to do new things, usually in group environments. Teaching strikes me as a process consisting of the communication of knowledge, performed by one who knows, enabling someone else to know, and enabling them to practice.

"I've always thought of coaching as advising and correcting on a very personal level, as one-on-one feedback. Coaching is ensuring that new information, which has been taught, is consistently and correctly applied in actual application. Coaching is fine-tuning what you've taught. Together, teaching and coaching bring our strategies to life and sustain and grow Certus. Just think about continuous learning and you can't go wrong.

"All you're interested in is making learning happen and making it stick to your people like pine sap. Does that answer your question?

"Sounds simple enough," one acknowledged.

"Don't oversimplify this though," Bert quickly cautioned. "Teaching and coaching are complex. Teaching is a huge and honorable profession in its own right. Coaching is also a huge and honorable profession, as we know from sports. There is a lot that we can learn from successful teachers and coaches. We are all the products of both professions. In the course of our own education we all have had some outstanding learning experiences, a few poor ones, and many that were fair-to-middling. Examine your own history all the way back to kindergarten—both formal and post-school. What teachers and coaches made an impression upon you, and why? How did they teach and coach? Why did you learn more in some environments than others? I'll bet there are some lessons there. Right?" Neither was listening. Ol' Bert could see they were both wrapped-up somewhere in their pasts.

"Good point," one finally said, clearly having uncovered something valued.

Bert continued, "People imitate their leaders appetite for learning. By the intensity of your thirst for knowledge and skills—and the subject matter you pursue—*you* are a learning model. The example you set—good or bad—is powerful." And Ol' Bert pushed *How Organizations Learn*, *Ten Steps To A Learning Organization*, *The Adult Learner*, and *Learning Organizations*, across his desk. "Here, why don't you go through these? They're all marked up with my own notes and that should help you. When you finish those, I've got more."

The two managers recoiled at the sight of the implied studying. One said, "Uh—great—thanks Bert. We're with you." Reaching for the books, they both got up to leave as if the session was over.

"Whoa, hold on folks. I haven't even started yet," Bert chuckled, reaching for his ice water. He drank ice water like an old generator consumed #2 diesel oil—drinking more, as the 'load' got heavier.

"I've got a pretty simple four-part philosophy for outrageous teaching and coaching," he continued. He slowly wrote the four words on his whiteboard.

FREQUENCY
REGULARITY
RIGOR
ACCOUNTABILITY

"First of all, what's frequent? That's ultimately for you to decide. Once a year? Of course not. Once a month? I doubt it. Once a week? That's better.

Daily? That's best, and that is my personal measure of teaching and coaching frequency. I make sure I teach or coach *something* every single day. It's a personal goal, or 'stake', as I like to say. The 'frequent' aspect of my philosophy comes from Saint Paul, who said in one of his letters to *constantly* teach and never lose patience. While he was referring to the faith, it made an everlasting impression on me.

"One of the biggest reasons for being frequent is *change*—change in markets, customers, competitors, products, services, and scores of other things.

"Some of my frequent efforts are formal teaching sessions—some are informal counseling and feedback discussions. It can be something as simple as a question-of-the-day e-mailed to everyone or a lesson imparted on the phone during a discussion about a touchy customer situation. The over-all business situation should have no bearing on frequency. That's how managers get in trouble. When times are good they slack off teaching and coaching, which of course is very bad. The business situation should have a bearing on teaching *content*, not on teaching *frequency*. Frequency is a measure of commitment. If teaching and coaching are not frequent what does that say?"

"It's certainly not an encouraging message," one of the managers agreed, back in the flow of the discussion.

"Second, what's regular? Regular means that major, or formal, elements of the teaching are executed on a timetable, that it's not sporadic. Since I've been here I've had a formal class session with my people once a week at a *fixed time* for a *fixed period*. I never permit it to be bumped—*never*. If teaching occurs randomly, it comes across as 'filler'. People think 'we must have a gap in important stuff', or, 'we must have time to spare', or, 'a program is being ram-rodded down from the top'. Randomness communicates that something is insignificant, that it's minor, peripheral, or secondary. That is certainly *not* the case with teaching or coaching. Don't you agree?"

And the two managers concurred, one saying, "I can see how a consistent pattern communicates consequence and underscores commitment."

"Third, rigor. Rigor means the teaching and coaching is thorough and tough, that it's deep and demanding, and that it presses your people physically and mentally. I want my staff to be able to react and respond correctly when they are under pressure and fatigued. Anyone can pop off an answer when they are fresh or not pressed. I like to create worst-case scenarios in my classes. Testing and quizzing are always a part of my teaching. Practice is always a part of my coaching. A good teacher and coach shouldn't serve-up pabulum and shouldn't accept mushy drivel for answers. I want my teaching and coaching to

126

be more intense than anything they will experience in the real world. I'm a proponent of the old Chinese proverb that says, *the more you sweat in peace the less you bleed in war*. If teaching and coaching are not rigorous, what does that say? It implies that your people can work at the same level of intensity at which they were taught, which of course is not my intent. Your teaching intensity level *sets the standard* for your work intensity level.

"File this quotation in your memory. '*We must remember that one man is much the same as another, and that he is best who is trained in the severest school*'. That little gem comes from an ancient history of the Peloponnesian Wars. I love it."

The two managers both wrote it down.

"Fourth, what's accountable? Accountable means holding your people responsible for what they've been taught. Your people must understand that they are liable to be called to account for their learning. Otherwise many will just go through the motions, cherry-picking what suits their fancy. Accountable means you're going to follow-up on the teaching, observing how and where stuff is being used, investigating and challenging its application, tracking the effects of what's been taught, watching outcomes, measuring the results—and your people understand this. It's your responsibility to hold your people accountable for what they are taught. Counseling sessions and performance reviews are the instruments of formalizing the accountability.

"Don't waste your time teaching or coaching something for which you are not going to hold your people accountable. Your people will pick-up on that and then your credibility as a teacher and coach is shot. Remember what I said yesterday about courage as a key element of leadership? Well, holding your folks accountable is an application of courage."

The two managers both raised their eyebrows on that statement, and vigorously kept taking notes.

"If teaching and coaching are not frequent, regular, rigorous, and accountable it says that you as a manager believe that teaching and coaching are unimportant, and by extension, that your people are unimportant, and perhaps expendable. Certainly a bad conclusion. Don't laugh. Employees can easily make that mental jump.

"Think about activities in your life that are done with frequency, regularity, rigor, and accountability. Dental checkups every six months. An annual physical. Going to church, synagogue, or mosque weekly. Eating. Working out three times a week. Personal hygiene. Going to work every day. Taking a vacation. Hmmm? Notice how they are all very, very personal activities. Those are also consequential activities, aren't they? Absolutely! Teaching and coaching are also very personal and consequential. Notice the variable time frames associated with each of my examples—some daily, some annually. Teaching and coaching are the same. Some subjects need daily attention, others not as frequent. The development of your people and yourselves must *never* be left to chance.

"Everyone okay on the coffee?" Bert asked.

"Coffee's terrific, Bert. I feel guilty I didn't bring doughnuts. You've already uncovered a couple of mistakes I make," one of the managers confessed.

"Good. Glad I'm helping. Once you're comfortable with those four philosophy points, the next step is to get organized by answering four imperatives."

Back at the whiteboard, he wrote:

WHAT are you going to teach
WHO is going to be taught
WHICH person will do the teaching
HOW will it be taught

"First—a preface to these imperatives. Let me start by sharing a personal secret about the order of learning. The first subjects I teach have always been a couple of short courses on thinking and learning—about multiple intelligences—plus mind-mapping, which is an organizational system. This preface prepares the ground for everything that follows. Here are some good guides," and Bert passed his copy of *Frames of Mind, Eight Ways of Teaching*, and *Mapping Inner Space* across the desk.

"These books were written for teachers. They will sharpen your teaching efforts by telling you how people learn. It's the strengths and weaknesses in our eight intelligences that affect how people learn. And we as teachers, and our people as students, must understand these intelligences. The eight intelligences are called verbal-linguistic, visual-spatial, bodily-kinesthetic, logical-mathematical, musical-rhythmic, interpersonal, intrapersonal, and naturalist. In other words, there are eight ways to 'be smart' and 'get smarter'. Everyone possesses these intelligences in varying degrees. These eight intelligences are the skills that solve problems—and create and contribute to what is valued within Certus and valued by our customers. Teaching and learning are not as simple as it appears, as you can see," Bert said gravely. "It takes understanding to do it right."

"Bert, whoa! You serious with this stuff? This is *heavy*," one of the managers responded with a gloomy sigh, sensing the work.

"Don't lose sight of the fact that we're talking about outrageousness," Bert reminded them. "There's a price to pay," he smiled.

"And here's more. Not only is it important for you and your people to know how to think and learn—your people need to know how to study. Look through *How To Improve Your Study Skills, How To Learn Anything Quickly*, and *Study Smarter, Not Harder*," said Bert, gleefully adding to their stack. "I've high-lighted all these books. And here are all my teaching notes to help you. My little preface-courses, which I call Pine Sap 101, help learning stick. I also gave each of my people a copy of these study books. They loved 'em!

"You both okay?" Bert tested.

"We're hanging in," one responded. "But barely."

"Good. You'll catch on. Back to the four imperatives.

"Let's first talk about 'what', ***WHAT are you going to teach***. I believe all teaching and coaching should start from *the customer's* perspective. Think about *their* expectations and values. Teach to plant the knowledge and develop the skills in order that your people can deliver what customers and sales partners expect and value. Coach to sharpen the aptitudes and personal qualities that customer's respect. My horses are 'horses' because they provide impressive value to our customers and as a result they are respected and liked by our customers.

"For example, it's been found that customers, above all, value a supplier's understanding of *their* business and how they *do* business. So I've been teaching how to accomplish that. Customers also expect suppliers to provide solutions to their problems and focus a spotlight on unseen opportunities. So I've been teaching what our products, services, and company can offer—and I don't mean superficial 'benefits', I mean second and third level impacts on *their* business.

"We also knew from planting our Mustard Seed strategy that our customers want specific information and support quickly. So I've been teaching everyone how to make that happen, ensuring that our computer skills are at the highest level. Another element of our strategy is the scientific research and basic technology associated with our products. Therefore I ensure that material gets emphasis. And—our customers' buying process relies heavily on a proposal. Therefore, I've taught the team to be outstanding proposal writers.

"Virtually everything I teach cascades down to customers. It's not for the salespeople's *direct* benefit that I teach how to do all this. It's all for the customer's benefit—*the customer's advantage and profit*. It's a matter of viewpoint. We have to look at teaching and coaching from the customer's shoes. My people and Certus benefit indirectly. We create customers before we make sales. Think about that."

"But—but Bert—our groups don't deal with customers," one of the managers protested gently.

"Yep—they do, they just don't know it," Bert responded softly. "All the work *everyone*—in *any* firm—does is for the benefit of the customer, client, or sales partner. Some employees, like salespeople, are just closer to the customer than others. Let me give you an example. The people in purchasing buy materials that go into our products. If they don't purchase top quality at the best price and get that stuff here on time, who suffers? The customer, first and foremost. And then we *all* ultimately pay for the problem. It's that way all around Certus. Would you like another example?"

"No, we get the point. We'll come up with examples of our own for our own departments."

Bert continued, "And don't teach what *you think* is needed, teach what *you know* is needed. Teach essential things first. Teaching-for-the-customer can cover hundreds of sales, service, support, product, technology, information, process, and application subjects. I don't have the time or the money for a crapshoot. But I know what our customers and partners want from Certus's sales team because I went out and asked a select few with whom we have both good and bad relationships. And more importantly, I even asked *non-customers*, which is a real eye-opener. I had some opinions beforehand based on my experience, but all their inputs confirmed my feelings and added new insights. Plus, they respected me for asking the question. People like to help. Here's a copy of what they told me," and Bert handed each some papers.

He let them study the comments for a minute.

"If you ask enough customers and non-customers, getting a fix on the issues and prioritizing their needs and expectations becomes easy," Bert chortled confidently.

"Once I knew where all those people stood, then the sales team and I assessed where we stood in relation to delivering on those expectations. The 'delta' between where we stood and what the customer base expected helped define the teaching and coaching I needed to implement. I certainly didn't expect customers to define everything, but my three horses and I heard enough and we are good enough at reading between the lines to figure things out. The bottom-line? Teach what is essential and helpful to E-X-C-E-E-D the customer's expectations. Just as I believe in exceeding the closer-in, the farther-out, and the over-the-horizon 'stakes' we've pounded, I believe in exceeding our customer's expectations. The teaching and coaching I execute based on the customer's expectations accounts for about 80% of my total teaching and coaching effort.

"You both okay?" he asked again, a little worry in his tone.

"Absolutely! Keep going, Bert", one acknowledged with heightened confidence.

"Next. You have to ask *what* needs to be taught and coached from *our company's* perspective. I need to fulfill Certus's corporate needs and expectations, lining us up behind the corporate agenda and following Certus's procedures, policies, and processes. It all must be taught and coached.

"The sales department also has many *internal* customers so we need to understand their expectations, and I need to teach my people how to *exceed* them as well. Order entry exactness, for example. Adherence to terms and conditions of sale, for example. Product specs and capabilities that marketing wants us to emphasize is another example. Compliance with US anti-trust laws is another example. It goes on and on.

"Sales departments are notorious for throwing sand in the internal gears. I can't tolerate that. I need to *grease* the gears, and that's what we have been doing.

"The bottom line? Teach what is *essential* to the smooth functioning of internal systems and strengthening teamwork. Again, you must be the judge of what's essential based on your understanding of other business functions and how your function integrates with all others.

"This accounts for about 10% of my effort," Bert said.

He then mentioned some teaching he had executed which related to both managers' own departments.

"Thanks—thanks for thinking of us," one offered, a bit surprised.

"My group gets blasted from time-to-time by other departments," the other admitted. "I've got to stop the problems we're causing. I've got your point, Bert."

Bert paused on that acknowledgment—then began again saying, "Next, you have to consider *what* needs to be taught and coached from your people's *personal* perspective. This is the hardest teaching and coaching to execute because it can strike at private, and possibly sensitive, gaps and aspirations that may or may not have to do with the business. Therefore, some managers don't even address this.

"Let me give you a spectrum of examples.

"Encouraging formal education where there are obvious deficiencies.

"Proposing a change in personal style.

"Pointing out perceptions of attitude left on others.

"Talking about career options in and outside the company.

"Suggesting the reading of a book that contains character elements.

"Asking a philosophical question that causes honest self-analysis.

131

"Engaging in a discussion about a matter that is hurting the person's reputation.

"Pointing out how a personal strength can be leveraged for greater benefit or how an unacknowledged weakness diminishes effectiveness.

"We as managers have an inescapable role in character formation. It is not an option. It's implicit in the manager-employee relationship. Our every action and word has an impact, whether intended or not. We should be proactive coaches rather than sluggish spectators simply letting accidental impressions occur and shortcomings fester.

"But Bert, can't some of that stuff be construed as an invasion of privacy or a little too personal?" one manager asked.

"No, not if you do it with tact and sensitivity. And with genuine concern—which is the mature response of those who recognize their duty towards others. Teaching and coaching that lack genuine concern may enter their ears but it will never reach their hearts and minds.

"Mutual trust also helps. So does personal courage. I believe this level of teaching and coaching is one of the secrets of outrageous success because when people see that you are sincerely interested in them—*them as individuals*—not just producers—commitment and results mushroom. They'll blow the walls down for you.

"Teach what is essential to making our people better people. That should account for about 10% of what you teach and coach. *A teacher affects eternity; he can never tell where his influence stops.* Fella by the name of Henry Adams, a historian I believe, first said that. I like it.

"That answers the first imperative, *what* to teach and coach. Okay?"

"Okay, whew, that's a load," said one of the managers.

"Yep—it is. But again, remember we're talking about outrageous success," emphasized Bert.

"Let me make a few points, as a breather, before jumping into the second, third, and fourth imperatives," Bert said.

"Identify and watch what *signals* the need for teaching and coaching. For me, those signals include a weak pipeline, poor results, business and personal problems, customer complaints, complaints from inside, mistakes, repetitive questions, poor morale, and dejection or despair. Identify and watch your own signals. Your signals may be unique to your department. Then, of course, leap on those signals.

"Teaching has got to be consistent with, and supportive of, our 'stakes', our Mustard Seed strategy, and the sales team plan. And I prioritize. I don't try to teach and coach everything at once. I suggest you do the same.

"Also—show your people what you're planning to teach. *Share* your teaching plan. Help them understand *why* you're doing what you're doing. Don't let teaching events 'just happen' out-of-the-blue.

"Okay—let's jump back into the imperatives. After addressing the 'what', the second imperative is 'who'—*WHO is going to be taught?* Confirming the audience sounds simple, but it isn't. The audience should also include other people, in and out of the company, who will be affected by the teaching you are providing. As teachers and coaches we sometimes tend to focus on the obvious, grooming our horses, making 'em look good, and neglecting the supporting cast. Certus delivers solutions as a marketing-sales-service *team* therefore I need to teach that way. That's why I've included folks from those departments in many of our sessions, and that includes management, even Mr. Pimm. It doesn't mean that the supporting cast needs the same breadth and depth of material and time involved, but they *must* participate to some degree. Teaching in that fashion embeds the team concept. To play as a team you must learn and practice as a team.

"And learning is important for *all* of a manager's direct reports. As you know I've got a couple of inside sales support folks. I hold them in the same high regard that I think of Leslie, Lance, and Luke. Include *all* of your direct reports in your teaching and learning efforts, regardless of their title or responsibilities."

"Bert, how do you handle those who may not be motivated for all this learning, or denounce what you're trying to teach and coach?" one manager asked.

"If you want to genuinely teach and coach you have got to make up your mind to do things that some people will shrug at or criticize. I have *no* patience and *no* compassion for the person who is lazy about learning. I offer *no* option. Our reality does not permit it. I never hire folks with that mind-set. I counsel those who develop that mind-set. And I cull-out those who persist in that mind-set," Bert said matter-of-factly.

"That sounds severe," one manager responded.

"The implications of tolerating any indifference for learning, or permitting 'slamming' of the learning agenda, are *more* severe," Bert said. "They're suicidal."

There was a hush. The two managers slowly and thoughtfully nodded.

"Finally, folks—as a sales manager it is also imperative for me to include sales partners in my teaching and coaching, which I've also done. You, also, may want to include people outside of Certus with whom you have close working relationships.

"The third imperative is 'which'—*WHICH person is going to teach*? It may sound self-evident, that it's always going to be you, but it doesn't always have to be you. Put your ego in your back pocket. Use your resources. Outsourcing, if you can afford it, is a good idea. So is having someone on your staff or someone from another department do the teaching. The possibilities are endless.

"Let me tell you what I think are the characteristics of an outrageous teacher," and Bert went to his whiteboard and wrote three more words boldly:

COMMITTED
KNOWLEDGEABLE
COMMUNICATOR

"Committed means the person doing the teaching really wants to do it *for the sake of the people being taught*, not for themselves. Their energy is unmistakable. He or she loves doing it and gets a great deal of self-satisfaction from the effort, like the time I had one of our Ph.D. managers from engineering explain a new production process. Boy, was he psyched about being able to share with us and make us stronger!

"Knowledgeable means a deep and broad grasp of the subject, a passion for the subject, and an understanding of the subject as it applies to *today's* business. Knowledge must be contemporary, not historic memory-lane excursions. Knowledge establishes unquestionable credibility," and he tapped his bookshelves to emphasize this point.

"Communicator means someone with good platform skills that can *project and transfer* the knowledge, someone that is articulate, has a good sense of timing, is a keen observer and listener sensitive to audience reactions, can share his or her knowledge with stories, anecdotes, or acting, and can be as inspirational or tough in delivery as the situation warrants. Like the time I brought in a local TV news announcer to discuss presentation skills. Wow, did *she* fire everyone up!

"Remember this famous saying from a teacher named William Ward—*the mediocre teacher tells, the good teacher explains, the superior teacher demonstrates, the great teacher inspires.*

"Pick your teachers carefully. Ask yourself who can best deliver the messages you want implanted. It's worth delaying your teaching to wait for the availability of the right—the *best*—teacher for a given situation. Your own learning experience has probably proven that, hasn't it?" Bert challenged.

"Yes, you're right, I've been in situations where a convenient alternate was clearly a compromise choice," one of the managers stated. "Those learning situations were always disappointing."

"Bert," one of them said, "I hear what you're saying, but I've read that the best teaching is teaching you author yourself because it helps both parties. What do you think?"

"Absolutely! I agree!!" Bert replied enthusiastically. "You benefit as well. *'Even while they teach, men learn'*, said the first century Roman statesman and philosopher, Seneca. To the greatest possible extent, create and execute your own teaching efforts. It sends a powerful commitment message. Reach for expertise only when it makes sense, when the subject matter is outside your realm or competency, not to cop-out.

"In either case, regardless who teaches, make it obvious to all that you have seized personal control of all teaching.

"Thanks for bringing up that point. And by the way—if someone else does end up doing the teaching you *must* be in the audience. After all, you're going to be the one doing the follow-on coaching.

"I'm not keeping the two of you too long, am I?" Bert asked.

"Heck, no. This is invigorating," one stated.

"Okay," said Bert. "The fourth imperative is design and delivery of the material. The 'how', *HOW will it be taught.* We must execute the teaching to the highest delivery standards.

"This 'how' stuff is the fun stuff, but I'm tired of talking," Bert said with a smile. "Why don't the two of you tell *me* what *you* think is important about delivery. I'll make notes on the whiteboard, and then I'll fill in any blanks."

"Fair enough," they both said, then they started popping-out thoughts—alternating back and forth.

"Make the teaching environment comfortable, not distracting."

"Provide some pre-class work to get everyone up to speed and in the mood."

"Customize as much as possible."

"Be highly interactive."

"Deliver in an enticing or engaging way."

"Use a lot of stories and real-world examples."

"Balance group and individual activities."

"Think about adding some variety and excitement with how things are presented and who presents."

"Develop some individual or group projects that require homework and teamwork."

"Make really creative presentations."
"Use a variety of different media."
"Throw in some games and competition."
"Require a lot of practice, make it action learning."
"Give people ample opportunity to ask any and all questions."
"Lighten up from time to time. Do something recreational."
"Use all the new presentation technology to the greatest possible extent."
"Think about how things should flow logically from one item to the next."
"Vary the speed of delivery. Don't be monotonous."
"Talk about concepts as well as hard facts and figures."
"Energize the group. Inspire."
"Provide good materials to which they can later refer."
"Practice before you present."
And then the well ran dry.

"You did *great!* Thanks," Bert enthused. "Let me close with one important point. People have different learning styles, what I like to call 'intake-pipes', and you must make sure you know your people's 'pipes'. The three learning styles are visual, auditory, and kinesthetic, or in other words people have a predisposition to taking-in information by seeing, hearing, or doing. One style always predominates in everyone, even though all three are used. For example, I've learned that Lance is a visual learner, Leslie an auditory learner, and Luke primarily a kinesthetic learner. My understanding of their preferred learning style, and my awareness of the eight intelligences I referred to earlier, helps the four of us."

"How did you learn about your horses' predisposition to learning styles, Bert?" one asked.

"I asked and I observed," Bert said. "Not hard to figure out.

"And here are some additional resources to help with your delivery," and Bert handed over *Intelligence Builders For Every Student, Creative Whack Pack, Games Trainers Play*, and *Even More Games Trainers Play*.

"This stuff will stir your creative juices," he laughed, knowing that he was really loading-up these folks. "I've got more when you're done with these."

"Discussion of learning styles leads me to make some points on coaching," Bert said. "Because coaching is primarily one-on-one, sensitivity to different learning styles and the eight intelligences is even more important.

"Teaching and coaching go hand in hand. They cannot be separated. As I said earlier, coaching ensures that teaching that has already occurred—*sticks*— and it identifies future teaching needs. Coaching is feedback on the application effectiveness of what was delivered in teaching sessions. If you fail to follow-up your teaching with coaching you're leaving money on the table—the money you invested in teaching and the money to be made in the market.

"I believe the attributes that make a great coach, *in addition to* the three words I wrote earlier on the board, include the following," and Bert turned his monitor and clicked his mouse on each of a dozen points in a file he had labeled Certus' Coachin' Canons.

"First. Be sensitive to the values and hot buttons of your people, sensitive to their micro-culture, and try mightily to understand them as individuals.

"Second. Project the appropriate attitude and image during the moment the coaching is delivered. Customize based on the situation. Sometimes you've got to be a bit of an actor or actress—so loosen up.

"Third. Always stress the fundamentals and the principles in which you— *and Certus*—deeply believe. As I like to say, enforce The Law of the Farm and The Law of the Garden. And do it in a structured way. No hip-shooting.

"Fourth. Be a fire-lighter, stoking peoples' inner furnace. Being an energy *giver* translates into confidence building, esteem building, enthusiasm building, character building, or whatever else needs to be built.

"Fifth. Set boundaries. The coach is a disciplinarian—as stern or tolerant as need be—exhibiting as much or as little patience as required.

"Sixth. Pick the right time —which should always be sooner rather than later. Let the emotion of the moment and the freshness of the situation work for you. Emotion and immediacy help embed coaching.

"Seventh. Be an amateur psychologist—a Zen master, a priest, a rabbi— whatever it takes to get inside your people's heads and hearts.

"Eighth. Possess microscopic vision and a finely tuned ear. Nothing should escape you. Be a sharp observer, listener, and recorder of details in people and in situations.

"Ninth. Be a quick, calm, and imaginative thinker. In the face of conflict or contention, or under pressure, or facing an employee's exasperation, turn insights and observations into understandable and doable guidance. Screaming needlessly siphons energy from your brain.

"Tenth. Be relentless with obsessed pursuit of what's good for individuals and what's good for the team—not accepting so-so execution. It's not right til' it's right. Right?" Bert smiled.

"Eleventh, delivery. Dispense suggestions frequently in 2-to-3 minute digestible mini-doses, not in hour-long harangues. And make those mini-doses interactive and collaborative.

"And twelfth, follow-up, to ensure that the coaching is applied. Employees will often have the feeling that 'this too shall pass'. Nip that thought in the bud with 'this too shall be done' supervision. Behaviors *must* change.

"Okay? Got those?" Bert quizzed.

"Yes! Thanks. Your points remind me of coaches I've seen in action, speeches I've heard coaches give, or books they've written," one of the managers responded, looking up from her note-taking.

Bert continued, "The coach sets the tone, but both the coach and employee have responsibilities. Candor, mutual respect, mutual effort to understand how the other person feels, and the employee using the manager's suggestions and having the courtesy to feed back the results characterize the best coach-employee relationships.

"You'll know you've become a very effective coach when your people come to you *voluntarily*—and frankly, until they do, you've got to work on your coaching skills and your relationships with your people.

"Coaching keeps your standards high and accelerates results. Coaching maintains *learning mo-men-tum*. I can't overemphasize the importance of learning momentum because it translates into outrageous results. And *you* control momentum.

"Accelerating your learning, or gaining learning momentum, means accelerating your results.

"Steady-state learning means steady-state results.

"Decelerating your learning, or losing learning momentum, means decelerating your results.

"Dead-stop learning means failure and bankruptcy.

"Do you know how much energy it takes to restart a tractor pulling a 40-foot grain drill if it loses momentum? A lot, believe me. You're the tractor—stay in motion.

"I'm going to say this again. Teaching and coaching are parallel activities. In other words, I don't do all the teaching before I start coaching. I jump back and forth. Picture the scene at baseball or basketball pre-season training. You've probably seen glimpses on TV or experienced it yourself. Teaching and coaching are parallel. They go together. I teach a piece of knowledge than I coach its application.

"Now—listen—you always need to determine if you hit the target. It is imperative that you confirm understanding, seek feedback, and obtain evaluations on all you're teaching and coaching—*as you execute*. How well *you think* you've done doesn't matter one iota. Your employees—*and* our customers—are the best judges of your teaching efforts, just as the guest at a banquet can better judge a feast than the cook. Confirm that what you serve satisfies their appetites and then adjust accordingly.

"Finally, I see teaching and coaching as preparing my people to be very successful people, not just very successful salespeople. I'm only going to have them for a short indeterminate time. I want them to look back on their time with me as a highlight of their career—*of their life*—where they learned valuable lessons. We, as a company and as managers, have both a business and a social responsibility for our people to thrive.

"What does all this teaching and coaching investment do for Certus?" he asked rhetorically.

"Aid the bottom line. Winning companies are teaching and coaching companies. But there's more. We have to stop and think about *all* the implications of our teaching and coaching investment.

"Here's what I mean," and he excitedly started pacing and gesturing.

"The credibility of our people, the firm, and our brand names improve. That credibility has value and often permits higher prices and margins.

"It enhances our reputation in the marketplace, the industry, and the financial investment community as an employee-focused company.

"It forces us to look harder and more frequently at the marketplace and customers—and our internal policies and processes.

"We become more capable of making changes, adapting, responding to threats, and implementing new concepts and ideas.

"It makes us a more attractive environment for 'horses'. It's much easier to recruit. We can point to specific programs and activities. And it improves retention of all employees.

"It gives us a competitive edge.

"And acculturation of our people to Certus occurs in teaching and coaching sessions. Let's not forget—our people *are* Certus.

"In summary, the feeling sometimes is 'why should I invest so much in these people? They'll be gone in 18 months or so. Company loyalty is an anachronism'. Well, I don't buy that gibberish. I'm committed to my people. I want our customers to be there in 18 months and our company to still to be there in 18 months and beyond. *That's* the bottom line. The plusses far outweigh potential people losses. Don't let anyone *ever* trap you in that 'personnel turnover' argument. It holds as much water as a pitchfork. Get out there and teach and coach," he said, slapping his hand on his whiteboard.

Startled, the two managers said, "Bert, this has been terrific, thanks so much," and they quickly got up to leave, staggering out with their load of books and notes.

"Hey—we're a team. I just may be coming to you for help tomorrow," Bert concluded with that twinkle in his eye.

"Thanks for asking me to share my thoughts. Remember what Frederick the Great said—*God is always with the strongest battalions*. It's our job to make this battalion, Certus, the strongest.

The company ended-up achieving a first quarter result of 110.7%—hitting its plan—and exceeding Ol' Bert's self-imposed 'stake' by .7%. The raw numbers weren't outrageous, but a deep-in-the-hole starting position had people respectfully acknowledging the progress.

More people were now thinking that maybe—just maybe—they could make it.

The company was slowly remaking itself. People could see that things were somehow different—but not completely sure what was causing it. Whatever it was—it felt good.

The sharing about teaching and coaching that Ol' Bert had executed reminded him of the next essential for outrageous success—a message he must share with Leslie, Lance, and Luke. He felt that a recent competitor-inflicted problem that was threatening the second quarter might be the means to convey that essential.

Essential #8
Ask The Neighbors For Help

The Wisdom Pantry was crowded with people from marketing, finance, and product development—plus Leslie, Lance, and Luke. Most were standing, leaning against the bookshelves, all quite somber. Ol' Bert had called the meeting the night before.

Certus's biggest competitor had recently made some product enhancements, lowered their prices, and extended their products' warranties. This was the biggest threat that Certus had faced since Ol' Bert had come on board. He had more than the competitor on his mind as the meeting started, knowing that everyone would closely watch his words and actions.

He started by giving an unemotional and factual account of the situation, sizing-up and scoping-out the problem as he saw it, and asked all those assembled for their initial impressions.

"I'm confident we can handle this. I don't know exactly what we need to do next, but I've got some ideas." With that, he offered his own initial suggestions.

The marketing director then facilitated the main discussion while Ol' Bert acted as note-taker, so specific plans could be sketched out.

At the conclusion of the discussion Bert intoned seriously, "Ladies and gentlemen, we need help, and you need help. We're here to help each other. Let me know what else the four of us can do to assist you." Glancing at his three horses to emphasize their commitment, he said, "We will continue to keep you all up-to-date with every bit of information we pick up in the market, and add our recommendations to your efforts. If we work together we can overcome this." He finished by urging all to read an engraved plaque on his memorabilia-filled wall.

Now, Brother, as for me I assure you I will press on, and the contrary winds may blow strong in my face, yet I will go forward and never turn back, and continue to press forward until I have finished, and I would have you do the same.

Chief Teedyuscung, Delaware Nation

141

Everyone nodded and murmured agreement. The meeting broke up with consensus and mutual resolve.

When everyone had left, Ol' Bert asked his three horses to stay for a few minutes. He said he wanted to share some thoughts about the value of collaboration, the synergy of people working together to solve problems and handle crises, and the necessity of each of them to reach for resources when they needed expertise or questions answered.

"Those are all great people," Bert said, motioning to the door, referring to all those who had just left. "I think of them as neighbors. I rely on them the same way we relied on our neighboring farmers and ranchers back home. When times were tough and we were scratching out a living, neighbors were the first people to whom my daddy and momma went.

"Neighbors can help us now. And when I say 'neighbors' I mean *every single* employee here at Certus. We're in this together.

"Think for a minute about your actual neighbors where you live. I don't know about yours, but where I now live they're sure a wild variety of people, all wonderful folks, but all very different. Some I naturally feel more comfortable with than others. The dangerous tendency when you need help is to go only to neighbors with whom you are comfortable.

"If you were in a bind at home and needed to borrow a wrench from a neighbor because of faulty plumbing would you only ask the one neighbor you liked? Heck no! You'd be pounding on everyone's door! Of course you could be stubborn—some would say stupid—and not go to another neighbor if your favorite neighbor didn't have a wrench. Don't laugh—many managers and staff members do that in business situations.

"I bet you'd go first to the neighbor *you thought* had the proper wrench, regardless of your relationship, wouldn't you? That's what I'd do. The same is true in business. Go to the person whom *you think* has the wrench. If that doesn't yield help then approach the other neighbors, one after another—all of them.

"Sometimes you're surprised. People who you *think* have nothing or know nothing—who *couldn't possibly* be of help to you—are fountains of knowledge and assistance."

"That's so true, Bert," Luke added. "We tend to make assumptions because of people's titles or style or how they look or how they talk, or even their sex, age, race, or education. And the sad thing is, the people you are avoiding know

142

or suspect you are avoiding them for those very reasons. And avoidance is like building a psychological fence."

"Well said, Luke," Bert acknowledged, shaking his head. "I call that intellectual discrimination. It stings individuals. It loosens team bonds. It punctures company potential."

"Whew, this is getting heavy," Leslie, piped in.

"Yep—it is, but it's reality," Bert said. "Asking people for help is a sign of *respect*, particularly junior people, new employees, and people who *in some way* are different than you. It is a fact often forgotten. Mutual respect is critical to the smooth functioning of any organization. You show me an organization where every single warm body is respected and engaged, and I'll show you an outrageously successful company," said Bert, with lips pursed hard.

"When you ask someone a question there is an assumption in the mind of the person being asked that *you believe* she has the answer. She feels that you respect her for having the information, or you wouldn't have asked. If she has the answer she's happy to help, and feels good in the process of giving you the information. If she doesn't have the answer she feels disappointed and will often bend over backwards to help you find someone who does. And as Luke said, title and other differences mean *nothing* when it comes time to ask for help.

"Maintenance people, top executives, and everyone in between have *a lot* to offer. Everyone—*everyone*—is a neighbor, a resource. Other people know much more than what we often give them credit for. Going to them for help is an essential for outrageous success."

Lance laughed. "You know, that's so true. Yesterday I was in a new account looking for the IT manager's office, and I stopped a guy who looked like a bigwig to ask for directions. He didn't know. And he was gruff about it. It surprised me. Then I stopped someone who was waxing the floor and got the right answer. Not only did he have the answer, but I could also tell from his expression that he was happy I asked. He even offered to escort me to the office."

Everyone else smiled and nodded, saying they had had similar experiences.

Bert then asked, "If someone gives you a good answer to one of your questions you're likely to go back to that source when you have another question, won't you? You'll also go back if you were treated in a professional manner. I'm sure Lance wouldn't hesitate to ask that maintenance man another question. Right, Lance?"

"Right, I'll probably go out of my way to say hello to him the next time," Lance confirmed. "And I'm sure he'll go out of his way to catch my eye."

"If the experience was *un*successful or *un*comfortable for any reason, it's not likely you'll go back to that person. If Lance were to see that bigwig again

143

JOHN W. CEBROWSKI

he may not ask him the time of day. But that's *not* the way to think about neighbors and help.

"Unfortunately, some folks that you *must* go to for information act like know-it-alls, or are condescending. Some have a superior, contemptuous attitude. Or they patronize you. Some will be snippy and snooty. If they're the only ones that have what you need, 'the wrench', so be it. Don't let other people's shortcomings—whether temporary or habitual—complicate *your* problem," Bert concluded. "Oftentimes those attitudes are exhibited unknowingly. Don't let initial responses permanently influence you.

"There is a real lesson here concerning people coming *to us* with questions—and that could be customers and sales partners as well as our Certus neighbors. Those people are also looking for a 'wrench'. Do you want to be a troublesome or a cooperative neighbor? Hmmm? The answer seems obvious, but how often does your own fatigue, agenda, or impatience color your response? It happens to all of us."

No one said anything. Ol' Bert had hit a hot button.

"I know there is often anxiety about asking someone for help. Vacillation, cold feet, embarrassment, and excuses are the enemies of approaching the neighbors. Pride—and the belief that others will think you are incompetent often get in the way of resource utilization. Asking for help is an emotional hurdle for many people. But remember, help means assistance—it means aid, support, guidance, advice, and backing. Those are all solid notions when you're pursuing outrageous success. So—don't be anxious! Don't equivocate! Delays can be costly, especially in our situation. It is not a sign of weakness—but rather, a sign of strength to ask for assistance. Or to put it another way—there's no disgrace in not knowing an answer or having an idea—there's only disgrace in not pursuing an answer or an idea.

"When someone comes to me, do I think they're weak? Heck no! I think they're strong and smart and have a little gumption. I respect them for their initiative."

"Yes, I feel that way also," Luke, added. "Frankly, I *enjoy* helping someone. I think we sometimes don't go to resources because we don't want to *bother* someone, or we feel we're intruding because they're busy."

Bert jumped-in, saying, "If someone I work with regularly feels 'bothered' it's clear I have an undesirable neighbor on my team, but you're right Luke, timing means a lot. You come across as a selfish, insensitive boor if you ask someone for help while he's in the middle of a crisis or on the run. Pick your spots. Confirm convenience. Watch and wait for lulls. Or make an appointment. My gosh—use your judgment.

"Engaging your neighbors to obtain help doesn't mean that you're asking others to do your work. And help doesn't mean laying a monkey on someone's back or sloughing off your responsibility. Be careful."

In the ensuing silence all that could be heard was Ol' Bert's clicking screen-saver. Everyone was thoughtfully nodding. Another hot button touched.

Just then, Mr. Pimm walked in breaking the silence, his face its normal shade of gray, his usual frown deepening when he saw the three salespeople in the office rather than out in the field.

"Bert, excuse me, I've got to prepare an interim report for the Board of Directors. I'd like you to proofread this for me, if you could," and he handed Ol' Bert a sheaf of papers.

"Happy to oblige. When would you like it back? Anything in particular you want me to zero-in on?" Bert asked.

"Quickly, and everything, to answer your two questions," and Mr. Pimm turned and left, glancing again at the three salespeople.

"That's the big boss. He's our neighbor and I hold him in high regard. We all understand the pressure he's under. But let's turn his request for my help into a little learning exercise," Bert suggested. "How would *you* have done that differently —and this stays in the room."

Ol' Bert then let the three of them exchange numerous options and tactics. Everyone got the point.

"*How* you ask for help is important. Style counts. Here are some key points," and Bert went to his whiteboard to write.

Storytelling

"Being a storyteller is a very effective way to describe your needs. Compress the essence of what you're looking for into an understandable little tale. Explain why you're asking the question, where else you've tried to get the answers, what you will do with the information, how quickly you need it, and who else will see or use the information.

Clarity

"Be crisp and specific, as opposed to being speculative and mushy. Hypothetical, theoretical questions result in slushy, soppy answers—and they can leave the neighbor feeling that he or she may have been toyed with.

Framing

"Communicate your question in the context of Certus's overall strategy and needs, being sensitive to profits, margins, return-on-investment, expenses and other key business metrics. Include any linkages or implications you sense in your question. Someone who can present a question in a macro-sensitive light comes across as a solid businessperson, not a narrow-minded opportunist.

Candor

"Be honest with your situation assessments. Embellishments and concealment reduce the credibility of your question. If you've created your own problem, or dug your own hole, be honest about it. 'Fess up!

Listening

"Don't be surprised if your question causes counter-questions for clarification as your neighbor tries to understand where you're coming from. Those questions are a signal that the person is trying to better understand your request. Treat his or her counter-questions with respect—regardless of your perception of their relevance.

Patience

"Go slow—calm down—because sometimes your questions take time to digest. A simple request to you may be complex to the other person, in spite of her expertise. She may not be familiar with all the details of your dilemma—and she also probably wants to respond with something substantive—so is taking her time.

Stand tall

"Don't falsely minimize or pooh-pooh your inquiry—and don't grovel. Belittlement doesn't play well with anyone. It comes across as phoniness.

Respect

"However, a little sincere deference is a good idea. Your courteous consideration of the opinion of another raises the position of that person—just like a child's seesaw. If you 'lower' yourself a little the other person goes 'up' proportionately.

Validating

"Many times you'll already have an idea or the answer, but you'll have a queasy feeling that there's a better way. That's good! Express that feeling clearly. Use the neighbors as a backboard in those situations, seeking their wisdom to strengthen what you already have in mind. I like to bounce my ideas off a group of two or three in those situations. The group dynamics fortifies the initial idea.

Sourcing

"When you ask the neighbors something also ask them where they got their answers or ideas in the first place—from policy statements, magazines, data sheets, websites, or wherever—so that you can do your own digging in the future. Or you simply may want to do your own digging now. An inquiry about sources fosters respect.

Bonding

"Finally, be alert to the opportunity to turn your request for help into a long term advisory relationship—instead of a transactional one-shot exchange. Your request can easily become a long-standing mentor-protégé relationship. Nurture it. By the way, I'd advise having mentors below you, beside you, and above you on the organization chart.

"Everyone okay?" Bert asked, checking for understanding. "I know I'm giving you a lot to digest. Here's a copy of my notes."

"Yes, we're okay. Bert, you're smooth," Lance acknowledged. "These fine points can professionalize us as neighbors and team members."

"Absolutely! Outrageous success is professionalism at the highest level of supportive neighborliness," Bert agreed. He paused and let them scan his notes.

"Ignorance of *who* your neighbors are can be a major problem", he continued. "Since I've been at Certus these few short months I've gone out of my way to say hello to everyone and try to get to know them. I suggest you do the same. Inquisitiveness and a craving for knowing whom the neighbors are, and seeking out the wisdom and skills of the neighbors, are desirable attributes in everyone. Those attributes are particularly important for anyone in a business who is providing solutions to problems or answers to inquiries. Solutions providers must be masterful researchers—crackerjack detectives of *sources*—and crackerjack *diggers* at those sources.

"Neither you nor I are paid to answer every question or spawn every idea. We are paid because we know *a lot* of the answers, we have *a lot* of ideas, and we know to whom to go for other answers and ideas when we're in a bind.

"Go to your neighbors when you need help, but on the other hand, don't become a resource junkie," Bert cautioned next.

"But how do you know when you've gone over the line?" Luke asked.

"When you haven't stopped to think. When you haven't paused—and believe me—*you'll know* when you haven't paused to think. It's mental laziness. It happens."

"Yes, yes, I know when my impatience leads me to do that," Luke said. "I think most salespeople are naturally impatient, I know *I* am."

"I know exactly what you mean," Leslie added. "Speed and pressure can cause us to react and say 'hey, who knows about such-and-such' without stopping to figure it out ourselves."

Bert added, "We live in an instant-gratification world where a dependency on spoon-feeding easily develops. So be careful—try to figure things out yourself. *Think.* Muck-around in your own mind a bit, but don't wallow excessively in your own mental thrashing. Think hard, not long. When you

147

ultimately go to someone for help they will hold you in higher regard for the thinking you've done. Preparation pays. If documentatibn helps explain your dilemma, bring it. It's like a sales call. Bring any aid that helps explain what you're struggling with and what you've considered to-date to try and solve the issue.

"A well-crafted, crisply-articulated question that's obviously been chewed-on most often generates some additional worthwhile chewing."

Leaning forward in his chair, squinting, Bert looked the three of them in the eye and said, "One other thing I want you to remember—we're 'family'. That's the way I think of this sales team. And like 'family' I expect each of us to go to each other for support in times of need because *we all* have very useable pasts.

"Think about *your* family a minute. Mine were all hard workers and many were pretty clever. Sure, they all had idiosyncrasies, and there were a couple of rambunctious cousins and uncles, but most would give you the shirt off their back. We stuck together like wet hay. In the lean years we pooled our physical and mental resources, and we survived. And *that's* what we'll do as a sales team—and as a company. Share your wisdom and resources with each other—share the answers and ideas you receive from our neighbors—and share with the neighbors in return. Voluntary sharing is a mighty powerful multiplier.

"I'm sure it hasn't escaped you that a significant element of our compensation plan and recognition program rewards team results."

They all smiled and nodded.

"And remember—I'm a part of the family. If you want to think of me as the daddy or the momma, that's okay with me. The boss is often a sorely underutilized family member. Don't do that to me—or to yourself. Use me directly for answers and ideas and indirectly to go to bat for you. The chances of success, of getting answers to knotty, complex questions is sometimes better if there is a balance of power between the person asking and the person being asked. Don't be afraid to let me carry the ball for you—on an exception basis. Try me. I was a good halfback in high school.

"And I can help on a personal level as well. I once read something from a fella by the name of Warren Bennis who said, *make sure you always have someone in your life from whom you can get reflective feedback.* It's true. If not me, someone else, but have someone to talk to—*please*!

"Mr. Pimm can go up, down, and laterally to seek help. He can go *up* to a Board of Directors, *down* to his management staff, and he can go *laterally* to clubs and associations to which he belongs where he can hobnob with other presidents and get their ideas. You should also think of your neighbors in those three dimensions.

"And let's not forget the distant neighbors, the ones in the next county, so to speak. Distant neighbors are our good friends outside the company. They can also help. Distant neighbors are associations, chambers of commerce, government agencies, trade clubs, various contacts inside your customers, suppliers, personal friends, counterparts in non-competing companies—anyone!

"Let me give you an example. One time when I was in the insurance business I asked a fellow in the same office building who was a sales manager for a medical supply company a question on how he kept customers from shifting to other providers. He gave me some approaches I would have never thought of. Whew, that saved my butt.

"I want collegiality to rule this roost." He glanced purposefully at each of the three.

"Remember these two gems, the first from the old Dutch scholar, Erasmus—*no gift is more precious than good advice.* The second from some old Roman—*many receive advice, few profit by it.* You profit by seizing and following the shared advice—the gift—not arrogantly discarding it or tinkering with it to where it's unrecognizable.

"*But*—there can be rare exceptions. Not all advice-givers are fountains of respectability. Knowingly or unknowingly soliciting questionable advisors can leave you tainted. *He who lies with dogs shall rise with fleas* is the way some old Welsh clergyman put it. It's a balancing act—you don't *have to* approach everyone—and you don't *have to* take all the advice you're given. Use your common sense folks. The best thing is to avoid the dogs—which fortunately I haven't seen at Certus—but they're out there in the weeds.

"Your judgment always plays a role. I've found that rock-solid sharings come from rock-solid people. Writer Tom Peters says—*getting the psychology and sociology of sharing right is more important than state-of-the-art electronic linkages.* I agree 100% with that clever young whippersnapper.

"Whether you took the advice or not, or whether the neighbor helped or not, always 'thank' the neighbor. It's basic civility—and it's the best way to keep the doors open for continuing and reciprocal visits.

"Public recognition is one of the best ways to give thanks. If you can acknowledge someone's contribution at a staff meeting—wow! Or send letters and e-mails of appreciation, or for extraordinary effort above-and-beyond write commendations, copying the contributor's boss. Or you could even give a small gift to a neighbor who helped with your efforts. Or you may even want to take someone out to lunch to say thanks. Be creative and expansive with your gratitude.

"Let the neighbor know how his or her advice played-out. Wouldn't you like to know if you were the one providing the help? That follow-up has the potential for enriching what you were told in the first place.

"Of course, it should go without saying to never take personal credit for the help of others, or let others think it was your idea. And don't point fingers for a real or imagined lack of support. I've learned that just because someone doesn't support you the way you want doesn't mean they haven't supported you with all they've got. Never say, 'I asked so-and-so for help, but he didn't offer a thing. That's why I failed'. It sounds like obvious advice, but people do that with body language, facial expressions, and inference more than they realize."

"Sometimes you'll get unsolicited help from the neighbors. Accept the help graciously, whether it's needed or not. Think about what was offered. Don't be too quick to dismiss it. Your neighbor may be *way ahead of you* seeing your need or problem well before you do, or coming at the problem from a perspective you personally never imagined. Your gracious acceptance of unsolicited help sets the tone for continuing sharing and cooperation.

"And when a neighbor or family member comes to *you* with a question or for help, *grab* the question with vigor. It is a subtlety that won't be lost on the other person," Bert admonished. "It immediately puts the inquirer at ease. Do it because it's the respectful thing to do, not to look like a know-it-all or set yourself up for a question of your own.

"Here are a couple of final comments.

"Your questions to our neighbors are often 'hidden messages' of deeper needs. Your question could be telling you—and me—that I have a teaching or coaching gap—or that there's a communications gap with another department. Let me know if you think either is the case.

"The benefits of going to the neighbors are more than what's obvious. You'll always pick up incidental information you would never have thought of. And this essential plays well up top. Neighborliness, not rugged individualism, is what business and industry leaders value. Or to put it another way, soloists are inspiring at the symphony but there is no place for them in organizations like this.

"Let me leave you with this one special thought from the Bible—I think it's from Proverbs. *For want of counsel a people will fall; but safety lies in a wealth of counselors.*" And Bert paused.

"Enough said. I've beat-up on this essential pretty well because I feel so intense about it. Let's get back to work," Ol' Bert finished, with his trademark smile.

"Thanks for the help and the sharing, Bert," Luke offered on behalf of the threesome that had been intensely soaking up the advice. "We sincerely appreciate it."

The relationship kept getting stronger.

There was a lot going on in the business. The place was percolating full steam.

The sales team, being continually rearmed with new marketing and sales tools—dubbed 'Pest Repellant Packets' by the marketing department— drove back the opposition's product, price, and warranty initiatives, regaining lost ground.

Corporate-wide planning had commenced for the annual industry trade show. Everyone knew the event had the potential to really put the little firm 'over-the-top'.

Other department managers were earnestly seizing Ol' Bert's essentials, tweaking them to meet their needs, and were folding them into their labors as fast as they could.

And Mr. Pimm was leaving for the Board of Directors meeting, confident that he could suppress the Board's normal flak. The numbers he was so fond of crunching were telling a more hopeful story—a story he hadn't been able to share with his Board in a long time. He was looking more like a pretty shrewd CEO for shepherding the little firm back towards respectability—and for his gutsy decision to hire this sales manager—a decision that had originally been hard to swallow.

Essential #9
Treat Folks Like Kin

Over four months had gone by. Time was short. The sales team was in Chicago for the industry's big annual trade show. The buzz and exhilaration that comes with attending such an event had infected them all. These horses were banging against the starting gate rarin' to go. Their confidence was heightened by the superb preparation job that had been done by the rest of the team back home.

This trade show had the potential of generating enough business for the sales team to 'exceed' the six-month stakes that they had set for themselves. The sales staff was staying in an economical motel out in the suburbs, having opted not to invest their limited funds at the posh downtown hotels.

They had spent the day before the show opened getting their booth in tip-top shape. That night, weary, but fired-up for what lay ahead, the four of them decided to get together for a little relaxation and one last briefing session.

Ol' Bert, Leslie, Lance, and Luke were sitting in one of those comfortable family restaurants that provide paper place mats and paper napkins. They didn't see themselves as having earned the right to be in the 'linen category' quite yet.

"I like to come to this restaurant because of the way they treat me. I used to come here years ago. Great memories. They treat me like kin," said Ol' Bert.

"Sorry, Bert, but I've never used the word 'kin'," tweaked Leslie. "It wasn't in common usage at Columbia, or back home in Hartford."

The three horses all hooted. They were as loose as can be.

"All right, you got me," Ol' Bert chuckled. "Kin, you know, c'mon, your extended family and relatives, or kinfolk. It's an old word—maybe that's why I use it. We used it a lot back home. When I think of kin I think of closeness and all the people we're going to meet in the next few days. Customers and non-customers—and our partners. We're going to want to get close—real quick—to the folks who visit our booth. We want to treat them like kin.

"Listen to me, the three of you. People do business with people, regardless of a buyer's casual attitude or what he or she says about product, price, or service. People are at the root of all transactions—even in this Internet age.

"Speaking of the words 'root' and 'kin' and munching on these dry breadsticks makes me think of another essential for outrageous success. I'll use tonight's dinner to share it with you. It's all about relationships, of course. I know you've figured that out. 'Root' makes me think of wheat, which we used to grow a lot of back in Kansas. Here, let me show you."

With that, Ol' Bert flipped over his place mat and began to painstakingly draw.

"This is going to be a wheat plant. Use your imagination. Leslie, you can make believe this is going to be a begonia in the garden, if you'd like," he teased lightly.

"I can go with wheat," she shot back. "You've turned me into a farmer. Is this going to be one of those old Kanred, Tenmarq, or Blackhull wheats, or the new Jagger that's so popular in Kansas?" she teased back, name-dropping for effect.

"How'd you know all that?" Bert quickly countered, very surprised—and pleased.

"Hey. I do my homework," Leslie said, nonchalantly. "It's a good idea to understand the boss's roots."

"Alright. You got me again. Let's make it Jagger. Let's make believe we're in Kansas."

"Bear with my drawing everyone," and he looked up and smiled. He certainly wasn't an artist, but everyone was patient. "Wheat is the most widely grown of all cereal grains. It is a grass-type plant. Wheat is the basic ingredient in this breadstick," and he detailed a small, young plant. "When wheat is young, wheat is green, and looks like grass, like this," pointing to his completed drawing. "When relationships are young they are *also* green and look like casual acquaintanceships. We'll see a lot of 'grass' at the show starting tomorrow. Right?"

"We *hope* we see a lot of grass," said Lance. And they all murmured affirmation.

Then Bert began to draw a mature wheat plant, saying, "Wheat may grow up to four or five feet, and it turns golden brown when it is ripe. But relationships can grow as high as the mythical stalk in the children's fable, *Jack In The Beanstalk*, and business relationships simply turn *golden*, as in cash flow, when they're ripe. We'll see a lot of gold starting tomorrow as well. Agree?"

"We *expect* to see a lot of golden opportunities," said Lance again. And the others grunted affirmatively.

"When mature, business relationships look like formal partnering compacts and deep friendships. They can, and should, become emotionally and strategically tied. We'll see that with many of our existing customers and sales partners who stop by to see us," said Bert, laboring on his drawing.

"The root system of a wheat plant is extensive and can reach down 15 to 20 inches or more," and he penciled in many scraggly roots. "Relationship roots are also extensive and can reach deeper, as deep as in the movie *Journey To The Center Of The Earth*. Roots feed both the wheat plant and our relationships.

"Relationship roots are *behaviors*—behaviors *valued*—and behaviors *delivered*. Our customers and sales partners *expect* certain behaviors from us, and the display of those valued behaviors shape relationships. So ultimately, our behaviors are powerful business building mechanisms."

"The roots of a strong relationship, like the roots of a wheat plant, are varied." Bert continued. The three salespeople were all leaning forward, watching carefully, as Ol' Bert began to label each of the roots he had drawn. He commented on each one.

"This root here, this behavior, is understanding. Understanding is a root in relationships. People expect you to make an effort to understand them, comprehending who and what they are and what they stand for. They want to see and feel your effort.

"This long root here is respect. Respect is a root behavior because all people expect to be held in high regard. Respect is holding them up with your words and actions. It is amazing what can be accomplished when you treat people with respect.

"This squiggly one is civility. Civility is a root behavior because people expect you to treat them with politeness, consideration, and common courtesies.

"This thick root is judgment. You know when to stay away and leave some space. You're not a hanger-on. And you know when to keep your mouth shut.

"And this curlicued root is support. Support is a root that means that you help, give ideas, provide advice, and go out of your way to offer something, particularly when the other person is in a bind.

"This fancy one over here is empathy. You try to know, or you endeavor to sense, how someone feels. As Obi-Wan Kenobi said to Luke Skywalker regarding 'The Force' in the original *Star Wars* movie, *'Your eyes can deceive you. Reach out with your feelings Luke, trust your feelings'*. Empathy is one of those roots that go down very, very deep.

"Some of these roots you might say look a lot like another. That's okay. Attention to the subtle differences between the roots will more clearly differentiate you and enable people to feel better about you."

And on he went.

155

"Thoughtfulness is here. Thoughtfulness is a root that shows your initiative. You do things that are nice that are not asked for.

"This perfectly straight root is openness because being matter-of-fact and easy to talk to enables you to cut right to the core of everything. Your frankness is appreciated.

"This complicated looking root I'll call interest. You can build more relationships in the little time we have left by becoming interested *in people* than in one year by trying to get people interested *in you*.

"This one here is listening. Listening is a big root. Listening is soaking up and retaining what we hear. I think listening should be one of the deeper roots.

"This one here is the sacrifice root. Sacrifice is giving of something or giving up yourself for the other person. The other person sees you forfeiting something on her behalf.

"Here's one called delivery. It means that both explicit *and* implied promises are kept.

"This one on the side here is gratitude. Gratitude is a root because sincere 'thank yous' and appreciation go a long way to keeping all the other roots fresh, like water.

"There are more roots than I've labeled though. Do any of you have any ideas of what we can name some other roots?" he asked, with a hint of a challenge.

"Yes, I'd say one is commitment," offered Lance. "You stick with this relationship through thick and thin—and the other person sees that."

"Investment is another one," snapped Leslie. "You pour visible energy and resources into the relationship."

"I'd call one of them responsiveness, leaping to action when you sense a need," Luke said.

"Yep—you're right, and we could add many more," Bert said. "Live and work according to the root behaviors, and you can't help but have outrageous relationships and outrageous success. In today's business environment these behaviors take on heightened importance because emphasis on e-mail and the Internet often mean fewer chances at personal contact. Also, because buyers have more options and choices they are less forgiving of slights and snubs.

"Deep roots anchor the wheat plant securely in the soil. When you think about the rough weather in Kansas and where Luke went to school in North Dakota you'll understand why anchoring is so important. These valued behaviors help anchor our relationships.

"Just as the roots of wheat plants vary in their depth, the depths of relationship roots vary from person to person. In other words, some customers and sales partners value and rely on these behaviors more than others—and

156

some sales and marketing people are better at delivering on these valued behaviors. I'll bet your personal experience has proven that, hasn't it?" he asked.

All three quickly agreed.

"Relationship root depth is synonymous with the ability to *establish* relationships—and—with the *sustainability* of those relationships. It's why some people's relationships never really grow or are easily torn asunder. And it's why other people's relationships can withstand incredible environmental forces. So I guess we could say 'deeper is better' for everyone concerned. Luke jumped in, saying, "Because root depth is a measure of *both* valued behaviors *and* delivered behaviors, it seems to follow that we can have a big impact on the depth of those roots. We can help drive the roots deeper!"

"You got it! Right on," said Bert. "It's a simple concept—but simple can be complex. The key word in your statement, Luke, is BOTH, because implicit in the word relationship is the number two."

"Which root is the most important?" Leslie inquired, her interest peaked.

"I don't know if any one is the most important, Leslie. I kinda think it depends on the customer and which root he or she values the most," Bert reflected. "You know, no two root systems are the same. If you pull up several wheat plants the root systems will all be very different. The same is true of relationship roots."

"Yeah, I guess you're right, Bert," Leslie said. "But aren't there priorities?"

"Great question!" and Bert beamed. "You made me think of something I forgot. Wheat plants *do have* both primary roots and secondary roots. Primary roots come first after the seed starts to grow, then the secondary roots take over. In relationships I think understanding comes first, I think it's a primary root. We *must* make an effort to understand our customers and sales partners—just as you, Leslie, made the effort to understand me with your wheat research.

"I know none of you are old enough to remember President Woodrow Wilson, but he once said something that is very relevant to our subject—*A man's rootage is more important than his leafage.* Wilson may not have been thinking of rootage exactly the same way I do—but his words are right-on.

"While you tend the roots of others your own roots are simultaneously on display. Your own rootage—*your* values—are displayed by the sensitivity and care you exhibit for the roots of others.

"But be careful! It's your *true* self that affects display of your own rootage. Matters of character and rootage have their indelible fingerprints all over you. External actions, as good as they may be, will not make up for an insincere or manipulative approach. There's a fine line between sincere schmoozing and

157

artificial gibberish. People can 'read' your inner thoughts and motivations—and don't fool yourself into thinking otherwise. Your rootage—*your behaviors*—must be truly embedded inside you, not flaunted as a fanciful facade. You cannot be what you are not—so don't even try.

"Now you have to feed and water peoples' roots," Bert admonished.

"What do you feed them with?" Luke asked.

"Attention. Attention is *providing* the valued behaviors. How can you have a relationship with someone you're never with or someone you make little effort to know? Different people require different types and levels of attention because their root systems and root depths vary, right? It's your job to figure out their root values and depths and figure it out quickly. Make every customer contact an attention-providing, root-tending event.

"Both roots and people are sensitive. Too little water or fertilizer and you'll notice that a wheat plant is withering or stunted—and the same goes for attention to people. Too *much* water and fertilizer with wheat and you'll notice limpness, rot, or mold—and the same goes for people. And of course, if you really overdo it one way or the other you'll kill the wheat plant. The same thing goes for relationships.

"Generally, you can consider that in the beginning a little more attention is better than a little less attention. Experience teaches us what is likely to be exactly right, but you must constantly observe and evaluate. It's that *exactness* in delivering attention to the roots that maximizes the wheat stalk's yield. And it's that *exactness* in tending a customer's rootage with
valued behaviors that help make a businessman or woman successful.

"But a word of reality here folks. In some cases you'll *never* figure it out. No one—absolutely *no one*—can be expected to develop and possess a satisfactory relationship with *everyone*. Don't let your ego get in the way. 'Fess up quick where you sense that's the case and let's figure out—as a team—who else should handle that relationship.

"And don't try to hide any questionable relationships. Remember, this is a 'boundaryless' organization so don't worry about turf protection or compensation. I know you're aware that our team-level rewards take such contingencies into account.

"Sometimes whole departments and whole companies will value certain behaviors because the leader of that department or company has instilled his or her values in the organization. In those cases that whole field of wheat needs attention with those certain behaviors.

"As you learn what behaviors individuals, departments, and companies appreciate—share that information with all our customer-contact colleagues so they can deliver the same behaviors. We *must* deliver attention—valued behaviors—as a team—not as individuals. Our consistency will have a multiplier effect. Inconsistency frustrates the customer and results in that sickening wail of 'you don't understand me'—and ultimate defection to another supplier."

Everyone nodded heartily.

"The next point I'd like to make is that root systems grow. They're always changing. Like wheat plants, you can't rip relationships out of the ground to examine the roots to see what's there, what's growing, and what's changing. Kills the relationship just like it kills the plant. You don't know exactly what's below ground. That's what makes this essential such an attractive and stimulating challenge for us. But hints are available! People's subtly changing and maturing vocabulary, attitudes, and actions—their leafage—give away what root behaviors they value. And that brings us back to the necessity to *understand* people. You see how this all fits?

"Yes, I do," said Leslie, excitedly. "Let's save that place mat, frame it, and hang it in the Wisdom Pantry."

"Done!" Bert committed.

"Strong roots make for a strong stalk. *THE LONG STALK IS THE RELATIONSHIP ITSELF*," Bert emphasized, filling-in the drawing with his pen. "Everyone can see and evaluate the health of the stalk, the relationship itself. It's not hidden like the roots. Just as the strength of the wheat stalk protects the wheat plant from hail, high winds, and dust storms, a strong 'relationship stalk' protects Certus from competitive threats, market gyrations, and economic disasters.

"That strong wheat stalk holds up the wheat head, or spike, that holds the kernels. A healthy wheat plant can produce an average of fifty kernels of wheat. A healthy 'relationship stalk' can produce an unlimited number of business transactions.

Drawing in some details on his place mat, he said, "The clusters of kernels in the wheat head cling tightly to the stalk until they are fully ripe, just as potential orders cling tightly to prospects, customers, and partners until our relationships are ripe."

The three sales people were deeply absorbed in Ol' Bert's drawing and analogy. But he wasn't sure if they were really listening.

"Wheat is the staff of life. I don't know who said that. I should know, but I forget," Bert slyly offered.

JOHN W. CEBROWSKI

"I think the saying is, 'bread is the staff of life', Bert," Luke quickly corrected.

They were obviously listening.

"Okay, okay," Bert smiled. "But may I please have the liberty of twisting that phrase?"

"Sure, go ahead," Luke agreed, willingly. "We know where you're going." And then the three of them in chorus said, "If bread is the staff of life, then relationships are the staff of outrageously successful business." They all laughed good-naturedly.

"Yep! You smart alecks got it. That's the bottom line. Now let's order something to eat before I pass out," Bert suggested. The three of them knew that Ol' Bert had a voracious appetite in spite of his small stature and his age. Fortunately, his favorite, chicken-fried steak was on the menu.

Ol' Bert wasn't done. After everyone ordered, he continued.

"You know it takes time for wheat to grow, just as it takes time for relationships to grow. Winter wheat planted in the fall is harvested the following spring or early summer—*if* all goes well. Wheat has its enemies just as relationships do. While insects, rust, smut, bad weather, and weeds are the enemies of wheat—indifference, laziness, assumptiveness, neglect, and a taking-for-granted attitude are the enemies of relationships. Those enemies can be beaten with constant real-time relationship assessment and exact doses of appropriate attention by the appropriate people.

"Just as that wheat stalk reaches out to the nourishing sun and vitalizing breeze to grow—gaining energy from above as well as the roots below—reach out with your relationship building efforts to the nourishing environments in which you find yourselves—gaining energy from people, resources, settings, and events surrounding the relationship. Healthy wheat stalks and healthy relationships take energy from *everything* healthy that surrounds them. You are the *manager* of our relationships—so *manage*—don't try to do it all alone."

"We'll do that," committed Luke. "Can you make relationships ripen more quickly?" Luke continued.

"*No*," Bert was quick to reply. "You can't make wheat grow faster than nature intended. It's in the genes. Now, one particular stalk may grow a little more quickly than another may grow, but the ripening takes place at virtually the same time.

"But one person is as different from another as wheat is different from barley, barley different from oats, and oats different from corn—each ripening in its own time. Differences remind me of the fact that people all over this

160

country and all over the world value these root behaviors even though what we see above ground can be very, very different. Therefore, as we grow and branch out into other markets all over the world we'll be running into rice, millet, sorghum, maize, and other grains that aren't as familiar to us, but we must remember that the *same valued root behaviors* are expected.

"*However*—some cultures—just as some individuals—need *more* of certain root behaviors than other cultures. So we'll have to research as we go, remembering that even though the roots are the same, some cultures may require greater emphasis on certain behaviors.

"Just remember wherever you are, and whomever you're with, that relationships ripen in their own time. Be patient Luke. It happens. Just take care of the roots," advised Bert.

"The synonyms for the word relationship, and some related words, are also a lesson on what relationships mean. Since we're eating dinner, chew on each of these words with me.

"First, affinity. I like the word affinity. It means you kind of like each other. There's mutual attraction. Like magnetism. Speaking of mutual—if relationships are not mutual—they are not relationships. Don't kid yourself.

"Next, connection, another good word. You're kind of tied together by something of common interest. A tangible or intangibles that act as bolts or screws fasten you to each other.

"Alliance, another good one. It reminds me of two people having made a strong compact to stick together through both the good times and through tough circumstances.

"Bond, yet another strong word. It makes me think of glue, holding things together for the long haul, holding to withstand outside pressure and tension. Bonding implies permanence.

"Knit. It reminds me of my momma knitting those warm sweaters out of different colors and plys of yarns. Knitting reminds me of our need to intertwine ourselves, our colleagues, and our customers together, weaving substance and enjoyment into our interactions, making warm partnerships.

"Kinship, my favorite. See, you knew I'd get back to kin again, didn't you? Those close interdependent family ties.

"All those synonyms and related words are powerful and say a great deal about what a relationship is.

"Finally, I have never heard relationships explained more beautifully than this," and he poetically recited, '*Oh, the comfort, the inexpressible comfort of feeling safe with a person, having neither to weigh thought nor measure words, but pouring them all right out, just as they are, chaff and grain together, certain that a faithful hand will take and sift them, keep what is worth keeping, and with a breadth of kindness, blow the rest away'.* A wonderful proverb of the great Shoshone people, isn't it?"

The three horses absorbed the elegance of the proverb in silence.

"Unfortunately, many people still don't understand. I think it's because relationship has gotten to be an over-used buzzword, a cliché. I also think it's because so many people are *into*, rather than *outside*, themselves.

"I hope this has helped you all. Just remember that relationships are the basis of long- term business associations—as opposed to deal-cutting and deception, which are often the basis of short-term transactions.

"When you think about growing relationships think about your *personal* business relationships as the foundation for growing *enterprise-wide* relationships. Personal relationships are between you and the customer's personnel—enterprise-wide relationships are between the customer's company and Certus. Enterprise-wide relationships are our ultimate goal, and must ultimately prevail. Foster them. Facilitate them. Remember, you're selling everything this company stands for and values—and selling all of our colleagues—along with selling our products, services, and yourself. Don't be afraid to take a backseat as necessary for the sake of the company. Our customers want to know *us*, who Certus is and what Certus is all about, as much as we want to know *their* company. They want an enterprise-wide relationship as much as we do. We'll all move on some day, but Certus and the firms who buy from us are here to stay—most of them anyway. People enter into business relationships because it is in *both* their personal and professional interests to do so. Companies enter into relationships because it is in their long-term business interest to do so."

"Bert, your comment about 'personal' triggered something. May I add a thought?" Lance asked.

"Absolutely. Anyone—jump in," Bert advised.

Lance began, "My grandma back in Louisiana always said the personal touch is important. She said that personal sharings, sharing the stuff inside you, must be mingled with the stuff about business. Like putting a lot of butter, salt, and pepper on your grits and stirrin' 'um up, she used to say. She said a measure of a relationship is the depth and frequency of those personal sharings, that mixing. Of course that can't happen right off the bat. It takes time. Talking about yourself a bit. Talking about business a bit. And so on. Both of you season those grits together, slow and steady."

"That's great advice. Sounds like you and your grandma were really close," Bert said.

"Yes. It's where I learned all about people," Lance said solemnly.

Leslie added, "I had a dear old aunt who once told me that in the best relationships you give more than you receive. You don't even think about any receiving. You just think about the giving. The receiving just 'sorta happens'. It's not expected, and you never even notice it, unless someone else brings it to your attention. And even then you say, 'oh yeah, I didn't realize it'. You don't treat the receiving as 'a big deal'—it's not anything you're consciously seeking."

"Sounds like your aunt was a generous and caring woman," said Bert.

"Yes, she loved people," Leslie agreed.

Luke chipped in, "My dad used to tell me that salespeople needed to work just as hard with their relationships inside the company as they did with their outside relationships, a fundamental that many forget. He always talked about how 1+1=3, where three is the unexpectedly surprising sum of strong external *and* internal relationships. So, since we'll have some of our marketing staff joining us in these next few days let's not forget *their* roots and the roots of everyone back home on whom we'll be relying to deliver everything we promise."

"Right on! Definitely! Absolutely," the others offered with enthusiasm.

Bert slowly leaned forward, saying, "Remember what I said earlier about kin? Did you notice how you all used 'kin' to emphasize this discussion about relationships?" The reactions of the three revealed their pleasant surprise.

"Touché," said Leslie, smiling broadly.

"We never used the word 'touché' back in Kansas," Bert giggled. They all laughed.

"I can tell we're going to have a fun and productive next few days," Bert said. "What do you say that we order some dessert for extra energy. They have some great apple crumb pie and homemade vanilla ice cream."

The show turned out great. Visitors seemed to enjoy the Certus booth more than other booths—and more than in years past. Customers, prospects, and sales partners couldn't put their finger on it, but the attention they received was somehow a little different—a little special—a little more memorable.

The sales staff ended up with more leads than they could handle themselves. When they got back home the folks in marketing and customer service began to immediately help with the follow-up. Everybody at Certus was hustling, but the jury was still out.

Mr. Pimm walked into Ol' Bert's office in the midst of the hustle, nervous as usual, and asked him if he thought they could make it.

Bert said, "I think we can make it," then paused with a scowl, having caught himself falling into a trap.

Reversing himself quickly, he said, "No! I know—I know we can make it. I could see it in the eyes of all the people who came to our booth in Chicago.

"Mr. Pimm you've given me an idea. I'd like to share what I saw in their eyes with everyone here at Certus. This may be a great opportunity to impart the tenth and last essential for outrageous success. Can you call an all-employee meeting for tomorrow?"

"You got it. Just tell me what you need," said Mr. Pimm, who suddenly sprang to life.

Essential #10
Dig In And Do It Right

Ol' Bert went up to Mr. Pimm's office prior to the all-employee meeting. He was feeling good—pumped up—and ready to pump up everyone else at the meeting. He walked in and closed the door. Mr. Pimm had an air of confidence about him that Ol' Bert hadn't seen before. There must have been some good-news numbers since yesterday's discussion. Numbers drove Mr. Pimm's mood.

"You look like I feel," Bert said excitedly. "We're coming to the end. This reminds me of running the mile when I was in high school. And that's one of the things I'm going to talk about today."

"I trust you, Bert. I know that whatever you say today will be more appropriate than what anyone else could say. I wanted to thank you for your help before we got to the end of this six months—this race for survival and outrageous success in which you and I have been entwined."

"I trust you, also. That's one of the reasons I came here over six months ago," Bert said, then added, "After the all-employee meeting, can we get the management staff together in the conference room for a few minutes? I'd like to share some thoughts appropriate for them. One of the things I'm going to talk about is trust."

"No problem. I'll announce it when we kick off the general meeting in a few minutes."

"Great. As you said many months ago, 'let's go do it'," Bert said with a grin. Then the two shook hands, with a vigor that conveyed a suddenly heightened confidence.

The all-employee meeting was held in the factory. Mr. Pimm, looking more enthusiastic than ever with microphone in hand, thanked everyone for their hustle and contribution. The finance director made a couple of quick comments on precisely how much volume needed to get out the door for the company to succeed—*to outrageously succeed*, she corrected herself. Then Mr. Pimm turned the floor over to Ol' Bert. All of the employees had been aware of Ol' Bert's impact and his activities. He was well known by the factory workers and office staff for all the before-hours, after-hours, and second-shift time he had spent in every department, supporting and coaching, answering questions, and sharing his infectious can-do attitude.

Ol' Bert stepped carefully onto a pallet on a big old Yale forklift truck. The motor whirred and slowly lifted him, high in the air. The whistling and the cheering were ear-splitting. Everybody had come to love and respect Ol' Bert. A few of the big guys from the factory moved in close to catch him in case he fell off.

He stood up there, microphone in hand, with his wispy white hair blowing, and gave everyone that trademark smile. For some reason he was wearing his best blue suit today, so his dashing figure suspended above the crowd looked like the epitome of a professional businessman. Everyone could see and sense Bert's energy.

"It's time to *dig in,* ladies and gentlemen. And..." The cheering interrupted him. "Thanks, everyone. We're in a race with the clock, you all..." And he was interrupted with clapping again. "I haven't had this much fun since I ran the tractor into a ditch when I was twelve years old," he said. And everyone whooped. "Let's get everything out the door clean and on time. We're going to be selling to the last day of the month. Leslie, Lance, and Luke aren't here with us today because they're out beating the bushes for every last order." The cheering and whistling interrupted Ol' Bert again.

"I'd like to tell you about the recent trade show we attended in Chicago," he started. "You need to hear what people are saying about *you* and about *our* products and services." Ol' Bert then proceeded to tell them specific stories related by customers, naming people and departments in the audience that had made an impression on customers and sales partners. When Bert finished with his fifth little vignette, he said, "I'm proud of you. You should be proud of yourselves. Thanks for all of your hard work." The cheering broke out again.

"I've got more. I've got more," he said with a big smile.

"Okay. Let me tell you what's ahead of us." That quieted everyone down. "Way back when I was in high school, I was a miler on the track team. I was pretty good. You know, Kansas has always produced some great milers. Remember Glenn Cunningham? How about Jim Ryun?" Except for a few old-timers, the crowd was quiet. It was too far back for most to remember. "The mile's tough. You need to put on a 'kick' at the end. You're bone-tired, and *then* you have to dig in and sprint. Certus is coming out of the last turn of the last lap right now. It's time for us to sprint. I know we're all hurting from all the extra effort we've already given, but we have to give *more*. I know your arms and legs feel like logs, but now is when we all have to turn on the extra energy.

"In the pursuit of outrageous success, there is no *final* finish line, there are only *interim* finish lines—mini-races within a great race. There is only the end of a lap and the beginning of the next. We run a lap at a time—and the race never ends. *But*—this lap will determine if there are future laps for us to run," Bert said earnestly. His understandable candor had always caused everyone to respect him.

"Everybody close your eyes. Make-believe with me. We're breathing as hard as can be. The wind is blowing in our faces. Why the wind always does that I'll never know, but it does, and it's aggravating, and it tries to sap our determination. But in spite of that, we're gritting our teeth and we're starting to really dig in. Ladies and gentlemen, we can hear competition breathing behind us, gaining on us. It's scary. But we can see the finish line for this lap. We can see the tape. Let's think about how good it's going to feel when *we*—all of us— break that tape together. If you keep your eyes closed, you can hear a lot of yelling and cheering—people urging us on. That's our families at home, our stockholders, and this wonderful community of which we are such a big part. This last hundred yards, these last few weeks, is where the work begins. When you are running, you are all by yourself, but we're lucky because we have each other. It's time to dig in, dig in hard. Let's dig, dig, dig!"

And then the crowd began clapping in unison.

After a minute, Bert started again, "Let me tell you one last story. I believe most of you know that my little office looks more like a mini-library than an office. Today I'd like to refer to one of my favorite books that fits our situation. Did you ever read the children's book called *The Little Engine That Could?*" Ol' Bert held up the book for all to see. Those familiar with the book got Ol' Bert's point immediately. "It's about a little engine that pulls a load of toys over a big mountain after many other bigger and more powerful engines pass up the daunting task. The little engine chugs and tugs and puffs and huffs and keeps saying 'I think I can,' 'I think I can,' 'I think I can,' 'I think I can' as it starts up the mountain.

"Well, Certus is a little company just like that little engine. But Certus is *the little company that will!* And we've got to keep saying, 'I know we can,' 'I know we can,' 'I know we can,' 'I know we can.'" And the rhythmic clapping began again.

Little by little, Bert began to pick up his volume and speed like a locomotive, saying, "When the little engine got to the top and started down the other side, it began to say 'I thought I could,' 'I thought I could,' 'I thought I could.' And, of course, the story ends happily ever after.

"At the end of this month, all of us will be saying, 'we knew we could,' 'we knew we could,' 'we knew we could.'

"Just as that little engine dug in its wheels, we've got to dig in ours and get

167

over the mountain." Then Bert yelled one last time at the top of his voice, "I —
KNOW — WE — CAN!" And the clapping increased in volume.

Before the lift-truck lowered him, Bert said to the group, "Let's recognize
Mr. Pimm for getting us this far, for his resolute leadership, investment, and
policies that have kept Certus on its feet during these challenging times. I
wouldn't be here if it weren't for him."

Everyone yelled, and Mr. Pimm, all red-faced, waved and acknowledged
the crowd. The applause was thunderous. Then their chant began—'I know we
can'—'I know we can'—'I know we can'—'I know we can'—'I know we can'!
Meanwhile, down on the floor, the marketing staff was handing out a copy of
The Little Engine That Could to every employee. When Ol' Bert finally walked
out of the factory, they were still chanting. Meanwhile, Mr. Pimm announced
that all managers and supervisors needed to gather in the conference room.

Back in the conference room, the mood was also effervescent. All of the
managers and supervisors were there.

"Bert, you sure were passionate out there," one of the managers
commented.

Bert calmly answered, "An old German philosopher by the name of Hegel
once said that *nothing great in the world has been accomplished without
passion.* Passion is implicit in this last essential for outrageous success."

Everyone offered thanks to Ol' Bert. From the small talk, it sounded like
everyone was 'pumped' and going in the right direction.

He was hoarse. "I appreciate it, ladies and gentlemen. Thanks. Before I
lose my voice, I'd like to just share a few thoughts about 'digging' and 'doing'
that strike appropriately at our personal efforts as managers and supervisors.
Then we can all go out and help make it happen.

"What I'm about to say is all about management style. Who knows how
much longer I'll be here. I think the timing is perfect to share this last essential
for outrageous success," Bert started.

At the hint of Ol' Bert leaving, everyone glanced furtively at each other.

His laptop was hooked up to the projector. "I call this presentation
Slathering on the Glue," he said solemnly. "We need to spread these notions on
thickly to hold the other nine essentials together."

Ol' Bert clicked to his first PowerPoint® slide. All it said was:

> **"They can because they think they can."**
> *Virgil*
> **"Plant the thought."**
> *Bert*

"I started the planting out there," Bert stated, and he pointed in the direction of the factory. "And I'm going to finish the planting in here. You all know I'm a pretty good planter," he said, smiling.

"Then it's up to all of us to bring in the harvest.

"Let's not let old, self-imposed boundaries block Certus's and our people's potential. Nothing is worse than having companies and people not reach their capacity. Companies and people are creatures of habit, and habit keeps companies and people within bounds. We're about to establish new boundaries and a new habit—outrageous success.

"People do not lack ability. They lack conviction that they *have* the ability. Have you ever watched someone discover that he could do something that he previously thought was impossible? Isn't the outpouring of joy and self-satisfaction a thrill to watch? I'm sure you've seen it. Capture that moment. We're about to reproduce it.

"Out there they're saying, 'I know we can,' 'I know we can.' Do we feel that same way in our guts in here? Do we have an assumptive, matter-of-fact winning attitude?"

"Yea!"

"Yo!"

"Yes, sir!"

"Absolutely," came the quick, spirited replies from around the room. Ol' Bert clicked to his next slide.

> **"Self-confidence is the first requisite to great undertakings."**
> *Dr. Samuel Johnson*
> **"Get it. Give it."**
> *Bert*

"We've communicated genuine belief to those people and among ourselves that we *can do* what is expected of us. Believable, positive expectations yield positive results. It's called the Pygmalion effect. *The powerful influence of one person's expectations on another's behavior has long been recognized.* I read that in an old *Harvard Business Review* magazine. *Achievement* mirrors expectations. We'll *achieve* outrageous success because we *expect* outrageous success. Isn't that so?" said Bert, breaking into a grin.

There was a lively chorus of agreement in return.

"To give your people increasing confidence is one of the greatest gifts a manager can ever present. Expect a great feeling of self-satisfaction from watching that confidence grow."

169

"Let's look further at the digging and doing."
Up popped the next slide.

> **"In all human affairs there are things both certain and doubtful, and both are equally in the hands of God, who is accustomed to guide to a good end the causes that are just and are sought with diligence."**
> *Queen Isabella of Spain*
> **"...and in our hands as well."**
> *Bert*

"We know we've got a just cause, as old Isabella reminds us.

"I'll start with the digging half of the diligence to which she refers. This is simple. It's work ethic—a *strong* work ethic—a superglue. A strong work ethic is characterized by a natural affinity for work—and consistent vigorous efforts that unceremoniously set an example. A strong work ethic is often revealed through a willingness to start something without being told, a willingness to put in as much time as necessary, a willingness to get your hands dirty, and a willingness to pitch in on things that aren't your responsibility. In these last few weeks, we need to exhibit a strong work ethic as never before."

Then came the next slide.

> **"No wise person wants a soft life."**
> *An old Anglo-Saxon king of Wessex*
> **"No honest manager takes pride in easy effort."**
> *Bert*

"While a strong work ethic may be simple to define, it is often hard to execute because it frequently demands sacrifices. Sacrifices remind me of getting out of a comfortable bed at four in the morning to face the snow and cold back on the farm. Sacrifices remind me about the necessity to stop what I'm doing and help someone else, to forgo a pleasure for the benefit of another, to tolerate infringement on my personal agenda, and unemotionally tolerate team-level diversions that are for the benefit of the organization."

Bert was picking up speed, saying, "Work ethic means execution with an inspired and contagious attitude. I personally make sure I'm inspired every morning because I'm in charge of my own inspiration. You're in charge of your inspiration. Don't look further than the mirror for a 'dig-in' attitude check.

"Work ethic also means execution in accordance with the highest quality standards, not creating an ugly wake for other people. We've got a great total quality management program here at Certus, and that's part of our work ethic. Top-quality execution makes the difference between outrageous success and plain-vanilla success. There isn't room for any mistakes or deviations from here on out.

"Working hard under intense pressure and keeping our composure is what the next few weeks are all about. From this point on, let's forever glue a strong work ethic—a 'dig-in' attitude—into our culture—and into our legacy.

"So let's dig in. Okay?" Bert asked. And then he walked forward, close to everyone, and said slowly, "Remember, the word outrageous, and the word success, come before the word work, *only* in the dictionary. I'm sure you've heard it before. It's worth repeating." He paused for effect.

No one said anything.

Ol' Bert clicked ahead to his next slide.

> **"The time is always right**
> **to do what is right."**
> *Martin Luther King, Jr.*
> **"Do right always.**
> **It will give you satisfaction in life."**
> *Wovoka – the Paiute Messiah*

"As we execute our work, we must not only think about what we should *do* and *how* we should do it—but also what we must *be*. Our work does not dignify us. We must dignify our work.

"And so, here's the other half of Isabella's diligence. We've got to do it *right*. Always. When we're exhausted and under pressure, our minds can sometimes lead us astray and suggest dishonorable or shortcut ways to get to outrageous success. We won't do that. We'll 'do it right'.

"Let me tell you about 'right.' Research says that the top two characteristics people want from their leaders and managers are integrity and trust. I believe that integrity and trust are industrial-strength adhesives that keep a company firmly together.

171

"Integrity *must* come before trust because it is the basis of trust. It is no accident that I refer to them in this order. A definition of integrity that has stuck with me says that integrity is a state of wholeness, of being complete, or unbroken.

"Personally, I've always seen thirteen fragile behaviors that lie within the 'whole' of integrity—like nestling thirteen fragile 'Grade A' eggs in a soft straw-lined basket—where the basket represents integrity itself. A combination of teachings, readings, observations, and experience fixed these behaviors in my nature. I know they are behaviors of consequence because a lack of any one of these behaviors suggests the opposite. It is human nature to suspect the contrary when these behaviors are not clearly evident. And contrary impressions all lead to needless grief. Ladies and gentlemen—the trick is to never let ugly questions develop. While one broken egg makes a mess of the whole basket—one broken behavior makes a mess of integrity."

Ol' Bert flashed up the first six behaviors. His only comment was, "Confucius once said, *if you lead the people with correctness, who will dare not be correct?*"

He waited while everyone read.

The Behaviors Within Integrity

Speed — *because delays can fuel foolish speculation, indifference, and waste.*

Fairness — *because partiality, prejudice, or unwarranted privilege can devastate motivation and psyches.*

Crisp and clear explanations — *because dancing, shading, and spinning signal gamesmanship or monkey business.*

Sincerity — *because duplicity is two-faced and deceitful to individuals—and can take the wind out of team unity.*

Care of details — *because lack of precision can feed suspicion and insecurity—or diminished concern about consequences.*

Seeking opinions — *because unilateral actions can arouse skepticism or spawn a what's-the-use attitude.*

172

"An author by the name of Joe Batten once said, *the actions of a responsible executive are contagious.* I suggest that we begin—and preserve—an integrity epidemic here at Certus." Then he flashed up the last seven behaviors and asked the group to read them aloud with him.

The Behaviors Within Integrity

Objectivity — *because subjectivity can smell selfish or fraudulent.*
Order — *because mayhem and messy mishmash can suggest sloppy let-ups—or even scheming cover-ups.*
Adherence to policies — *because disregard signals disrespect for authority and laws.*
Judgment — *because faulty choices of topics, tone, timing, and words can be disparaging and deflating.*
Firmness — *because a lack of resolve can communicate weak resistance to suspicious outside pressures—or moral laziness.*
Consistency — *because flip-flopping and shot-gunning foster disbelief and create discrepancies and doubt.*
Honesty — *because lying and cheating permanently stain people, institutions, and organizations.*

"Gnawing, nagging questions of motive linger in situations when one or more of these thirteen behaviors are missing or abused," Bert said.

"Spreading integrity generously into our work lives and personal lives requires that we strengthen our grasp on the thirteen behaviors and consider potential challenges *before* we find ourselves in the intensity of a fray—because frays tempt with compromise. With no firm grasp, integrity can fade in the heat of challenges as sure as prairie grass will wither under blazing sun. Integrity demands that we live and work to its obligation, not compromising for convenience' sake, standing firm for what is right, even in the smallest of daily issues.

"Every day, choices between the right behaviors and the contrary behaviors are presented to us in simple ways. The choices we make define our integrity.

"Integrity also demands that we recognize that there may be costs. However, the costs, which *can* get to be heavy, are always outweighed in the end.

"Integrity is very personal. I'm not going to preach to you. You know what's in your own heart. Collect your own eggs—using some or all of mine. Live and manage according to your own 'Grade A' collection. And carry your basket of eggs with care. In the end, make sure you're doing it right."

The group sat quietly, almost mesmerized, many heads slowly nodding. It was easy to sense their concurrence.

"Trust? It's unquestioning faith in the values, intentions, decisions, and actions of others. Trust is confident reliance on people and things. Trust is the opposite of doubt. As soon as doubt creeps in, anxiety and fear take root like vicious weeds, and trust is choked.

"Developing trust means shifting our mental models from contention, suspicion, and cynicism to collaboration, confidence, and optimism.

"Trusting others starts with trusting yourself. So relax. You are who you are. We know who you are. So *be* who you are. That's authenticity—which is unmistakable to others. Then, be easy to get along with. Loosen up. Be reasonable. A feeling of what's-the-use resignation festers in situations where you're a pain in the butt to deal with.

"Next, allow yourself to be vulnerable. You accomplish that by permitting appropriate degrees of risk, encouraging novel ways of doing things, admitting you don't have all the answers, and accepting that nobody is perfect and that mistakes will be made. Vulnerability is a magnet, drawing people closer to aid and contribute—and it also makes them feel more powerful.

"It's a pleasure to watch trust unfold and flourish.

"Along with trusting others and trusting yourself, don't forget to trust in God. He or she who trusts at all three levels can do all things.

"As with integrity, your *behaviors* build trust. I'd like to highlight fifteen behaviors—five at a time," and Bert went to his next slide.

Trust-Building Behaviors

↗ *Your sensitivity to—and your respect for—who people are and where they came from.*
↗ *Careful listening coupled with sincere concern—then reacting to what you hear.*
↗ *The perceived effort you make to build understanding of the values of others.*
↗ *The genuineness of the attempt you make at relationship building.*
↗ *Living up to your word—doing what you say you will do.*

"Managers must work to build trust among their staffs and among each other. These are the things that other people need to *see and feel* from you to build trust. Remember—they need to *see and feel*. It's not a case of your personal impression of what *you think* you're doing—it's their *seeing* and *feeling* that counts. I hate to keep taking you back to the farm, but have you ever picked tomatoes, or watched people buy tomatoes at the supermarket? Notice the intense eyeballing and gentle handling. It's a combination of what they see and feel that determines their selection. You, ladies and gentlemen, *you*, are the tomatoes. Woe unto you if you are not 'picked.'

"I'm not going to give a lecture on the meaning of each of these points. It's too late for that. I just want to remind you of these imperatives."

Ol' Bert clicked ahead to his next slide.

Trust-Building Behaviors

↗ *Your acceptance of the word of others.*
↗ *Open-minded dealings with all people.*
↗ *Your own self-convincing competence.*
↗ *Quick and honest admission of mistakes.*
↗ *Giving responsibility freely—but with accountability.*

JOHN W. CEBROWSKI

"Trust has a funny way of making people feel freer. Somehow it unburdens them, and lets them do more. I think it's the absence of negative imaginings that clears the mind and the spirit. All the internal energies can be directed positively. People begin to tap into their potential and talents and create outcomes that will literally amaze you.

"Certainly there are exceptions. A few will abuse your trust. There never is an act of trust without risk. That's the reality, but it's a small price to pay for overwhelming benefits. And those benefits are outrageous success and your inner peace. The scale always tilts in favor of trust."

Ol' Bert clicked ahead to his next slide.

> **Trust-Building Behaviors**
>
> ☒ *Recognizing and utilizing the talents—and acknowledging the contributions—of everyone.*
> ☒ *Providing quick, honest, and useful coaching and counseling.*
> ☒ *Maintaining personal and professional confidences.*
> ☒ *Consistency in direction, support, and disposition.*
> ☒ *Truthfulness, thoroughness, and frequency of communication about situations.*

"True trust is heartfelt and unfeigned. It implies that people will not fail. Bestowing trust imparts confidence, fosters empowerment, heightens commitment, and improves performance. When trust is present, people can feel it very easily. When it's not, it's not. Trust is binary, a '1' or a '0.' You're either a wholesome tomato that gets carefully picked, or you're a blemished tomato that gets hastily snatched for the ketchup factory. Your choice.

"Trust must be given before it can be expected in return, and trusted employees feel obligated to meet expectations. If trust does not emanate from the top," and he glanced at Mr. Pimm, nodding in grateful recognition, "the reciprocal emotions are likely to be fear and suspicion.

"Unfortunately, we live in a world where trust has deteriorated into widespread cynicism. Scandals and improprieties reinforce the belief that

176

playing by The Golden Rule is now passé. That belief is nonsense, but it has made our job harder.

"Trust is also a very personal subject, but whatever you end up with, live and work by it. Trust will intensify the flow of energy, effort, and enthusiasm to get this little train over the mountain.

He paused to let it all sink in.

"That represents my thoughts on integrity and trust—on 'doing it right.' These are my guidelines. Internalize them as is, or tinker with them to your liking.

"An emphasis on 'doing it right' is best made with attitudes and actions. Employees are alert to the tiniest clues of evidence—or voids. I invite you to assess your own level of integrity and trustworthiness—of both evidence and voids—and then to react accordingly."

Ol' Bert clicked ahead to his last slide and stepped aside.

EXECUTE.
"Only those who will risk going too far
can possibly find out how far one can go."
T.S. Elliot
"I Know We Can."
Bert

"Thank you, ladies and gentlemen," Bert said. "Let's glue it together. Let's 'dig in' and 'do it right'. A culture is demonstrated by its habits. Let's all commit to slathering on 'dig-in' and 'do-it-right' habits, stepping up to a higher level of productiveness and rightness.

"And on the highest plane, let's remember that 'digging in' and 'doing it right' are not so much about protecting this business or any business as they are about preserving opportunities and environments for our children in this wonderful community and this great nation, and leaving them an outrageously enviable legacy."

The managers and supervisors smiled, shook their heads in agreement, and clapped. Mr. Pimm handed out a copy of '*Slathering on the Glue*' to everyone. The room emptied quickly as everyone rushed back to their tasks with heightened determination.

Mr. Pimm, the finance director, and Ol' Bert went back to Mr. Pimm's office to double-check some figures. They lingered, sensing the history of the moment and exchanging observations.

"Bert, we've all noticed that you've spent an awful lot of time with your people and the rest of the management staff in the past months. Personally, I've sincerely appreciated your help, and the manner in which you did it. Is there a special secret there?" the finance director asked.

"Yep. Unless these ten essentials are pulled together by a collaborative team, individual efforts won't be as effective," he said. "Thanks for implementing them in finance. If I had just implemented them in sales, sure we would have seen improvement, but not at a level to save this company, and not at a level commensurate with outrageous success. It would have been selfish just to think of myself."

"How'd you stay so calm throughout all this, Bert," she asked. "You always seemed unflappable."

"Personal confidence. Deep belief in the essentials. And reliance on all the people around me and the powers above me. I don't think anyone can shoulder anything in life alone."

"You really believe we're going to make it, don't you?" she inquired gingerly.

Bert, recognizing that there are always laggards, said reassuringly, "Yep! The only question is by how much. Our ultimate success level is set by the weakest of the ten essentials, so I've been constantly vigilant and have worked steadfastly to shore up any wobbly essential in sales, and I've coached other managers on buttressing their efforts. The essentials have never looked better— in all departments. What I've seen throughout the company reminds me of a beautifully manicured public garden or the picture-perfect farms or orchards you'd see in California, Indiana, or South Carolina.

"But just as the weather can wreak havoc on those alluring scenes in a minute, so can our situation be ravaged. Now is the time for all of us to be most vigilant and most steadfast."

"Amen," concluded Mr. Pimm.

The last few weeks were a whirlwind of activity. Everybody in the company had dug in and was doing it right. Outrageous success seemed to be just around the corner.

It Ends

The conference room was dead-quiet as the management team waited for the final figures. Everyone felt optimistic, but the end-of-period numbers were still being crunched in the finance department. The atmosphere was reminiscent of the lively tension of children waiting for Christmas morning. The whole company was motionless for the moment, not a bit of work going on anywhere.

Then the finance director burst into the room! Her expression made it unnecessary for her to say a word. The place went crazy.

She slapped an overhead on the projector for all to see. The first line read—The Little Company That Could - Did!

There was momentary quiet as everyone absorbed the figures. All revenue 'stakes' had been exceeded—every single one of them! The backlog and pipeline figures were also robust, promising that the next reporting period would be healthy.

The combined feeling of relief and exhilaration was indescribable. Certus had done it! A supernatural buoyancy enveloped the room. Some ran out to alert all the employees. Others picked up phones to alert various people who had been following Certus's progress.

The lines on Mr. Pimm's charts could take another step upward.

At the end of the jubilation Ol' Bert quietly announced his intent to go back to rocking on the front porch of his retirement home. He said he always knew when it was time to leave—and now was the time. The senior staff had been forewarned. Many others had suspected his announcement. His message dulled the celebration somewhat, but he did it in such a professional, understated way, heaping credit on the staff that all anyone could say was that Ol' Bert was a man of class, a true gentleman.

A grand farewell was quietly mentioned and agreed-to by several managers.

In the end, Ol' Bert and Certus had succeeded outrageously, coming back from the brink of disaster. The mission had been accomplished, but a lot more than anyone had expected had been achieved.

Beyond the current results, morale in the company was high, and esprit de corps in the sales unit was exceptional.

The company's culture oozed teamwork, respect, pride, integrity, and trust.
An audacious 'we-can-do-it' attitude had permeated the organization.
Leadership and followership were integrated and finely tuned.
Expectations were well understood throughout the company.
Creative strategies and crisp plans for the future were in place in all departments.
An atmosphere of continuous-learning had job knowledge and skill levels soaring—from the top to the bottom of the organization.
Processes were smoothly humming throughout Certus.
The relationships with customers, sales partners, and suppliers were chipper.
And—all those achievements paid some serendipitous dividends quickly.

The earlier e-business investments were clicking beyond expectations.
The previous initiatives in new-age business concepts popped into place.
A measurable improvement in quality was noted in all areas.
There was a buoyancy of spirit throughout the company—everyone knew he or she was carrying a bigger load than before—but feeling lighter in the process.
Bad attitudes, clumsy procedures, and incompatible people seemed to be self-ejecting of their own volition from the company—as if the new culture was somehow magically casting out infections.
Word from the street was that a special mystique had enveloped Certus and that its reputation had brightened. The stock went to an all-time high.
The HR office began receiving unsolicited inquiries and résumés from 'horses' for all departments.
The local community was bursting with pride about its rejuvenated corporate citizen.

All of Ol' Bert's essentials—including *The Attack of the Mustard Seed*—had worked!

Our Closing Scene

It was time for the grand good-bye. The factory was the only place big enough to hold the crowd.

All employees were present.

The banker was there.

The Board of Directors was there.

Dignitaries from the local community were there.

Many sales partners and major customers had flown in for the event.

The local and national business press was in attendance, scrambling for comments from everyone.

A photographer had been brought in to record the occasion.

And Mr. Pimm had secretly invited Ol' Bert's sisters to come and share in the jubilation. He had sent the grandest limo you can imagine to bring them in.

A luncheon of chicken-fried steak and mashed potatoes for all had been prepared by Ol' Bert's favorite restaurant in Chicago—flown in at company expense. Homemade apple crumb pies—which his sisters had made—were brought out for dessert.

Then the ceremony began.

The three horses were sitting in the front row, beaming.

Mr. Pimm stepped forward to the podium, clearly touched, never dreaming that what he had started back at Ol' Bert's retirement home would turn out this way. It was the first time employees had seen this poised man show such emotion. His words of thanks and recognition were crisp and well chosen. Employees would later say that it was the best speech Mr. Pimm had ever given.

Mr. Pimm then asked that the trophy cup be brought in. It was so big it needed to be carried by two people.

All was quiet as Mr. Pimm called Ol' Bert up to the front and took the covering shroud off of the trophy cup—and then the room erupted in joyous ovation. Cameras clicked, and flashbulbs popped all over the place.

The cup was engraved with Ol' Bert's essentials for outrageous success.

*In recognition of your outrageously
inspirational leadership and management.
Thank you for teaching us
outrageous success.
Presented by all the outrageously grateful
people of Certus.*

**Put The Horses In The Barn
Pound Some Stakes Into The Ground
Plant Somethin' Special
Know How To Git Where You're Goin'
Use The Best Ways For The Best Yields
Lead With Heart, Brains, and Courage
Aid Everyone In Learnin'
Ask The Neighbors For Help
Treat Folks Like Kin
Dig In And Do It Right**

Certus, Inc.

Mr. Pimm discretely pulled him aside and slipped him an envelope that Bert knew contained his bonus check—but *didn't* know also contained the title to the '93 Chevy. Ol' Bert stuffed the envelope, unopened, into his jacket, and then stepped forward to speak, barely visible over the podium. The room was hushed.

It was obvious to all that he was flustered by the recognition. There were humble thanks to Mr. Pimm for the opportunity. He thanked all employees profusely for their support and dedication. He acknowledged his horses with great passion.

He then divulged the ten simple secrets of sustaining outrageous success.

"First. Remember that the responsibility for outrageous success lies with *everyone*—*all* the leaders and *all* the followers—just like it did with every single one of us kids and grownups back on the farm. Some will carry more responsibility than others will, but that's never an excuse for *anyone* dropping their share of the load. There's no room for benchwarmers or spectators.

"Second. Talk about outrageous success all the time—like a never-ending town meeting. Chatter. Argue. Challenge. Listen. The give-and-take gabbing fuels the effectiveness of all the essentials.

"Third. Think 'outside-in', always paying close attention to the market, but don't be falsely beguiled. The market instructs not by seduction and success, but by pain and disappointment.

"Fourth. Regularly take a leisurely far-off view of the company—surveying what you see—like driving down the road on a Sunday afternoon to inspect your farm from afar. Your relaxed manner and the distinctive perspective will provide surprising insights.

"Fifth. Don't create ruts. Constantly challenge your day-to-day methods with a leery, never-be-satisfied attitude—being a nitpicker of details and doing.

"Sixth. Be vigilant for creeping contentment, poisonous agendas, stinging motives, and biting rascals—and wipe out those varmints with the speed and efficiency of a barnyard owl.

"Seventh. Guard and protect the company's intellectual assets, brands, market reputation, and customer base with a sheepdog's stamina and dedication.

"Eighth. Emphasis on these ten essentials demands metrics to match. Continue to develop and refine them. Then let others trumpet your success—being humble as they do. There is no lack of people, organizations, and market mechanisms that love to keep score with you. *They* will always have the greatest credibility.

"Ninth. Enjoy your success. Wallow in it. Celebrate it all together—and with vigor. Invite all the stakeholders, as you've done here today, to share in your jubilation. Recognition and reward will whet your appetite for further success.

"Tenth, and finally. Reflect on your success carefully and intently, constantly remembering the true source of your success, saying thankful prayers for it.

"When I first told Mr. Pimm of the ten essentials for outrageous success many months ago he astutely said to me—'Sounds simple—yet serious and intricate'. Well—so are the secrets for sustaining it. But—I KNOW YOU CAN!" he zestfully finished.

The audience acknowledged with light laughter that signaled understanding.

He then bequeathed the contents of his 'Wisdom Pantry' to the company.

Ol' Bert concluded, saying, "Ohiyesa, a famous Santee Sioux once expressed parting this way. *Each soul must meet the morning sun, the new sweet earth, and the Great Silence alone.* I now await that meeting with joy."

His eyes glistened. The applause spoke sincere gratitude.

JOHN W. CEBROWSKI

Shortly after Ol' Bert had first announced his retirement the three horses had each voluntarily declined to step into Ol' Bert's shoes. Rather, each were given and accepted additional major responsibilities. Those were big shoes to fill, and Mr. Pimm had been fretting about finding a replacement ever since Ol' Bert's announcement to leave.

While talking to the press, board members, and other dignitaries at the conclusion of the farewell party—soaking in the glory—Mr. Pimm continued 'poking around' in earnest for a replacement. He asked if anyone knew of possible candidates. He told folks to keep their eyes open for a 'horse-of-a-manager'. He suggested they spread the word to all managers out there who felt qualified to follow in Ol' Bert's huge footsteps and who were committed to outrageous success.

Watching Mr. Pimm 'work' the crowd, applying one of his twelve 'Ps', Ol' Bert smiled in deep self-satisfaction. He was very happy that he had made the decision to come out of retirement. 'The Farm' seemed to be in good hands. All the seeds that he had sown were now flourishing—*but*—he knew that in business, as in farming and gardening, the story is never really 'over' because time and the seasons mandate regular renewal.

To be continued...

There is a master key to success with which no man can fail.
Its name is simplicity.
Sir Henri Deterding

A Summary of Key Points

Essential #1: Put The Horses In The Barn
- Ol' Bert's special 'Twelve-P-System'

1. Preparation	2. Position description	3. Profile
4. Process	5. Poking around	6. Persuade
7. Precautions	8. Pick	9. Priming
10. Plan	11. Prevent	12. Pruning

Essential #2: Pound Some Stakes Into The Ground
- **Destination stakes:** Remember that there are three time frames associated with stakes because you always need to 'roll-the-clock'.
  - **1. Operating stakes for the current, or close-in period**
  - **2. Positioning stakes for the next farther-out period**
  - **3. Surveying stakes for the next over-the-horizon period**
- **E-X-C-E-E-D** the stakes you pound.
- **Boundary stakes:** Communicate what you expect from your people—and communicate what your people can expect from you. Then have your people communicate their expectations.

Essential #3: Plant Somethin' Special
- Remember the 3 'D's of strategy:

Demand	Differentiation	Dominance

- And keep in mind the fundamental nature of strategy…**"The essence of strategy is choosing to perform activities differently than rivals do."**

Essential #4: Know How To Git' Where You're Goin'
- Start with hard, squirmy questions—because planning is more thinking more writing—and then turn your plan into a document.
- The three common threads that run through effective plans…

Dual-duty for Format	Quilting for Content	Buttonhole twist for Style

- Plans are always works-in-progress. Keep your plan in-hand as you execute.

Essential #5: Use The Best Ways For The Best Yields

- Understand your customers' buying process before you put your selling process in place.
- Create a silver-bullet tool for each step of your sales process.

Apply the four 'S's of Sensational Service…

1. Shorter	2. Speedier	3. Sweeter	4. Simpler

Implement the four key sales management tools…

1. Pipeline	2. Forecast	3. Activity Report	4. Asset Budget

Essential #6: Lead With Heart, Brains, and Courage

- Effective followership comes before effective leadership.
- Leadership is defined by valued behaviors.
- Outrageously successful leadership is characterized by one or a few behaviors expressed to the fullest possible degree.
- Practice your leadership in view of everyone and by engaging challenges and needs.
- Create your own leadership model and lead by it.

Essential #7: Aid Everyone With Learnin'

- The four-part philosophy for outrageous teaching and coaching,

1. Frequency	3. Rigor
2. Regularity	4. Accountability

- Organize your teaching by answering these four imperatives:
  WHAT-are-you-going-to-teach
  WHO-is-going-to-be-taught
  WHICH-person-will-do-the-teaching
  HOW-will-it-be-taught

- **THREE CHARACTERISTICS OF THE BEST TEACHERS**

1. Committed	2. Knowledgeable	3. Communicator

Essential #8: Ask The Neighbors For Help
- Your 'neighbors' are everyone around you.
  Never hesitate to ask them for help.
- The eleven pointers on 'how' to ask for help include:
  Story telling, Clarity, Framing, Candor, Listening, Patience, Stand tall, Respect, Validating, Sourcing, Bonding.

Essential #9: Treat Folks Like Kin
- Build an understanding of the root behaviors that people value.
- Deliver the behaviors that people value...by providing attention
- Remember that different people value different root behaviors.

Essential #10: Dig In And Do It Right
- Consider and evaluate your work ethic.
  Is it as strong as it *can* be?
  Is it as strong as would *like it* to be?

- The thirteen behaviors within integrity:
  Speed, Fairness, Crisp and Clear Explanations, Sincerity, Care of Details, Seeking Opinions, Objectivity, Order, Adherence to Policies, Judgment, Firmness, Consistency, and Honesty

- With trust—it's a case of what people *see* and *feel* in you that counts.

187

Bibliography
Selections from Ol' Bert's 'Wisdom Pantry'

You will find all of these titles helpful in your pursuit of outrageous success. All the books that were highlighted in the story are here. Those books, plus numerous others, are listed under their most appropriate Essential.

Essential #1 Put The Horses In The Barn
96 Great Interview Questions To Ask Before You Hire, by Paul Falcone, from AMACOM
> The book tells you why to ask various questions and how to analyze the answers. It also teaches how to evaluate candidates, how to reference-check, and how to make an offer.

Hiring the Best, 4th Edition, by Martin Yate, from Adams Media Corporation
> A guide to effective interviewing that contains techniques, strategies, and scenarios—and over 400 questions.

Hire With Your Head, by Lou Adler, from John Wiley & Sons, Inc.
> Five steps to getting hiring right—the POWER staffing system™. Addresses the necessity to start with defining superior performance, to use reason instead of emotion to guide hiring decisions, and the inconsistencies in hiring.

Interviewing and Selecting High Performers, by Richard H. Beatty, from John Wiley & Sons, Inc.
> Discusses the forgotten relationship—people and profit. Contains a predictive model that clarifies the key qualifications needed by candidates. More than 500 behaviorly based questions. For the manager who wishes to upgrade organizational effectiveness.

The Evaluation Interview, by Richard A. Fear and Robert J. Chiron, from McGraw-Hill
> Effective interviewing techniques. Helps you develop job descriptions and worker specifications, establish rapport, probe for clues to behavior, control the interview, and determine the candidates mental ability, motivation, and maturity.

Essential #2 Pound Some Stakes Into The Ground
DNA Leadership Through Goal-Driven Management, by James R. Ball, from The Goals Institute Inc.

The author is an authority on goal power who provides methods for selecting and achieving goals, and the secrets of succeeding within a goal-structured environment. Will easily help you put your company's ideas to work.

First Things First, by Steven Covey, A. Roger Merrill, and Rebecca R. Merrill, from Simon & Schuster

A book that can help you escape the tyranny of the clock and rediscover a principle-centered compass-based approach to work and life.

The One Minute Manager, by Ken Blanchard, from Berkley Books

A story that describes how people work best with other people. Helps manager and staff get more done in less time, reduce stress, find peace of mind, produce valuable results, reinforce expectations, and feel better about themselves.

The 22 Immutable Laws of Marketing, by Al Ries and Jack Trout, from HarperBusiness

An easy read that will cause you to think about basic truths early in your stakes-strategy-planning process—so as to avoid difficulty and disappointment down the road.

Essential #3 Plant Somethin' Special

Competitive Advantage, by Michael Porter, from Free Press

Takes strategy from broad vision to an internally consistent configuration of activities that gains a firm an advantage over its rivals. The book's value chain concept enables isolating the underlying sources of buyer value that will command a premium price.

Strategic Skills for Line Managers, by Michael Colenso, from Butterworth-Heinemann

This book will help you develop and implement a strategy at the team or business unit level. It emphasizes the fact that you need to operate your own unit strategically. Fits well in horizontally structured organizations.

The Balanced Scorecard, by Robert S. Kaplan and David P. Norton, from HBS Press

The book describes a management system that channels the energies, abilities, and knowledge of people towards achieving long-term strategic goals. It shows how the strategy can be tested, measured, and updated.

Essential #4 Know How To Git Where You're Goin'

A Whack on the Side of the Head, by Roger von Oech, from Warner Books
>It's about the ten mental locks that prevent you from being more creative and what you can do to open those locks. Contains bright ideas and originality boosters that will innovate your planning process and your final 'roadmaps'.

Crossing The Chasm: Marketing and Selling High-Tech Products to Mainstream Customers, by Geoffrey A. Moore, from HarperBusiness
>The chasm theory identifies and addresses the key challenges in getting from early market success to mainstream market leadership. The book is intuitive, makes sense, and contains easy to implement recommendations.

Gardening Basics, by Ken Beckett, Steve Bradley, Noel Kingsbury, and Tim Newberry, from Sterling Publishing Company, Inc.
>Yes, gardening. Whether you're starting from scratch or improving what is already there—here's how to design, plant, and maintain your garden. Lots of color, pictures, and illustrations. Look for linkages and parallels to your business plans in the themes and concepts that are in this big book.

Leading Change, by John P. Kotter, from Harvard Business School Press
>The book offers a compelling framework to eliminate or correct the eight common mistakes associated with change management—and since plans always contain changes—it will clarify and focus your direction and implementation.

Marketing Channels, 5th edition, by Louis W. Stern, Adel I. El-Ansary, and Anne T. Coughlan, from Prentice Hall. A classic textbook that focuses on how to design develop, and maintain relationships among channel members so that sustainable, competitive advantages can be achieved.

Marketing Management, 9th edition, by Philip Kotler, from Prentice Hall
>A classic. The most comprehensive textbook by one of the world's leading authorities on marketing. Use it as a reference. It will cause you to think about innumerable analysis, planning, and implementation subjects.

Export / Import, by Thomas E. Johnson, from AMACOM
>An outstanding reference book for the manager leading international sales efforts. A clear overview of the entire export/import process with actual sample documents and step-by-step procedures.

Management of a Sales Force, 10th Edition, by William J. Stanton and Rosann Spiro, from Irwin McGraw Hill

A comprehensive classic textbook—probably the best ever written for first-line mangers. It covers all of the essentials and addresses the realities of the 21st century.

The Market Planning Guide, by David H. Bangs, Jr., from Upstart Publishing Company

A comprehensive workbook of practical ideas and processes—with accompanying forms that you can modify to meet your needs.

The One-Day Marketing Plan, 2nd Edition, by Roman G. Heibing and Scott Cooper, from NTC.

A concise, well-thought-out guide that breaks down the complex planning process into ten critical steps. Includes sections on business review, problems and opportunities, sales objectives, target markets, strategies, and personal selling.

Who Moved My Cheese, by Spencer Johnson, M.D., from Putnam Books

A wonderful story that talks about how to deal with change in your work and in your life. Teaches you how to plan for 'your cheese' being moved.

Essential #5 Use The Best Ways For The Best Yields

Consultative Selling, 6th edition, by Mark Hanan, from AMACOM

Focuses on the issues of financial results by selling improved customer profits rather than products and services. Transactions with you should either reduce costs or increase revenues. Long-term continuing relationship-oriented sales process.

Customer Centered Selling: Eight Steps to Success from the World's Best Sales Force, by Robert L. Jolles, from Free Press

Teaches you the secret of the Xerox eight-step sales training program— focusing first on your customer's needs and decision-making process. A systematic approach that teaches you to anticipate and influence customer behavior.

Solution Selling, by Michael T. Bosworth, from McGraw-Hill

Offers a process—a model—to take the guesswork out of difficult-to-sell intangible products and services. Will help you become aligned and stay aligned with your buyers.

SPIN Selling, by Neil Rackham, from McGraw-Hill

Based on extensive research, the SPIN Model provides a precise question-asking process to manage the larger sale.

The Book of Excellence, by Byrd Baggett, from Rutledge Hill Press

Lists 236 habits of effective salespeople—in a bite-sized format.

The New Conceptual Selling, by Stephen E. Heiman and Diane Sanchez, from Warner Books
> Focuses on the effective management of the individual sales call. Expalins why customers really buy. Explains a unique questioning process that enhances information flow, provides competitive differentiation, and heightens confidence and credibility.

The New Strategic Selling, by Stephen E. Heiman, Diane Sanchez, Tad Tuleja, and Robert Miller, from Warner Books
> Offers proven, visible, repeatable skills. A good methodology for people who don't consider themselves 'salespeople', but who indeed sell. A very professional, low-pressure, ethics-based approach to selling.

The Sales Manager's Troubleshooter, by John Cebrowski and Charlie Romeo, from Prentice Hall
> The Troubleshooter gives you everything you need to handle 87 critical management problems—from performance to personnel to sales partners to your boss and more—thus improving your yields.

You Can't Teach a Kid to Ride a Bike at a Seminar, by David H. Sandler and John Hayes, from Dutton / Signet
> A guide to the Sandler Sales Institute's 7-Step system for successful selling. Filled with examples of success and failures.

Essential #6 Lead With Heart Brains and Courage

Leaders, by Warren Bennis and Burt Nanus, from HarperBusiness
> The book discusses the significance of the role of character, creating a culture capable of generating intellectual capital. a strong determination to realize a goal, vision, conviction, or passion, the necessity to generate and sustain trust, enrolling people in your vision, and a bias towards action.

Leadership, compiled by Robert A. Fitton, from WestviewPress
> Provides quotations from the world's greatest motivators. A great reference for speaking and writing—and examples for your own personal behaviors.

Secrets of Break-Through Leadership, by Peter Capezio and Debra Morehouse, from Career Press
> Focuses on identifying the characteristics of self-directed leaders. Demonstrates how you can develop and improve these skills through exercises and practice opportunities.

The Founding Fathers on Leadership: Classic Teamwork in Changing Times, by Donald T. Phillips, from Warner Books
> Successful leadership is deliberate and purposeful. Goal-setting, communication, and risk-taking are just a few of the traits to be learned by studying Washington, Jefferson, and their colleagues. Our early history suggests many ways to achieve success.

Tough-Minded Leadership, by Joe D. Batten, from AMACOM
> Helps you make the transition to tough-minded leader by explaining thirty-five essential conversions you must make in your attitudes and the fifteen challenges you must learn to confront.

The 21 Indispensable Qualities of a Leader, by John C. Maxwell, from Thomas Nelson Publishers
> A small book that will help you become the person others will want to follow

Essential #7 Aid Everyone In Learnin'

The Adult Learner, by Malcolm S. Knowles, Elwood F. Holton III, and Richard A. Swanson, from Gulf Publishing Company
> The book highlights the latest perspectives on adult learning and its application in adult education and human resource development. Covers methods of developing effective adult learning programs.

Eight Ways of Teaching: The Artistry of Teaching for Multiple Intelligences, third edition, by David Lazear, from Skylight Publications
> Everything you need to know about the different "intelligences".

How Organizations Learn: An Integrated Strategy for Building Learning Capability, by Anthony DiBella and Edwin C. Nevis, from Jossey-Bass Publishers
> A readable and detailed presentation on learning that provides a way to understand and develop learning capability in teams and organizations. For those interested in transformation, it provides a practical framework.

Learning Organizations, edited by Sarita Chawla & John Renesch, from Productivity Press
> Contains essays by thirty-nine of the most respected practitioners and scholars on this topic. Rich in concept and theory as well as application and example. Will help you develop a culture for tomorrow's workplace.

Sales Coaching, by Linda Richardson, from McGraw-Hill

You need the skills of a great coach to empower rather then micro-manage a sales unit or a business.

Transformational Learning: Renewing Your Company Through Knowledge and Skills, by Daniel R. Tobin, from John Wiley & Sons
> Explains how to align employees' learning initiatives with the long range goals of the company, create a personalized learning system, and develop partnerships with key company leaders. Contains checklists, evaluations, and guidelines.

Stop Managing, Start Coaching, by Jerry Gilley & Nathaniel Boughton, from McGraw-Hill
> This book highlights performance coaching. It demonstrates how managers can balance the roles of trainer, career coach, confronter, and mentor to improve performance. The chapters on confrontation and conflict, and on self-esteeming, are particularly useful.

Ten Steps to a Learning Organization, by Peter Kline and Bernard Saunders, from Great Ocean Publishers
> The book provides a means for developing a culture of high performance learners. Major subjects include; assessing your learning culture, making the workplace safe for thinking, and helping people become resources for each other.

Masterful Coaching Fieldbook, Robert Hargrove, from Jossey-Bass/Pfeiffer Publishers
> Contains an excellent five-step coaching model. Includes seven chapters written by seven masterful coaches that match coaching to seven different jobs. Also emphasizes thinking and teamwork.

Teach Yourself How To Study, by Paul Oliver, from Teach Yourself Books
> Although written for students, the chapters on improving your study techniques, developing your learning skills, identifying your learning resources, and considering your long term plans, make this book very valuable.

How To Learn Anything Quickly, by Ricki Linksman, from Replica Books
> Helps everyone find the learning or memorization method which best suits their personal learning style and implement the method to learn material easily and thoroughly. Gives everyone the opportunity to improve retention and recall.

Study Harder, Not Smarter, by Kevin Paul, from Self-Counsel Press
> The book explains how people learn and how you and your staff can take advantage of natural abilities. The strategies are very practical.

Creative Whack Pack, by Roger von Oech, from United States Games Systems

This is a creative thinking workshop-in-a-box—64 cards—each
featuring an idea on places to find new information, others providing
techniques to generate new ideas, some lending decision-making
advice, and some giving you the kick in the pants you need to get your
ideas into action.

Games Trainers Play, by Edward Scannell & John Newstrom, from McGraw
Hill

100 different games, activities, and exercises that have been field-tested
and proven highly effective by some of America's most innovative
trainers in teaching a variety of important business skills that are
challenging and fun for participants.

Even More Games Trainers Play, by Edward Scannell & John Newstrom, from
McGraw Hill

More of the above.

Essential #8 Ask The Neighbors For Help

Building A Dynamc Team, by Richard Y. Chang, from Richard Chang
Associates, Inc.

A simple teamwork guide to help create or rejuvenate a team. It will
help you change a group of individuals—a group of neighbors—into a
collaborative team.

Six Thinking Hats, by Edward de Bono, from International Center for Creative
Thinking

White, red, black, yellow, green, and blue hats provide direction labels
for thinking. Wearing the right hat at the right time results in everyone
looking and working in the same direction, saving time, eliminating
confusion, and helping each other.

Team Training from Startup to High Performance, by Carl Harshman and Steve
Phillips, from McGraw Hill

This will help you transform a traditional department or workgroup into
a confident, productive, fully self-directed work team. The 23 self-
contained skill-building training modules deliver an easy-to-use lesson
plan and reproducible handouts.

Working Relationships, by Bob Wall, from Davies-Black Publishing

The simple truth about getting along with friends and foes at work.
Solid advice and practical tools for making things better for everyone

EXECUTIVE ETIQUETTE IN THE NEW WORKPLACE, BY MARJABELLE YOUNG
STEWART AND MARIAN FAUX, FROM ST. MARTIN'S GRIFFIN

A practical and reassuring sourcebook that offers businesspeople at every rung of the corporate ladder, the guidelines they need for handling the increasingly complex relationships of office life.

The Dilbert Principle, by Scott Adams, from HarperBusiness

Full of workplace wisdom and humor. This is the reality of your neighbors cubicle life—which you must understand. It may all sound far-fetched, but much of it is true.

Essential #9 Treat Folks Like Kin

Customer Connections, by Robert E. Wayland and Paul M. Cole, from Harvard Business School Press

The authors reveal a comprehensive system that places customer relationships at the center of your business and shows you how to use this system to discover and tap new sources of value. It also unveils a model for fostering collaboration.

How to Win Friends & Influence People, by Dale Carnegie, from Pocket Books

A classic oldie but goldie. You'll learn six ways to make people like you, twelve ways to win people to your way of thinking, and nine ways to change people without arousing resentment.

Put Your Best Foot Forward, by Jo-Ellan Dimitrius, Ph.D., and Mark Mazzarella, from Scribner

This book will teach you how people judge you, and why. It will help you understand how impressions are made and how to accentuate the positive qualities that appeal to others. You'll learn how to project the 'four compass qualities' that are the foundation of every great impression—trustworthiness, caring, humility, and capability.

Riding the Waves of Culture, by Fons Trompenaars and Charles Hampton-Turner, from McGraw-Hill

Dispels the notion that there is 'one best way' of managing and treating folks around the world, provides a better understanding of your own culture and cultural differences in general, and supplies insights into 'global' versus 'local' dilemmas.

The Power of Simplicity, by Jack Trout and Steve Rivkin, from McGraw-Hill

Boils the chaos around us down to essential business elements. Will help you see through the management fads, jargon, and over-hyped ideas that impede business and relationships. Application of simplicity will provoke respect and aid understanding.

The Farming Game, by Bryan Jones, from University of Nebraska Press

Yes, farming. A small practical guide that's full of wit and the reality of farming. An opportunity for urban-dwellers and suburban-slickers to look through the author's (and Ol' Bert's) sharp eyes at the detail in his portraits of farming people—and find links to business people.

Essential #10 Dig In And Do It Right

Don't Sweat The Small Stuff, by Richard Carlson, from Hyperion
> A small book that contains 100 pearls of wisdom. Simple ways to keep the little things from taking over your life—so you can keep 'doing it right'.

Making Choices, by Peter Kreeft, from Servant Books
> Useful wisdom for everyday moral decisions. Aspects of practical morality most forgotten and most needed.

The Book of Virtues, by William Bennett, from Simon & Schuster
> A treasury of great moral stories that enhances moral literacy about self-discipline, compassion, responsibility, friendship, work , courage, perseverance, honesty, loyalty, and faith.

The Greatest Generation, by Tom Brokaw, from Random House
> Want to know what makes Ol' Bert tick? Read this superb collection of stories of individual men and women who came of age during the Great Depression and the Second World War and went on to build modern America. These are stories of a generation united by common values—values shared by Ol' Bert.

The Little Engine That Could, by Watty Piper, from Platt & Munk Publishers
> Chug, chug, chug. Puff, puff, puff. I think you've got this one figured out already.

The Soul of a Business, by Tom Chappell, from Bantam
> This book is about the two sides of all of us, the spiritual and the practical, both helping to achieve whatever business goals you set for yourself.

Printed in the United States
3442